AMARNA LETTERS

5

AMARNA LETTERS

Essays on
Ancient Egypt
ca. 1390 - 1310 BC
Volume Five, Summer 2015

5

Dennis C. Forbes, Editor

KMT Communications, LLC
Weaverville, North Carolina, USA

Publisher: Carl J. Kojis
Editor/Designer: Dennis C. Forbes
Distributed by Amazon.com

Front Cover: Black-granite life-size staanding statue of King Nebkheperure Tutankhamen,
found in the Karnak Cachette in 1904 and today in the collection of
the Egyptian Museum, Cairo, Egypt. Photograph: Kmt/Forbes

Frontispiece: Pigmented sunk-relief portrait of Nebmaatre Amenhotep III,
on a reused block from his memorial temple, today displayed at the
site of the Memorial Temple of Merneptah, the west bank at Luxor, Egypt.
Photograph: Kmt/Forbes

Contents Page: Small limestone head of young Tutankhamen, from
a pair-statue with the god Amen. Provenance unknown but today in
the collection of the Metropolitan Museum of Art.
Photograph: Kmt/Forbes

contents

Dennis C. Forbes
& George B. Johnson
"GIVEN LIFE FOREVER"
The Funerary Monuments of Amenhotep III

Arielle P. Kozloff
BUBONIC PLAGUE
In the Reign of Amenhotep III?   28

George B. Johnson
RECONSIDERING THE QUEEN TIYE-AS-SPHINX PLAQUE
in the Collection of the Metropolitan Museum of Art   50

Francisco Martin Valentin
& Teresa Bedman
PROOF FOR AN AMENHOTEP III/AMENHOTEP IV COREGENCY
Found in the Tomb Chapel of Vizier Amenhotep-Huy   66

Dennis C. Forbes
CIRCUMSTANTIAL EVIDENCE
for an Amenhotep III/Amenhotep IV Coregency   80

Arielle P. Kozloff
CHIPS OFF OLD STATUES
Carving the Amenhotep IV Colossi of Karnak   96

W. Raymond Johnson
SAME STATUES, DIFFERENT KING   114

Earl L. Ertman
SMITING THE ENEMY IN THE REIGN OF AKHENATEN   122

Rolf Krauss
NEFERTITI'S FINAL SECRET
A Forgery in Exchange for the Bust of Nefertiti?   132

Aidan Dodson
WERE NEFERTITI & TUTANKHAMEN COREGENTS?   150

Marianne Eaton-Krauss
SEATS OF POWER: The Thrones of Tutankhamen   162

W. Raymond Johnson
TUTANKHAMEN-PERIOD BATTLE RELIEFS AT LUXOR   180

Dennis C. Forbes
BEYOND THE TOMB: The Historical Tutankhamen   198

Earl L. Ertman
SYMBOLISM IN THE DECORATION OF THE   212
TOMB OF KING AY (WV23)

Notes to the Essays & About the Authors   230

"Given Life Forever"
The Funerary Monuments of Amenhotep III

**by Dennis C. Forbes
& George B. Johnson**

Photography by the Authors

N ebmaatre Amenhotep-Ruler-of Waset, ninth pharaoh of the Eighteenth Dynasty, wore the Double
Crown of the Two Lands for thirty-eight years
(1391-1353 BC), dying in poor health at no more
than fifty years of age. The third Amenhotep's time on the
throne of Egypt was called the "zenith of its magnificence" by
Egyptologist Sir Alan Gardiner,[1] the empire established by his
forefathers in the dynasty stretching from as far south as the
Fifth Cataract in Nubia and north to the Eurphrates River border of Syria-Palestine. Never before had the coffers of Egypt
been so full of foreign tribute; and Amenhotep III was able to
control his vast hegemony by diplomacy rather than militancy,
even arranging marriages between himself and the daughters
of the kings of Mitanni, Arzawa and Syria.[2] Relieved of the pre-
occupations and expense of military campaigning, Amenhotep
turned his vast resources to great building programs up and
down the Nile, but with special focus at Waset (Thebes, Luxor)
the southern capital of the Two Lands and cult center of the
state god, Amen-Re.

In particular he added to the great temple (mansion) of
that deity, Iput-Iset, modern Karnak, by erecting as its entrance
façade the Third Pylon (in the modern numbering sequence),
dismantling several earlier structures raised by his ancestors,
to make room for this huge gateway — especially a large portico forecourt built only a few years earlier by his father, Thutmose IV. The decorated blocks from these older monuments
were incorporated as filler in the new pylon, thus ensuring
their survival and reconstruction today in the Open Air Museum at Karnak.

A few kilometers south of Iput-Iset, also on the east
bank of the Nile, Amenhotep III dismantled an earlier temple
(perhaps dating back to the Middle Kingdom) and in its place
erected the much larger Temple of the Southern Opet, better
known today as Luxor Temple. This structure was the focus of
the annual Opet Festival, when the divine trinity of Waset —
Amen-Re, his consort, Mut, and son, Khonsu — traveled in
their barque shrines via barges on the Nile, in procession from

*Opposite, Detail of raised-relief depiction of Amen-
hotep III receivng "life," on a block from his mortuary temple reused in the Temple of Merneptah & today in a magazine on the site of that monument.*

Photo: Forbes

Karnak to the Southern Opet, where they remained "on vacation" for two to four weeks. During this time festivities celebrated the myth of the royal *ka*, or the divine kingship. It was in a chamber of the Southern Opet that Amenhotep III had a relief carved on the walls proclaiming he was conceived when his mother, Mutemwiya, was visited in her bedchamber by Amen-Re himself (in the guise of King Thutmose IV, of course).[3]

These temples, Iput-Iset and the Southern Opet (and one Amenhotep III built for the war god Montu, also at Karnak), were intended for the direct benefit the local deities, and by extension all of Egypt. But Amenhotep-Ruler-of-Waset also followed in a tradition established early in his dynasty, erecting a structure on the west bank of the Nile at Waset (West-of-Waset) to ensure his own eternal existence, a memorial (mortuary or funerary) temple, where his royal *ka* would receive offerings for all time in the Afterlife, where he would be "Given Life Forever" by the gods. Previously, from the beginning of the dynastic period, the cult chapels of deceased rulers were directly associated with their tombs, clearly marking the locations of the latter. With Amenhotep I there was a break in this tradition, however, the royal memorial chapels (now temples) being widely separated from the actual places of burial — which were secreted away in the desert wadi known today as the Valley of the Kings. By Amenhotep III's time several of these

Opposite, The Great Dedication Stela reerected in front of the peristyle court of the Amenhotep Memorial Temple at Kom el Hettan, as it appeared in 1988. Note Colossi of Memnon in the distance. Photo: Johnson

Above, The Colossi of Memnon still in situ, where they flanked the First Pylon entrance to the Amenhotep temple. Below, Detail of the Southern Colossus with the figure of Queen Tiye by the king's right leg. Photos: Forbes

Opposite, During the ongoing excavations begun in 1997 at Kom el Hettan on the Luxor west bank, a number of damaged Amenhotep III sculptures have been unearthed, including a double diad (top). The crocodile sphinx (bottom) has been visible for some years, but now is moved to ensure that it will not suffer further from the high water-table in the area.

Left, General views of the recently excavated peristyle court of the Amenhotep III memorial temple, with column bases & fragments of colossal granite statues of the king.

Above, The colossal red-granite head of Amenhotep III excavated at Kom el Hettan in 1957 & today displayed in the Luxor Museum. All photos: Forbes

structures were standing at the edge of the Nile flood-plain and beyond (in the case of Hatshepsut's unique memorial temple built at the base of the tall cliffs at Deir el Bahari). To the north of this row of royal memorial temples, also on the edge of the cultivation (modern-day Kom el Hettan), the third Amenhotep built his own structure, by far larger and more richly decorated and endowed with statuary than any raised by his predecessors (or his successors, for that matter).

On an immense dedication stela within the temple — today rerected where it had fallen in antiquity — Amenhotep recorded: *"I made it in excellent work of fine white sandstone. ...My Majesty filled it with monuments, with my [statues] from the mountain of gritstone* (quartzite). *When they are seen [in] their place, there is great rejoicing because of their size. ...My Majesty made a double pylon, seeking excellent things for my father* [Amen-Re]. *...Great was that which I made, of gold, stone and every splendid costly stone without end...."*[4]

The statues referred to are the "Colossi of Memnon," a pair of seated images of the king which still mark the first-

Recycling Nebmaatre

Excavations by the Swiss Institute of the Luxor west-bank site of the Merneptah memorial temple during the 1990s revealed that the elderly fourth king of the 19th Dynasty had massively quarried the nearby Memorial Temple of Amenhotep III for ready-cut stone, no doubt to build his own structure as quickly as possible. That this could be done suggests that the funerary cult of the 18th Dynasty king was no longer being maintained and his temple had been abandoned. In their reuse the decorated Amenhotep blocks were faced inward and the backsides carved for Merneptah. Thus a great deal of the highly refined original raised-and-sunk painted reliefs were inadvertently saved for posterity. Examples of the Amenhotep III images shown here are now in a storage magazine at the site. Others are displayed in the small museum there. Photos: Forbes

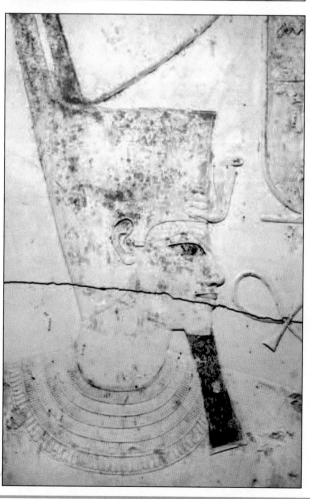

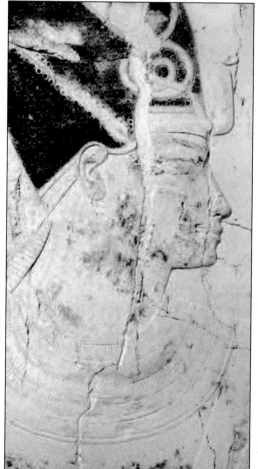

 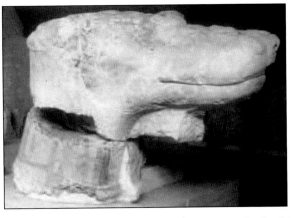 

In addition to blocks of relief-decorated limestone, Merneptah's builders stripped the Amenhotep III temple of architectural elements, such as small columns (above right) and architraves, and sculptural elements as well, such as a number of colossal couchant jackals (head of one above center). These are now housed in a magazine on the site of Merneptah temple (above left).

One of the Amenhotep III stelae appropriated by Merneptah is displayed in situ (above). The unusual abrading of the figures (details above & below) suggests these may have been gilded originally. Photos: Forbes

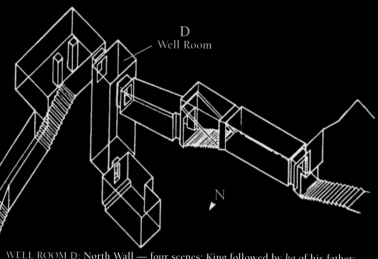

WV22 -The Tomb of Amenhotep III

Only the walls & ceilings of Well Room D, Antechamber G & Burial Chamber H are plastered & decorated. A *kheker* border was begun on the south wall of Chamber N but never completed. All the walls of Burial Chamber H are decorated with the *Book of Amduat*; the six pillars are painted on each of the 4 sides with a total of 24 scenes of the king before a god (most are damaged).

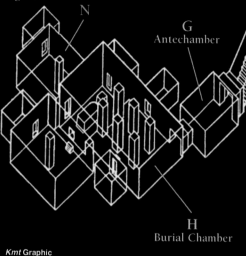

D
Well Room

N

G
Antechamber

N

H
Burial Chamber

Kmt Graphic

WELL ROOM D: North Wall — four scenes: King followed by *ka* of his father; Thutmose IV embraced by Hathor; King receiving life from Anubis; King receiving life from Western Goddess; King receiving life from Osiris.West Wall — four scenes: King before goddess (destroyed by door); King embraced by Hathor; King offered life by Anubis; offered life by Western Goddess. South Wall – King presented by *ka* figure of his father to Nut; King offered life by Anubis; offered life by Western Goddess; receives life from Osiris.

ANTECHAMBER G: West Wall —— six scenes: King receives life from Hathor; receives life from Nut; receives life from Western Goddess; receives life from Anubis; receives life from Hathor; receives life from Osiris. East Wall – six scenes, five destroyed; King in blue wig with applied curls; North Wall – three scenes: King in black wig with applied curls embraced by the Western Goddess; receives life from Anubis; King and Hathor, followed by King and Thutmose IV *ka* figure (destroyed by Burial Chamber door).

Above, Entrance to WV22 in the West Valley of the Kings. Photo: Forbes *Opposite, Scene on the left north wall of the well room (D) in WV22, showing Amenhotep III embraced by Hathor & followed by the ka figure of his father, Thutmose IV.* Photo: Johnson

pylon entrance to Amenhotep III's memorial monument. Originally over twenty meters high and carved from single blocks of quartzite quarried at Swenet (Aswan), the Ruler-of-Waset is accompanied by much smaller figures of his mother, Mutemwiya, and Great Royal Wife Tiye, standing by the colossi's legs. The northernmost of these great statues was partially toppled by an earthquake in 27 BC, but later restored (as much as possible) by the Roman emperor Septimus Severus. Recent excavations at Kom el Hettan have revealed the fallen (and broken) smaller colossi of the king which fronted the temple's second pylon. One of these has been re-erected.

Amenhotep's further description of his memorial structure is recorded on a second, black-granite, stela which originally stood in the temple and today is housed in the Cairo Museum: "*He made it* [the 'House of Amen on the West-of-Waset']...*an eternal, everlasting monument of fine white limestone, wrought with gold throughout; its floor is adorned with silver, all its portals with electrum, it is made very wide and large...and adorned with this very great stela. It is numerous in royal statues, of Elephantine [Swenet] granite, of costly gritstone [quartzite], of every splendid costly stone.... It is filled with male and female slaves, with the children of the all the countries of the captivity of His Majesty.... Its storehouses contain all good things, whose number is not known. It is surrounded with a settlement of Syrians...its cattle are like the sand of the shore, they make up millions.*"[5]

Above, The king presented by the ka of his father, on the south right wall of the well room (D). Note Amenhotep's head cut away in the 19th Century & today in the Louvre, Paris (below). Above photo: Johnson

Little is known of the state of the Memorial Temple of Amenhotep III during the reign of his successor and son, the heretic Akhenaten, except that the structure was not spared in the latter's campaign to hack out the name and images of Amen-Re throughout Egypt. When the orthodox religion was re-established following Akhenaten's death, the succeeding kings began the long task of reopening and repairing the damaged temples. As an act of piety, King Seti I restored the texts and god's images in the "House of Amen on the West-of-Waset." Whether the mortuary cult of Nebmaatre Amenhotep was also resumed there is not known.

But within 100 years of its completion (if, in fact, it was ever fully completed), the Mortuary Temple of Amenhotep III

Above, West wall of the antechamber of WV22. Below, Detail on the same wall of Amenhotep III greeted by Hathor. Photos: Johnson

was being employed as a quarry by King Mernepath, fourth ruler of the Nineteenth Dynasty, a close-by resource for ready-cut stone to be used in the building of his own memorial temple (which, given that king's advanced age when his turn to rule finally came, had to be accomplished as quickly as possible). The carved and inscribed blocks of Amenhotep III were faced inward in their reuse, the backsides newly carved for Merneptah. Architectural elements (such as small columns, architraves, etc.) and a good deal of the earlier king's stone statuary that was not of a portrait nature (for example, colossal crouching images of Anubis) were also removed and reused in Merneptah's temple, as almost certainly was all the metallic (silver, electrum) decoration — unless this was recyled as bullion for Merneptah's treasury. (See sidebar, "Recycling Nebmaatre.") It was that king who removed the black-granite dedication stela of Amenhotep III and inscribed the back with new texts, for reerecting in his temple. This stela, toppled to the ground, was found by Flinders Petrie in 1896, during his excavation of the totally ruined Merneptah site.

By Roman times all that remained of Amenhotep III's "House of Amen on the West-of-Waset" were a few scattered ruins and the two still-standing colossal statues, which were popular tourist attractions for wealthy Greek and Roman visi-

17

North wall of the WV22 well room, with view through a doorway to undecorated chamber E. Note area left by conservators to show condition of wall before cleaning. Photo: Johnson

tors sailing the Nile to see Egypt's "ancient" wonders. It was at this time that the earthquake-ruined northern statue was given the name the "Colossus of Memnon," due to a noise it purportedly sometimes emitted at sunrise, which was thought to be the voice of the Trojan War hero greeting his mother, Eos, goddess of the dawn.

During the Nineteenth and Twentieth centuries, fragmentary statuary of Amenhotep III was recovered from the site of Kom el Hettan — in 1957, the colossal red-granite head of the king in the White Crown which today is displayed in the former foyer of the Luxor Museum. Other colossal heads unearthed at the memorial temple are to be seen in the British Museum, the Louvre and the Fine Arts Museum, Boston, as well as *in situ* at Kom el Hettan. And a great many of the granite Sekhmet statues scattered in museum collections around the world were recovered there, as well. It has been estimated that there were as many as 400 of these images of the lion-headed goddess standing in one of the forecourts of Amenhotep's temple.

Now, beginning in 1997 and continuing today, extensive new excavations at Kom el Hettan — with Swiss funding and under the direction of the German husband-wife team of Rainer Stadelmann and Hourig Sourouzian — have revealed the complete plan of the Amenhotep III memorial, exposed a good deal of its peristyle court (with surviving column bases) and recovered a large quantity of fragmentary statuary, including the fallen southern colossus of the king that fronted the temple's second pylon (see *Kmt* 14:1, spring 2003, "Digging Kom el Hettan: The Colossi of Memnon & Amenhotep Temple Conservation Project," 34-43; plus updates, *Kmt* 14:4, fall 2003, and *Kmt* 25:2, summer 2014).

Swiss excavators reclearing the totally ruined Merneptah mortuary temple in the 1990s recovered a great deal of the reused architectural elements, statuary and decorated blocks originally in the Amenhotep III structure; and these are now displayed at a small museum and in tourist-accessible storage magazines at the Merneptah site neighboring the Ramesseum

Next two pages, Two detailed views of the King's head with applied curls in plaster. Photos: Johnson

Below, Two scenes on the WV22 antechamber north wall of the king with the Western Goddess & Anubis. Wig of the king at left has applied curls in plaster, giving a relief effect. Photo: Johnson

The only undamaged scene of a total 24 decorating the all four sides of the six pillars in the burial chamber of WV22. The king is given life by the Western Goddess. Note the small area left on the kheker frieze to show the state of the painted decoration prior to cleaning.

Detail of the Amduat *text on the east wall of the WV22 burial chamber, showing the evolution of the "stick-figure" style seen in the earlier tombs of Thutmose III & Amenhotep II.* Photo: Johnson

(see sidebar).

Amenhotep's great mortuary temple was only one-half of the theological complex needed to ensure the king's eternal life. The second part lies about 2.5 kilometers away, beyond the cliffs at Deir el Bahari, in the barren, rock-strewn West Valley of the Kings, a less-familiar offshoot of the more famous eastern valley. In this remote place, Nebmaatre Amenhotep III had cut for himself in the limestone bedrock the largest royal tomb up to that time. Today this is numbered (in the Valley of the King's tomb sequence) WV22 — or, as the Theban Mapping Project has it, KV22. It was the first tomb situated in the West Valley (if not the last) and broke with the tradition of his dynasty's previous rulers, who had all located their final resting places in the East Valley (save Ahmose I and Amenhotep I, whose tombs are not known for certain).

The plan of WV22 is based on that of KV43, the Tomb of Thutmose IV, Amenhotep's father and predecessor, but expanding and elaborating on that design and decoration, in a progressive evolution of Eighteenth Dynasty royal-tomb architecture, first seen in KV38, the Tomb of Thutmose I. It differs chiefly from KV43 in its overall greater size — especially the wider corridors and the addition of two double-room suites off the burial chamber, intended for the interments of Amenhotep's Great Wife Tiye, and his daughter-wife, Princess-Queen Sitamen — and in its more extensive painted decoration.

23

WV22 was looted in antiquity and the king's battered mummy removed in about 1063 BC (during the reign of Smendes in the Twenty-first Dynasty), ultimately being placed along with other rescued royal mummies in the Tomb of Amenhotep II, KV35, known today as the Second Royal Mummies Cache — where it was discovered by Victor Loret in 1898. The tomb itself was apparently standing open (if choked with rubble) when the West Valley was visited by the savants of Napoleon's campaign in Egypt in 1799. They mapped the tomb and included it on a plan of the New Kingdom royal necropolis published in the massive multi-volume *Description de l'Egypte*, along with engravings of fragmentary ushabti's of Amenhotep III, which they had carried back to France. Other Nineteenth Century French adventurers cut out small sections of the tomb's decoration, and these are now displayed in the Louvre.

Following this cursory exploration by the French, WV22 remained standing open to the elements and determined explorers and vandals, but was archaeologically ignored throughout the Nineteenth Century. In his 1910 *Guide to the Antiquities of Upper Egypt*, English Egyptologist Arthur Weigall wrote of the tomb that: *"...it lay open until a few years ago, when*

The peculair slanting lines of Amduat *text on the south wall of the WV22 Burial Chamber.* Photo: Johnson

24

an iron door was affixed to the entrance. It is not open to the general public." He continued with a short, but accurate, description of the tomb plan: "One first passes down a long passage cut in three sections which slopes rapidly downwards.... ...around the walls [of the well room] there are paintings showing the king in the presence of various gods. Crossing this well [into an undecorated two-pillared hall, a stairwell] leads down to further chambers, exactly as in the case of the XVIIIth dynasty. This presently brings one to a small chamber on the walls of which are some much-damaged paintings representing the king before the gods. One now passes into a pillared hall, at the far end of which, in a sunken recess, the broken fragments of the sarcophagus are to be seen. One or two much-damaged chambers complete the tomb."

From February 8, 1915, to March 8, 1915, Howard Carter — while on a short leave from his war duties in Cairo — excavated in WV22 on behalf of his patron, Lord Carnarvon, who had been awarded the Valley of the Kings concession when Theodore Davis ceded this in 1914. Carter recorded only a brief summary of his work in the tomb: "I made a complete clearance of the interior of the tomb of Amen·hetep III.... In the course of this work we made the interesting discovery, from the evidence of intact foundation-deposits outside the entrance, and then from other material found within the tomb, that it had originally been designed by Thothmes IV, and that Queen Tiyi had actually been buried there."[6] Carter's letters and papers clarify that, due to the short time he worked in the tomb, his excavation was limited to the upper corridors and the clearance of the well shaft.[7] Carter's statement that Queen Tiye was buried in WV22 was based on ushabti fragments he found in the tomb, although it is still not clear whether her mummy had ever been interred there.

The burial chamber of WV22, with lid of the king's quartzite sarcophagus in situ. Photo: Johnson

During her long-time research in the Valley of the Kings and environs — which she privately published in 1966 as *The Royal Necropoleis of Thebes* — American Elizabeth Thomas visited and "measured" WV22. She reported that the tomb: "...is now entirely accessible, but boulders and debris in quantity lie in the well and its lower adjunct, as well as turab to a lesser degree in the rooms off the [burial] Hall and in the small pit in the last. ...The tomb was evidently completed and decorated by Amenhotep III; inside no suggestion of another owner, prospective or otherwise, seems to occur."[8]

The first complete documentation, excavation, mapping and epigraphic survey of the Tomb of Amenhotep III were begun 1989 by the Institute of Egyptology of Waseda University in Japan, under the co-direction of Sakuji Yoshimura and Jiro Kondo, with the work continuing over the next ten years. All of the corridors and chambers were thoroughly cleaned and planned. Beginning in 2000, in cooperation with UNESCO, the painted walls of the tomb — in the well room, antechamber and burial chamber — were cleaned of 3,300 years of dust and grime (such as bat guano), and the surfaces conserved. Its location in the West Valley, where tour groups seldom visit, makes it likely that WV22 will remained closed to the public, to keep the fragile condition of these freshly revealed painted walls from further damage.[9]

While the scenes in WV22's well room and antechamber (of the king being welcomed into the Netherworld by various deities) are closely imitative of those same scenes in Thutmose IV's tomb — if perhaps painted with more refinement, or at least greater skill — there are some interesting differences. Three of the scenes uniquely depict Amenhotep III being accompanied by the *ka* of his father (identified by Thutmose IV's *serekh* or Horus name, Kanekhttutkhau). In two scenes of the antechamber, the king wears a Nubian-style wig to which moulded-plaster curls have been attached — perhaps to be seen as an early antecedent to the raised-relief decoration employed in later Valley of the Kings royal sepulchers, beginning with KV57, the Tomb of Horemheb. Although the columned hall and burial crypt of Thutmose IV's tomb were left unfinished (the only decoration being on his massive quartzite sarcophagus), in WV22 the pillars of the burial chamber are painted with scenes of Amenhotep III before various deities (as in Amenhotep II's KV35, except with greater sophistication and fully colored); and the walls are thoroughly decorated with texts and figures of the *Amduat*, but rendered semi-realistically in simple red or black outline against a papyrus-colored ground, rather than as the *Amduat* "stick figures" seen in the tombs of Thutmose III (KV34) and Amenhotep II. Interestingly, on the burial chamber's south wall, multiple adjacent narrow columns of the funerary text start out on the vertical and progress increasingly to a pronounced diagonal!

Unlike his principal temples raised to the gods, Amenhotep III's two funerary monuments did not survive intact for more than a century or two after his death. Although his mortuary temple was spatially the largest and most grandly embellished ever raised on the Theban flood plain, it was largely built on a core of mud-brick, inviting the stonework facades to be shamelessly plundered by the elderly Merneptah, who did not have the time to quarry blocks for his own memorial monument from scratch. Even though Amenhotep's rock-cut tomb was the largest and finest created to that time, it was greatly surpassed both in scale and decoration by the royal tombs of the next two dynasties. Promised him by the gods, it is only through the efforts of modern excavators and conservators that Nebmaatre Amenhotep-Ruler-of-Waset has been "Given Life Forever."

Opposite, Well-preserved painted raised-relief depiction of Nebmaatre Amenhotep Heqawaset, on a limestone block from his Mansion for Eternity, reused by Merneptah in the 19th Dynasty for construction of the later ruler's own memorial temple. Photo: Forbes

Bubonic Plague
in the Reign of Amenhotep III?[1]

by Arielle P. Kozloff

Some Egyptologists fall in love with the field because of the intricacies and mysteries of the language, some because of the beauty of its art, and others for the romance of its archaeology and the dream of unearthing new treasures. No matter the path to ancient Egypt, the traveler can not fail to be impressed by the greatness of this civilization — its millennia as a world superpower, its technical sophistication, its monuments that impress the world even today with their enormity and style. At every turn one is so overwhelmed by Egypt's greatness and its grandeur, that the inevitable moments of weakness are quickly passed over — and sometimes denied.

This is the case with the reign of Amenhotep III, one of the richest periods in all of Egypt's history. When there is an eight-year lapse in the written record — despite the fact that Amenhotep loved to memorialize his every action, when there are major anomalies in religion, art, burial and marriage practices — excuses are made instead of recognizing them as part of a larger, darker picture. Contrary to the current-day Western business mantra that change is good, in ancient Egypt change was bad. Stability and tradition were good. And so, as disappointing as it might be to think that the reign of Amenhotep III was not completely idyllic, these deviations from custom indicate that he had some very difficult years, indeed.

The most obvious evidence arises from the unprecedented attention Amenhotep gave to the goddess of war and pestilence, Sekhmet, who, before his reign — even during times of major military action, such as the reign of Thutmose III — was a relatively minor deity.[2] Amenhotep III commissioned more monumental statues of Sekhmet than of all the other gods put together.[3] Aside from his own Year 5 campaign in Nubia, a second small campaign years later and perhaps a skirmish in the Near East around Year 12, there was little war during his thirty-eight-year reign. So we are left to assume that these statues refer to Sekhmet's other realm — pestilence. The ancient Egyptians did not like to record bad

Opposite, Pigmented raised-relief depiction of Amenhotep III on a sandstone block from a dismantled monument of his at Karnak. The "juvenilizing" style of the king's features & particulars of his costuming date this representation of Amenhotep to the last decade of his nearly 40-year reign. Photo: Kmt/ Forbes

news, and attestations of major contagious disease events in Egypt around the time of Amenhotep III's reign are scant. A rare, though indirect, mention occurs in an Amarna letter (EA 11) from Burnaburiyas, King of Babylon, to Amenhotep IV, responding to the pharaoh's report that his father's wife (not Tiye) had died in a plague.[4] A famous, but inconclusive, Amarna letter (EA 23) dated Year 36, to Amenhotep III from his brother-in-law, Mittani king Tushratta, announces the visit of an image of the goddess Ishtar to Egypt.[5] As Ishtar was both a healer and a fertility goddess, both reasons for her visit have been offered,[6] and both apply in the context of the thoughts presented in this article.

References concerning Egypt's neighbors are more numerous. The king of Cyprus complained in an Amarna letter (EA 35) that the hand of Nergal had slain *"all the men of* [his] *country,"* especially his copper workers, and even one of his own young wives.[7] Near Eastern texts suggest that plagues attacked the Hittites at this time, and that King Suppiliumas died in one of these events.[8] If there was plague among Egypt's neighbors, in-laws and trading partners, then we have to take the above suggestions and intimations of plague in Egypt at this same time much more seriously.

While direct textual evidence is scarce, cultural clues abound. What are they? In 1951 Millard Meiss published the

landmark study of painting in Florence and Siena before and after the Black Death.[9] This classic work outlines in detail the changes in cultural patterns caused by a devastating epidemic. In 1996 C. Smith published a brief discussion of the geographic and cultural characteristics of several ancient plague events from Thucydides to Justinian.[10] John Julius Norwich has described the effects of plague in Byzantium.[11] Thucydides wrote a history of Athens that included his first-hand account of the Fifth Century BC Athenian plague, which he contracted and miraculously survived.[12] Many of the changes noted by these authors resonate in the reigns both of Amenhotep III and Amenhotep IV/Akhenaten, and even later in the dynasty. Below is a summary of the common cultural, historical and geographic traits exhibited by these five pre-Renaissance epidemics.

NOTABLE PRE-RENAISSANCE PLAGUE EVENTS

Epidemic #1: The "Black Death" of 1347-1350 AD

The cause of the Black Death has been identified as *Yersinia pestis* (Bubonic Plague),[13] possibly imported from central Asia.[14] It spread from the Caspian Sea to all of Europe via Italy, which in the Fourteenth Century AD was the center of world trade and banking; and it affected other population centers along the Mediterranean rim, including Egypt.

About one-third of the continental population died within three years, but the "Black Death" did not disappear in 1350. *"Between 1347 and 1517, there were 55 recorded plague outbreaks, among them 20 epidemics."*[15] In other words, a new epidemic occurred on average every 8.5 years for 170 years. Bubonic Plague characteristically recurs in waves,[16] but as the non-resistant population diminishes, each bout is less remarkable because fewer and fewer people die.

Dense populations were hardest hit in the early waves. The clergy was severely affected; many monasteries, where inhabitants were particularly closely quartered by nature of their profession, were wiped out. Armies were also hard hit, affecting the Hundred Years War, which was in its tenth year when plague broke out. *"It was no wonder that truces were concluded, which lasted for over two years; and were renewed — despite some local bickerings and raids by both sides — till 1354."*[17]

Urbanites fled to the countryside in search of plague-free land.[18] Formal funeral practices were abandoned, partly because of the loss of clergy and partly because of the huge number of corpses. In a plague the issue is not one of ritual and mourning, but of disposal.[19]

Meiss noted major changes in Tuscan art at this time: (1) the orderly development of Fourteenth Century art in

Italy was interrupted around 1350[20]; (2) the new art that emerged was more ritualistic and *"bound up with an expression of the authority of the enduring Church"*[21]; (3) before the Black Death, the predominating subject of Italian art had been the Madonna and Child, whereas afterward it was the majestic adult Christ and the Trinity, this change springing *"from an intention to magnify the realm of the divine while reducing that of the human"*[22]; (4) deliberate archaizing trends emerged — efforts to recreate Byzantine art[23]; and (5) the cult of St. Sebastian, the patron-saint of plague, suddenly became important in Tuscany after 1348.[24]

Three additional after-effects of the Bubonic Plague in Europe are notable: (1) a sharp increase in marriages, as the remaining population strove to replenish itself[25]; (2) euphoria among the survivors for having cheated death and for suddenly finding themselves inheriting — in the short term — a great deal of material wealth from the large numbers who had died[26]; and (3) longer-range economic depression and famine as a result of the loss of significant numbers of the labor force.

Epidemic #2: Justinianic Plague, Mid-Sixth Century AD

The Byzantine emperor Justinian was almost constantly at war, be it with the Goths or Persians, and thus his realm was vulnerable to contagious disease. The Justinianic plague *"is thought to have been imported from East or Central Africa and spread from Egypt to countries surrounding the Mediterranean."*[27] It has been identified, but not confirmed, by scientists to have been caused by *Yersinia pestis*.[28]

At the height of the plague in Constantinople, the death toll rose to 10,000 per day. *"The proper burial of the dead soon became impossible; the corpses were carried off to a huge abandoned fortress where they were piled up until they reached the roof."*[29] Close-knit populations, in particular monasteries and the military, were hardest hit by the plague. By the end of Justinian's reign, there were no men to volunteer for the army, only barbarian mercenaries. On the other hand, there was little need for an army, since the enemy Persian empire was also decimated by the same plague.[30] Coincidentally or not, the rise of Islam is dated a few decades later, to Mohammed's *Hegira* in 622 AD.

Epidemic #3: Mid-Third Century AD Plague of the Roman Empire

The third plague broke out in Egypt in 251 AD, and from there infected much of the Roman empire.[31] It recurred repeatedly until the early Fourth Century, causing heavy damage to the Roman army. Incursion from outside groups into both Europe and Africa required Third Century Roman military ranks to be augmented by mercenaries and provincials, who were promised precious Roman citizenship after having completed a term of service. At the end of this plague period, in the early Fourth Century, Emperor Constantine converted to Christianity (312 AD).

Epidemic #4: Antonine Plague of the Late Second Century AD

The Antonine plague of the late Second Century AD was brought back by Marcus Aurelius's soldiers returning from Seleucia *"and before it abated, it had affected Asia Minor, Egypt, Greece, and Italy. The plague destroyed as much as one-third of the population in some areas, and decimated the Roman army."*[32] After that time art production decreased dramatically and there was an extreme style-change in portraiture, which became far more spiritual.

Epidemic #5: The Athenian Plague of 430-426 BC

In the later Fifth Century BC, after wars with Persia and Sparta, Athens was one of the world's great capitals, attracting visitors and trade from far and wide through its seaport at Pieraeus. In 430 a plague invaded Athens. It was thought by the Greeks to have started in "Aethiopia" spreading through Egypt to Greece. It killed the great statesman Pericles and infected the writer Thucydides, who miraculously survived and left a detailed account of the symptoms, the panic and the after-effects.[33] Typhoid fever has now been proven by scientific testing to have been the cause of this plague.[34] Bodies of the thousands of victims were buried in mass graves, no one observed customary funerary rites and people fled into the countryside to escape.[35] In 427 Athens made its first expedition to Sicily, to found a new province.

In Greece, production of bronze statuettes suddenly declined,[36] as did vase painting.[37] Vase painting never recovered in Greece, but flourished in new centers in South Italy and Sicily; while bronze and other metal-work thrived in provincial areas to the north and east, such as in the areas of the Scythians and Thracians, and around the Black Sea.

The popularity of Athena, goddess of war, declined and that of Aphrodite, goddess of love, rose. Fourth Century BC Greek cities blossomed with temples and statuary dedicated to Aphrodite; and a new, more fluid artistic-style unfurled.

SHARED CULTURAL, HISTORICAL & GEOGRAPHIC CHARACTERISTICS OF THE PRE-RENAISSANCE PLAGUE PERIODS

1. Egypt was involved as a suspected source, carrier or victim in most, if not all of the pre-Renaissance plagues.

2. The plagues and epidemics cited occurred during

periods of increased international trade and/or military movement.

    3. Plagues, in particular Bubonic Plague, ravaged dense populations. This included monasteries or priestly groups, military and other highly concentrated populations, such as artisans, causing noticeable changes in religious and military activity, and in artistic output and styles.

    4. Panic caused flight from infected sites to "clean" areas.

    5. Mass burials and other non-traditional methods of burial were practiced among diminished populations needing to dispose expediently of large numbers of corpses. Mass graves where there is no evidence of foul play provide circumstantial evidence for the occurrence of mass death by disease even though most infections leave no specific trace upon the bones.[38]

    6. In religious life severe plagues caused a disaffection for old beliefs and support for new belief-systems. In some cases, this meant the death of prominent cults and the rise of new or minor cults.

    7. Artistic representations changed both in style and subject matter after plague episodes. In some cases entire artist colonies died out along with their artistic production. Where art continued to be made, it became more ritualistic and spiritual.

    8. After plagues, marriages increased as part of efforts to replenish the population.

OBSERVATION OF SIMILAR CHARACTERISTICS IN THE REIGN OF AMENHOTEP III
Characteristics #1 & 2: Plagues in Periods of International Activity

The reign of Amenhotep III was a high point in international commerce. Not only were goods exchanged, but human chattel, as well — including royal princesses from the Asia Minor with retinues numbering in the hundreds.[39]

    In the Amarna letters and in other sources cited above, it is clear that plague existed in Western Asia and the Mediterranean. If it existed among Egypt's trade partners, then it existed in Egypt as well; and Burnaburiyas's response to Amenhotep IV's mention of one of his father's wives dying of plague needs to be taken seriously.

Characteristic #3: Devastation of Dense Populations

In most plagues priesthoods were hard hit because large numbers of their members lived and/or worked in close quarters, providing opportunity for contagious diseases to spread easily. After an eight-year total lapse in the written record of Amenhotep III's reign, the first text to appear is the Year 20 record of the promotion of a temple official, Nebnefer, which

occurred in the presence of four high priests of Amen.[40] This extremely important document is not inscribed on a large and expensive grandiorite stela or statue, but rather around the sides of a small, poorly executed limestone statuette, giving the impression that the best hard-stone sculptors and engravers were not available, a point to which we will return later.

Perhaps related to this event is a text of the pharaoh's most trusted and most powerful official, Amenhotep Son of Hapu. Near the end of his life he recorded a long biographical inscription on one of his scribe statues from the south side of the east wing of Karnak's Tenth Pylon. Included is the statement: "...*The King has placed me to record the house of*

Amen. I set priests in [their] *places* [...]*back/after*[...]*in the entire land.*"[41] In other words, Amenhotep Son of Hapu was ordered to make a census of the Amen priesthood and to fill (presumably empty) ranks after *something (had occurred)* throughout the Nile valley. If the last lacuna in the inscription had originally referred to a positive event in the king's reign, then there would likely have been texts devoted to that event, and there are none. The existence of a lacuna at this point in the inscription suggests that the expunged word(s) was (were) dangerous and required erasure to destroy its (their) power.[42]

These two inscriptions — one on Nebnefer's statuette and the other on Amenhotep Son of Hapu's statue — taken together fit the scenario of a closely quartered priestly group being wiped out and their numbers having to be replaced. Therefore, the lacunae probably held words referring to setting priests in their temples *after plague in the entire land.*

The rise and fall of populations is difficult to document in Egypt. The only sign in the reign of Amenhotep III is the exponential decrease in numbers of jar labels for the successive *Sed*-festivals in Years 30, 34 and 37. These decreases may also have been signs of depression and famine following loss of field workers.

About Lower Nubia, which was nearly an extension of Upper Egypt during the third Amenhotep's reign, T. Säve-Söderbergh wrote, *"Everything indicates a decreasing population from the middle of the XVIIIth Dynsty and finally...*[Lower] *Nubia seems to be more or less depopulated."* He cited an impoverishment of tombs from the reign of Amenhotep III onwards,[43] and reported reasons given by several scholars for this depopulation (such as floods), none of which has been found satisfactory. The depopulation of Lower Nubia occurred simultaneously with the decrease in amounts of gold shipped from Egypt to Amenhotep III's and his son's royal in-laws in the Near East, if we are to judge from the increasingly strident complaints in the Amarna letters.

Gold working, including most of the separation of ore from rock, as well as the washing and smelting of the gold, occurred in relatively small, highly fortified settlements along the Nile.[44] These close-knit settlements on one of the world's most highly trafficked trade routes were prime targets for epidemics. And they also would have made ideal vectors for the transmission of disease from East or Central Africa to Egypt.

As plagues wiped out entire armies at other times in history, was Amenhotep's reign of peace forced upon him in the same way a two0-year truce was forced on the Hundred Years War by the first wave of Bubonic Plague? And if disease was rampant in Fourteenth Century BC Egypt, were her

On one of his scribe statues found at Karnak (above), Amenhotep Son of Hapu recorded that he had been ordered by Amenhotep III to make a census of the Amen priesthood, after "something" had occurred throughout the Two Lands — possibly an indication that said priesthood had been decimated by plague.

Photo: Cairo Egyptian Museum

37

Mud-brick ruins of Amenhotep III's palace-town at the Luxor west-bank area known today as Malkata. It is possible that relocating the royal residence to a "clean" site at the desert's edge during the king's third decade reflected abandonment of an urban setting due to plague. Photo: Kmt/Forbes

neighbors also unable to raise large armies? During other plague periods, for example during the Roman empire, armies were pieced together with mercenaries and other foreign recruits who were promised citizenship in exchange for service. If, however, the entire Nile Valley and all of western Asia were deeply affected, a large-scale war would have been impossible for some period of time, perhaps for several years.

Interesting changes occurred among the survivors of plague episodes. Immediately after a plague, Meiss noted, a greatly diminished population exhibits certain behaviors such as euphoria and celebration among the survivors, partly due to an overabundance of goods such as clothing and food, since the needs of a greatly reduced population are lower, and so much has been left behind in the estates of the deceased.[45] In this regard, the question arises whether the overabundant harvests recorded in Years 20 and 30 were superfluous only when measured against a smaller population's requirements.

Characteristic 4: Flight to Clean Areas

If this reign was a plague period, the question arises whether Amenhotep III's relocation of his palace from Karnak across the river and miles off to Malkata was inspired by a desire for a clean site. Malkata palace was demolished after the first *Sed*-festival, its lake greatly enlarged, and then it was rebuilt for the second jubilee. While the reasons may have been ceremonial or even structural, in the light of all the other evidence, one wonders if the real reason was cleansing after another bout of disease. Aldred felt that Akhenaten's move to Akhetaten was an attempt to find an area free of plague.[46]

Once ensconced in the new capital, Akhenaten stayed within its boundaries, eschewing the standard practice of kings to travel from town to town, and festival to festival, instead concentrating on home and domestic life.

Characteristic 5: Mass Burials, Non-traditional Burial Methods, & Poverty of Grave Goods

There is more evidence of mass or, at least, multiple burials from the reign of Amenhotep III than from any of his recent predecessors. Most of these burials occur in roughly cut and/or undecorated tombs. Somehow this seems incongruous with our long-held view of Amenhotep III's reign as one of tremendous luxury and unprecedented wealth.

The largest and most important evidence of mass death was an undecorated Theban tomb-chamber discovered by A. H. Rhind in the mid-Nineteenth Century.[47] Sealed with the name of Amenhotep III and a date of Year 27, it was devoid of bodies when found by Rhind but contained burial artifacts of the king's sister, Tiaa, his granddaughter, Nebetia, numerous other princesses, and a contingent of butlers, guardians, accountants and an embalmer.

Many of the Rhind objects had been made for other individuals, the names scratched out and re-inscribed. Rhind and other students of this find have been surprised by the poverty of goods placed within this royal cenotaph. Poverty of grave goods is typical of plague. A mass burial dating to about 426 BC, in Athens, according to archaeologists, also

The discovery by the University of Basel Valley of the Kings Project in 2011, in previously unexplored KV40, of a greatly plundered mass-burial (below) of princesses & princes (many of them children), plus several foreign women — all dating to the reigns of Thutmose IV & Amenhotep III — may reflect the consequences of plague in Egypt during those years.

Photo: Univ. of Basel VOK Project

"did not have monumental character. The offerings consisted of common, even cheap, burial vessels.... These factors point to a mass burial in a state of panic, quite possibly due to a plague."[48] A. Dodson and J.J. Janssen felt that the Rhind grave must have been a re-burial. This author suggests something similar: a cenotaph, the actual bodies having been disposed of in a more expedient manner.

In 2011 the University of Basel Valley of the Kings Project opened known-but-unexplored KV40 and found the greatly ravaged remains of some fifty individuals, identifiable as princesses and princes (many of them children) dating to the reigns of Thutmose IV and Amenhotep III, plus several women with foreign names. While analysis of this group interment is not complete, it is possible that it reflects the consequences of multiple deaths in the royal harims over a relatively short period of time, and attributable to plague.

Another interesting group-burial is that of two artists, Nebamen and Ipuki. It is rare to find two artists buried in the same tomb, and unexpected in a cemetery populated by important officials of the realm. The style of painting in the tomb is the latest style that occurs in the reign of Amenhotep III. Did they prepare their tomb before the onslaught of disease? Or were they — undoubtedly two of the most venerable artists of their day — among the first to die, and their tomb quickly prepared by colleagues?

There is an unusual number of married-couple burials in the reign of Amenhotep III, as though husband and wife died nearly simultaneously. The most famous of these are the royal parents-in-law, Yuya and Thuya, who were given pride of place in the Valley of the Kings, but their tomb was not decorated.[49] There is also Henutwedjebu, whose coffin is preserved in St. Louis, and who was buried in a rough cave with her husband Hatiay and two less richly coffined ladies, Siamen and Huy.[50] Turin's elderly Kha, who had served three kings, was buried simultaneously with his somewhat younger wife, Merit.[51] Simultaneous burials of elderly couples, where no foul play is suspected, suggests death by infectious disease. All of these tombs are either undecorated or meagerly decorated, despite the high status of the tomb owners, suggesting that there had been little time to plan or that there were few artists available to decorate.

The cache of coffins (at least one apparently of Amenhotep III style) found in summarily cut, undecorated Kings Valley Tomb 63 by Memphis University excavators in 2006, is also worth mentioning here.[52] No bodies were found, only coffins filled with miscellaneous funerary debris. This is a very peculiar, even unprecedented situation. While it may indicate a reburial, or a robbed tomb, it is also reminiscent of the unusual handling of bodies and effects in times of plague. These

KV63 (views above & below), discovered in the Valley of the Kings in 2006, proved to be a cache of several coffins & some two-dozen large white-painted amphorae filled with a variety of funerary rubbish, all dating to the late 18th Dynasty. Perhaps this unique assembly was in some way related to the plague conditions of the time. Top photo, G.B. Johnson; below, H. Alexander

repurposed coffins may have originally belonged to plague victims, for whom the lengthy process of mummification was not possible.

Burial practices changed in Nubia, as well, during the reign of Amenhotep III. According to S. Smith, by the mid-Eighteenth Dynasty acculturated Nubians had begun to copy Egyptian burial practices, including a number of elite burials; but, by late in the dynasty, *"all of the burials are relatively impoverished and the elites drop out altogether."*[53]

Characteristic 6: New Cults & Changes in Religious Affiliation

The sudden blossoming of the cult of St. Sebastian during the Black Death in Tuscany is reminiscent of the sudden popularity during Amenhotep's reign of Sekhmet, who was of minor significance before this time.[54] Her consort, Ptah, both punisher and healer, as well as, ironically, patron of craftsmen, also increased his popularity during this time.[55] Towards the end of Amenhotep III's reign vast resources went into expanding and redecorating his temple at Mennufer (Memphis). The little dwarf-god Bes, protector of hearth and home and warrant against disease, also gained new levels of attention during the reign of the third Amenhotep.[56]

The child moon-god Khonsu ("The Traveler"), son of Amen and Mut, also rose in popularity during the reign of Amenhotep III.[57] This pharaoh's avenue of ram-sphinxes at Karnak probably refers to Khonsu. At Soleb and at Luxor, His images wear ram's horns associated with this god. Khonsu was an ancient deity, often mentioned in Old Kingdom texts as a bloodthirsty god, for example: *"Khonsu, who slew the lords, who strangles them for the King, and extracts for him what is in their bodies."*[58] By the end of the New Kingdom, he was a healing deity.

As yet incompletely understood is Amenhotep III's self-deification sometime before his first *Sed*-fesitval in Year 30, most notably celebrated in the reliefs and inscriptions at Soleb temple. The king was no longer merely the intercessor between humanity and the gods, but a new and unique god in his own right.

The most obvious change, of course, is the rise of Atenism and Amenhotep IV/Akhenaten's vaunted monotheism. It is intriguing to wonder if Akhenaten's religious revolution was simply the reaction of a ruler desperately recoiling from plague. If so, he has been badly maligned in modern times, for he was neither a heretic nor a madman, but rather a terrified monarch trying desperately to save his realm. It becomes much easier to understand why he instituted such a monumental change in the cultural life of his country if the traditional gods had failed him. And it is easier to understand

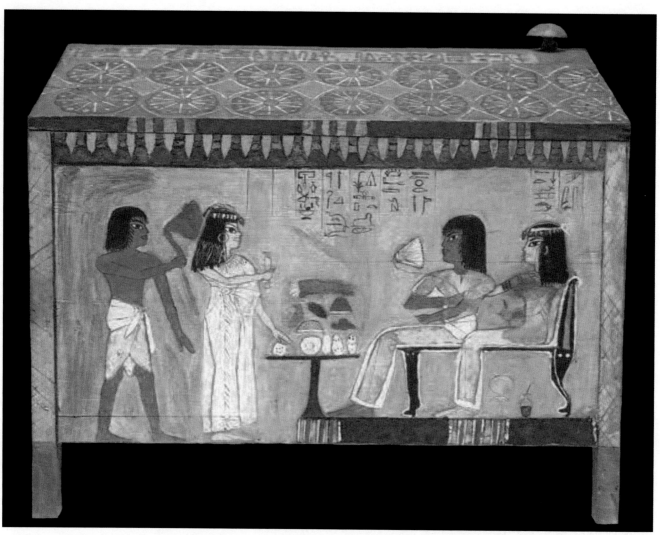

One of several relatively crude painted-wood chests from the Amenhotep III-era undecorated Tomb of Kha & Merit, at Deir el Medina. A chief architect, designer of three rulers' Valley of the Kings tombs, Kha could have afforded far-better work, if it had been available. Childish features of the figures would seem to reflect the "juvenilizing" style of Amenhotep's final decade of rule. The entire contents of the intact tomb, TT8, are housed today in the Museo Egizio, Turin.

how he implemented such a change if the traditional priest-hoods were greatly diminished in numbers. If these priests and support staff, who must have numbered in the thousands, did not die off in an epidemic, then what did happen to them?

One of the few temple officials whose career can be followed is Ipy (Apy), son of and successor to the Chief Steward of Mennufer Amenhotep, who followed his king to Akhetaten, becoming palace steward there.[59] Thus, previous allegiance to another god can not have been cause for banishment during the Aten's reign. Some priests and their subsidiary work force may have converted to serving the new Aten temple at Iput-Iset (Karnak), as well as at Akhetaten, itself; but there were not enough Aten temples in Egypt to absorb all of the priests of all of the temples that were placed out of service by the new religion. And there is no evidence for the banishment of thousands of priests and their families. In a plague scenario, a huge percentage — at least one-third in the first wave — would have died off. So much of the labor force having been wiped out, many of the remaining numbers of priests and kin would have been forced to work in the fields to survive.[60]

Characteristic 7: Changes in Artistic Subject & Style

Changes in artistic style during the reign of Amenhotep IV/ Akhenaten have been studied endlessly, and are mentioned here perfunctorily only because our primary subject is Amenhotep III. Changes in belief during our king's reign were reflected in the art of the time; as W. Raymond Johnson has shown,[61] Amenhotep III's art became more spiritual, more ritualistic. His personal accouterments also changed, and multiple sun-disks became part of his costume. This change is not unlike the shift of Christ the son of God to Christ the Saviour in Tuscany after the Black Plague.

There is evidence that the artistic community also was restructuring — perhaps under stress — at this time. Two styles of Theban tomb painting decorated dozens of tombs early in Amenhotep III's reign, attesting to lively activity in this medium.[62] Around the middle of the nearly four decades of rule, there was nearly a complete cessation of tomb-painting, and the few later tombs that are decorated have walls carved mostly in relief, with very little painting, Ramose's mourning scene (TT55) being a rare exception.[63] Instead there seems to be an increase in painted-wood boxes and chests, executed by artists of lesser skill than the earlier tomb painters. The decrease in skill level of artistry is typical of plague times; it suggests that the tomb painters died out, or at least declined in numbers, several years before the end of Amenhotep III's reign.

Deir el Medina, where the tomb painters lived, was destroyed by fire either during the reign of Amenhotep III or during the Amarna period.[64] While some scholars suggest that the painters moved to Akhetaten, where a similar artists' community was set up, there is no artistic evidence of this, inasmuch as tombs at Amarna were relief-decorated.[65] Only the palaces and houses at Akhetaten were painted. These painters in the land of the living would have come from an entirely different class of artisans from the "unclean" Deir el Medina group, and it shows in their entirely different style of working. If there was plague at Deir el Medina, then fire was the best way to cleanse the site.

The subject matter of Theban tomb decoration changed. Earlier in the reign, tomb owners favored traditional scenes of fishing and fowling, counting large numbers of fat, smiling bulls, and joyous, elaborate banquets full of extended family enjoying music and dance entertainments, and abundant offerings. Later tombs emphasize hierarchical scenes with the king. There is minimal entertainment. The numbers of friends and family represented are limited.[66] Mourning scenes become large and central, as in Ramose's tomb.

Fragmentary serpentine statuette of Princess-Queen Iset, in the George Oritz Collection, Geneva. She was one of Amenhotep III's two daughters by Queen Tiye whom the king made his Great Wife at the beginning of the last decade of his life, whether in a real or symbolic marriage is not known. Photo: Cleveland Museum of Art

In earlier Theban tombs, owners are shown with pet dogs, cats, birds, even antelope, under their chairs or nearby. During the reign of Amenhotep III this practice diminished, perhaps as a result of these animals having been banished, some as carriers of disease, or because of a more serious and spiritualistic approach to tomb wall subject matter in general.

The highly specialized glass-vessel industry also declined towards the end of the reign of Amenhotep III. It died out completely during the reign of Akhenaten, and was not revived until early Ramesside times.[67]

Characteristic 8: Increase in Marriages & Family Size: The Increased Importance of Women in Amenhotep III's Reign

Amenhotep III's marriages to his own daughters before his first *Sed*-festival of Year 30 fit this sixth characteristic. As far as we know, this was an extremely rare event in Egyptian history. The ancient Egyptians shunned incest, and most authors have decided that these marriages were merely symbolic or ceremonial.

If this was, indeed, a plague period, then a much more serious reason for Amenhotep's intra-familial marriages becomes apparent. Devastation of the population has been described above, and certainly among the losses would have been members of the royal family — such as sons and possible successors — as well as court officials. The kingdom needed to be repopulated.

Amenhotep III's self-deification would have set his conjugal relationships on a par with the gods', allowing him to have marital relations with his own daughters (his sisters being too old). This was hardly a matter of base incest. It was the divine responsibility of the god to insure the fertility, regeneration and well-being of his land, and to replenish his people after disaster.

The divine king did not stop with his own daughters in his efforts to repopulate his empire. By Year 30 Amenhotep was *"either bargaining for or already married to* [his Year 10 Mitannian wife Gilukhipa's] *niece Tadukhipa, two Babylonian princesses and the daughter of the King of Arzawa."*[68] These foreign marriages can not be attributed entirely to plague response because such alliances had been joined before the Eighteenth Dynasty; however, the number of Amenhotep's foreign queens far exceeded the norm.

Great emphasis was placed on Amenhotep's conjugal relationships in general. His father Thutmose IV had elevated his own mother, Tiaa, promoting her from concubine (presumably) to Royal Wife, thereby. Amenhotep III had done the same in his own early years for his mother, Mutemwiya.

In both cases honoring and promoting the mother bestowed legitimacy on the son. In his later years, however, Amenhotep emphasized his conjugal relationships as no other king had done before, seating Tiye beside him in colossal statuary and even building a temple to her in Nubia. Promoting his Great Wife emphasized his own virility and fertility.

In Year 30 Amenhotep decreed harim girls and songstresses for the Amen estate, as well as *"free women who were servants since the time of his [Amenhotep III's] forefathers"* exempt from taxes.[69] The result of this would have been to make a large number of nubile women, particularly in Waset, financially secure enough to be able to marry men who might otherwise not have been wealthy enough to support wives and children. This tax, which has been difficult for scholars to understand, makes sense as a marriage incentive at a time when the empire needed to be repopulated.

Queen-Princess Sitamen (above), Amenhotep III's eldest child by Queen Tiye, was also married to her father prior to his first Heb-Sed; additionally she was provided with a suite adjacent to the burial chamber in the king's tomb, WV22. Photo: Kmt/Forbes

POSSIBLE CAUSES OF EPIDEMIC IN THE REIGN OF AMENHOTEP III
Polio

The Syrian doorkeeper Roma shown on his stela in the Ny Carlsberg Museum, Copenhagen, has been diagnosed as most likely a victim of polio.[70] Polio affects motor nerves in an asymmetric fashion causing atrophy over a period of time, and so Roma's withered right leg appears to be the result of polio. Roma, his wife, Imaya, and her son, Ptahemheb, worship the Western Asian goddess Astarte, who was considered to have particular powers of healing. Roma's stela can be dated by the style of the faces and Imaya's coiffure, jewelry and costume to late in the reign of Amenhotep III.

Polio is only fractionally as virulent as some other diseases, causing death in about ten percent of contracted cases, as opposed to ninety percent for Bubonic Plague. Most of the post-plague cultural phenomena cited above would not have resulted from an outbreak of polio. This disease does not transfer from species to species, making both the contagion and the cultural effects less severe.

Bubonic Plague

The most obvious clinical manifestations of Bubonic Plague are the enlarged lymph nodes or *buboes* from which the disease takes its name, but those occur in the relatively few victims who are bitten by the flea carrying the disease. The pneumonic form of the disease starts *"in patients with Bubonic Plague, of whom as many as five percent develop secondary lesions in the lungs. These individuals may provide the starting point for a person-to-person epidemiologic cycle of airborne primary pneumonic plague. It is a fulminating infection accompanied by great prostration, cough, dyspnea [an abnormally uncomfortable awareness of breathing] and, in the later stages,*

The painted-limestone "Polio Stela of Roma," depicting the crippled doorkeeper, his wife & son making an offering to the Western Asiatic goddess Astarte. Style of the stela dates to late in Amenhotep III's reign.

Photo: Ny Carlsberg Glyptotek, Copenhagen

cyanosis [bluish color of skin and mucous membranes]. *The sputum is abundant, blood-stained, and teeming with Y. pestis [Bubonic Plague]....plague pneumonia invariably ends fatally within 1 to 5 days.*"[71]

In an article previously cited, Achtman and others studied the emergence of the pathogenic species *Yersinis pestis*, which they found to be a clone of *Y. pseudotuberculosis*. The latter is an enteric food- and water-borne pathogen, transmitted by the fecal-oral route, and it rarely leads to death. They concluded that *Y. Pestis* emerged from *Y. Pseudotuberculosis* "recently" (in geologic, not historic, terms), i.e., 1,500 to 20,000 years ago, with a median date occurring at 8750 BC. In other words, it is likely that Bubonic Plague was present in the Nile Valley and in Egypt throughout recorded history.[72]

Many Egyptologists — with the notable exceptions of Hans Goedicke and Cyril Aldred — have insisted that *"no proof of its [Bubonic Plague's] existence [in ancient Egypt] has yet been produced."*[73] Goedicke's discussion of the "Canaanite illness" became entangled with other issues and has been mostly discounted.[74] Aldred never wrote a full account of his idea. Scientists spending their careers studying Bubonic Plague, however, feel that it most likely has been present in the Nile Valley since before the onset of Egyptian civilization. E. Panagiotakopulu, writing in the *Journal of Biogeography*, in 2004, made a strong case for the existence of Bubonic Plague in Eighteenth Dynasty Egypt, in particular at Akhetaten (El Amarna). Small samples from the Workmen's Village there give evidence of high levels of ecto-parasitic infestations combined with cramped and squalid living conditions providing the perfect environment for the spread of epidemic disease. Panagiotakopulu notes several citations in her field attesting to the fact that the Nile rat (*Arvicanthis niloticus*) provides a natural reservoir of Bubonic Plague throughout the Nile Valley and into East Africa. *"The species carries both flea (Xenopsylla cheopis) and plague but has a high level of immunity."*[75]

The means of transmission from the immune host to the human population is not clear. Panagiotokopulu suggests that although the Nile rat is immune, new species of rat [in particular the black rat, (*Rattus rattus*)] introduced into the Nile valley by ship trade from the Near East was susceptible.[76] The Nile rat's flea would easily have infected the new arrivals. When the black rats died, their fleas had to find new hosts, moving on to other animals, including humans. It has been shown that *"as few as 20 infected animals can trigger plague in the human population."*[77] T. Schwan is less sure exactly what route the organism took, stating that fleas have discriminating taste in hosts, and might not like other species

Left, Large sandstone sarcophagus of the pet cat of Crown-Prince Thutmose, on which she is named & depicted as an Osiris. Collection of the Egyptian Museum, Cairo. Photo: Kmt/Forbes *Above, Schist statuette of Prince Thutmose on a bier, in the collection of the Ägyptisches Museum, Berlin. Dying prematurely, Amenhotep III's first heir & priest of the Apis Bull was possibly a plague victim.* Photo: A. Dodson

of rodent or even humans. He and K.L. Gage state, however, that cats are highly susceptible, and have been shown to transmit the disease to humans by biting, scratching or sneezing.[78]

Prince Thutmose's (Amenhotep III's first heir and priest of the Apis Bull cult) pet cat was given a special burial in a large sandstone sarcophagus, with inscriptions naming her an Osiris.[79] Since many of her species would have died in contact with the rat-and-flea-borne disease, giving her this special burial and merging her with Osiris, allowed her, too, to regenerate her numbers. This seems rather endearing to Twenty-first Century cat-lovers, but in the Fourteenth Century BC, it must have been quite a serious thing to equate a cat with Osiris — almost blasphemy — unless some cultural upheaval had occurred to make it sacred.

Hooved animals, including cattle, are resistant to Bubonic Plague.[80] One wonders what connection this has, if any, to Amenhotep's founding of the Serapeum for Apis Bull burials.[81] While there are many examples of animal inhumations in Egypt and in Nubia, creating a cemetery for a particular species, and endowing its tenants with coffins and burial equipment, raised it to a different class. Did the mighty bull — the perennial symbol of pharaoh — seem divine because of its resistance to the disease?

Schwan confirms that in East and Central Africa Bubonic Plague is currently a disease of "grasslands" or "sylvatic" rats, as opposed to desert rodents.[82] Thus, Karnak temple would have been a prime location for an early outbreak When informed of Amenhotep III's move to Malkata and Akhenaten's move to Akhetaten, both desert sites, he suggests that these may have been inspired by observation of severe infestations in the green areas. Eventually, however, desert sites, too, would have been infected by human-to-human pneumonic transmission.[83]

Finding evidence of Bubonic Plague on mummified remains is difficult. Once a full-blown epidemic was underway, the numbers of dead would have been so great — the embalmers being among the first groups to go — that the long process of mummification must have been abandoned, and bodies more likely would have been cremated. This is what may have happpened in the case of Amenhotep III's harim, represented by the Rhind burial and KV40 (?); and it explained the presence of funerary equipment belonging to an embalmer in the former.

Even where mummies exist, diagnosis is difficult. Many Bubonic Plague victims — those in contact with infected individuals rather than with the flea itself — died coughing up blood from their lungs before there was time for their bodies to develop *buboes*. If these victims were mummified, their lungs were removed, placed in canopic jars, and the mummies retain no obvious signs plague. What *buboes* would have existed may also have been compromised in the mummification process or simply decomposed.[84]

A new method has been employed successfully in Europe, and shows promise for Egyptology. Scientists recently used "'Suicide PCR' and Sequence Analysis" to examine the dental pulp of three victims of the Fourteenth Century AD European pandemic in Montpellier, France.[85] *"These skeletons showed no macroscopic signs of infectious disease and there was no anthropological evidence that these people could have died as a result of the plague."* Y. *Pestis* was identified in the dental pulp of all of the victims, however. This was also the method used to identify typhoid fever as the culprit in Fifth Century BC Athens.

CONCLUSION

Throughout history plagues have been cataclysmic events in pre-modern populations. They affected every aspect of culture and society. Written records of such times occur from classical Greece onward, but not from pharaonic Egypt. On the other hand, Egypt has often been either the source or a vector for infectious disease, so it makes sense to examine Egypt's monuments and history for more subtle traces of hard times. The eight-year gap in an otherwise verbose royal record, the new cults, marriages, art styles, the changes in habitation and in burial practices, and so on in the reign of Amenhotep III are uncharacteristic of a culture and a king who honored tradition — and therefore stability— above all else. They are typical of reaction to a plague.

If this hypothesis is correct, the first epidemic may have occurred between the textless Years 12 and 20 (probably early in that period), following a dynamic time of communication and trade with Western Asia. It would have become necessary then to commission great numbers of over-life-sized hard-stone statues of the plague goddess, Sekhmet, leaving fewer artisans of high caliber to provide monuments for courtiers like Nebnefer. Infants and small children would have perished in great numbers, resulting in a short supply of individuals reaching child-bearing age by Year 30.

The second bout could have broken out around Year 27, following Viceroy Merymose's Nubian campaign of Year 26.[86] This would fit in with Year 27, the date of the Rhind burial of a group of harem women and staff. Amenhotep III's self-deification and marriages to two of his daughters before Year 30 is also compatible with this scenario. His increasing emphasis on the importance of women — including his enhancement of the goddess Mut's temple at Karnak — fits with a time period when regeneration of the population was an urgent matter. His Year 30 exemption of three classes of women from paying taxes was aimed at the small number of youngsters who survived the first spell of plague, and now were young women reaching their child-bearing years.

Another bout may have occurred in the *Sed*-festival years, causing a revision of the Malkata palace area, inviting a visit by Ishtar and bringing about a diminuation of food gifts to the king. Yet another may have occurred early in the next reign, causing the death of one of Amenhotep III's queens, Amenhotep IV's move to a new capital, his name change to Akhenaten and the empire's forced conversion to Atenism, with the hope that the new god would save the world, the old gods having failed to do so.

The possibility that the contagion was Bubonic Plague can no longer be ignored, and steps should be taken to find direct evidence. Panagiotakopulu notes that it would be helpful if archaeologists working in areas of high ancient population would sieve their sediments to recover small mammal bones and to identify such. Furthermore, detailed palaeoecological and pathological research would be extremely helpful in finding direct evidence of Bubonic Plague. More evidence of unusual burial methods — such as impoverished mass graves — would also be of interest. Molecular research of the type performed on the Montpellier plague victims should also be applied.

Even without direct proof, circumstantial evidence builds to suggest that disease epidemics made the reign of Amenhotep III less idyllic than we have pictured it in the past. Before Year 30 Amenhotep III deified himself — and rightly so, for it is likely a miracle that he, Tiye, at least two daughters, and his son and second heir, the future Amenhotep IV/Akhenaten, survived.

Circa 1365 BC or 1912 AD?

Reconsidering the Queen Tiye-as-Sphinx Bracelet Plaque

in the Collection of the Metropolitan Museum of Art

by George B. Johnson

Three semiprecious-stone bracelet plaques in the Egyptian collection of the Metropolitan Museum of Art, New York, were purchased in 1926 from the estate of George Edward Stanhope Molyneux Herbert, the fifth Earl of Carnarvon. These plaques were originally acquired for Lord Carnarvon by Howard Carter in October 1912, who paid £350 for the lot from Luxor antiquities dealer Jusef Hasan.[1] All three plaques — MAA registration numbers 26.7.1339, .1340 and .1342 — are of similar size and shape; two are gem-quality red carnelian, finely carved in relief, showing Amenhotep III (1391-1353 BC) in ceremonial scenes. The third plaque — the subject of this essay — is sard, a dark-brownish variety of carnelian, cut in intaglio and open work, showing an image of a winged female-sphinx holding a cartouche inscribed "Nebmaatre," the prenomen of Amenhotep III.

Carter believed the plaques were pilfered in early 1912 by workmen, during Theodore M. Davis's brief examination of the Tomb of Amenhotep III (WV22). When Davis gave up the Valley of the Kings concession, it was awarded to Carnarvon; and, in early February 1915, Carter began a re-excavation of that same tomb. Although it had been standing open since antiquity, Carter was able to recover objects inscribed with the names of Amenhotep III, his father, Thutmose IV and Great Wife Tiye. In the rubbish from the well and a small room cut into the west side of the well, Carter found *"...One corner of a bracelet plaque in blue faience from the same series that had started Carnarvon and Carter on the search."*[2] Two additional Amenhotep III carnelian plaques were purchased by the MMA in 1926 and 1944.

During these early years of the Carnarvon-Carter collaboration, their excavations — though at considerable cost — produced only relatively minor discoveries. So Carter sought objects on the then-open Luxor and Cairo antiquities markets, to build a fine assembly of small artifacts for Carnarvon's personal collection; and he purchased other items that could be resold to collectors or museums, to partially defray

Opposite, Very-much-enlarged detail of the MAA bracelet-plaque depicting Q. Tiye as a winged sphinx, which reveals the crudeness of the cutting of the sard, a form of carnelian. Inset shows the plaque at actual size.

Images adapted from the Metropolitan Museum of Art

51

The three bracelet-plaques purchased by Howard Carter for his patron, Lord Carnarvon, as first published in the Journal of Egyptian Archaeology, *Volume III, 1916, 73-75. They have been mounted in modern settings patterned after the silver bracelets of Queen Tausret in the Cairo Museum.*

the Earl's excavation expenses. With Carnarvon's financial backing, Carter was often able to purchase items pilfered by workmen employed by other excavators, and thereby record the provenance of pieces that otherwise may have been lost.

The names of several dealers are mentioned in Carter's correspondence: Jusef Hasan, Mohamed Mohassib, Panayotis Kyticas, Maurice Nahman and retired American diplomat Ralph H. Blanchard (a Cairo-based dealer and sometimes bidder against Carter for choice artifacts). Because Carter was able to pay premium prices for objects, he formed a close business-relationship with many dealers. But this did not protect him from auction fever, when canny dealers set two or more buyers bidding against each other for special pieces. This was the case with the carnelian bracelet-plaques, when Jusef Hasan pitted a representative of the Berlin Egyptian Museum against Carter. Without the need to depend upon a tightfisted museum-director for funds, it was Carnarvon's deep pockets that assured the plaques' purchase by Carter.

After acquiring the bracelet plaques, however, Carter wrote a letter assuring his patron: *"I shall buy nothing unless it is very fine but please tell me if I am over spending. Everybody (the dealers) are sick with me over the cameos and say that I paid too much etc., etc."*[3] The dealers may have known another reason for telling Carter he "paid too much."

The three plaques were first published in *The Journal of Egyptian Archaeology*, Volume III, 1916, 73-75, by *JEA* editor Alan Gardiner. This initial description and a photograph of the objects show them in gold frames, as Carnarvon had them mounted by a Paris goldsmith.[4] This gave the impression, probably not unintentionally, that the plaques had been made *en suite*.

Soon after Carter's purchase of the plaques, his contacts with Luxor antiquities dealers brought him an even-greater opportunity. In 1914 men from the Qurna Village discovered a hidden cliff-tomb containing a fabulous treasure of gold jewelry and other artifacts belonging to three foreign wives of Thutmose III.[5] Later, Luxor antiquities dealer Mohamed Mohassib began offering pieces of this treasure for sale; and Carter became involved, acquiring seven lots of objects, which took five years of negotiations. He purchased most of the treasure for the Metroptolitan Museum and was paid a commission that ensured his future financial security.

The bracelet plaques remained in Carnarvon's collection until after his death in Cairo on April 5, 1923. In 1926 they were sold to the Metropolitan. Two additional Amenhotep III carnelian plaques, purchased by the Museum in 1926 and 1944, were from the MacGregor and Walters collections.

Since their accession by the MAA, the three plaques have been published and briefly analyzed by several scholars:

1959 : William C. Hayes (*The Scepter of Egypt, 1675-1080 BC*, 242-243) stated *"...we see Teye, represented as a winged female sphinx, holding in her extended hands the praenomen cartouche of her royal husband. Her strange floral headdress, springing from a piled-up coiffere bound with a ribbon, reminds us of that of the cataract goddess Anukis, and the generally Nubian appearance of the head is heightened by the massive earring and the dark, purplish brown color of the stone. It is perhaps a significant fact that a standing version of the sphinx of our bracelet gem occurs in the decoration of Teye's temple at Sedeinga in the northern Sudan."*

1971 : Alex Wilkinson (*Ancient Egyptian Jewelry*, 104) also accepted that the plaque represents Queen Tiye: *"Queen Teye is alone on the last plaque. She is represented as a sphinx holding a cartouche with the king's name. The sphinx motif of this type is less usual at this time than in the relief carving of the Amarna and post-Amarna periods."*

1971 : Cyril Aldred (*Jewels of the Pharaohs*, 216) described the plaque: *"...a winged female sphinx wearing bracelets and a cap surmounted by a plant motif, supporting the prenomen of Amenophis III. This may represent the lion goddess Tefnut who accepts the king's name in certain coronation scenes."*

1991 : Arielle P. Kozloff, Betsy M. Bryan and Lawrence M. Berman (*Egypt's Dazzling Sun*, 442-445) offered a more-detailed discussion of the sphinx plaque: *"The winged female sphinx, probably to be identified with Queen Tiy, is couchant and holds in her hand the prenomen of Amenhotep III. The sphinx wears a broad collar and an unusual headdress. This hairstyle or crown appears to enwrap the head and is banded by a fillet. Vegetation springs up from the top, and a nearly imperceptible sidelock, in the shape of an upsidedown question mark, descends over the ear. This lock, seen on other examples of female sphinxes, has been misidentified as an earring.*

"Although little prepares us for this image of the queen, there are winged sphinxes known earlier in Egypt. ...Despite suggestions that this representation is related to the iconography of Anukis and Nubia generally, it most probably combines purely Egyptian imagery with that of Asia.

"Two other images of Tiy as sphinx are known: one on her throne in Kheruf's tomb, the other in relief at her temple of Sedeinga in Sudan. The latter is a prowling image but wears a tall, flat-topped headdress from which Nefertiti's tall crown derives, complete with the fillet tied around it. It is not, however, Anukis' crown, being instead that of an Asiatic goddess.

"Apparently in Dynasty 18 there were two traditions for the foreign female sphinx. The plaque here portrays, instead, a foreign hairstyle which troublesome Asiatics now brought into

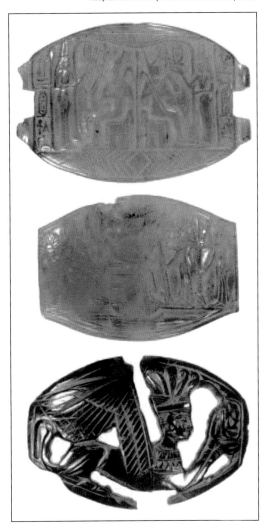

The bracelet plaques as they are today at the Metropolitan Museum, removed from Lord Carnarvon's mountings. They are shown here to relative scale, but larger than actual size.

Adapted from Metropolitan Museum of Art photos

Horemheb's queen, Mutnodjmet, is depicted as a winged sphinx on the throne base of a pair-statue of her & the king in Turin's Museo Egizio (above right, Author's graphic). A reversed engraving of the scene was published by Champollion le Jeune in 1824 (above, Champollion, Au Musée Royal Egyptien de Turin, Paris, 1824).

a protective and guardian status."

1997 : Dorothea Arnold (*The Royal Women of Amarna,* 107) identified the female sphinx as Queen Tiye and discussed the headdress: *"Scholars have pointed out how crowns similar to Nefetiti's headgear are first seen on Queen Tiye, when she is represented as a powerfully striding sphinx in a relief from the Nubian site of Sedeinga and as a winged sphinx on a carnelian bracelet plaque in The Metropolitan Museum of Art. In the bracelet, the plants that top the crown provide a link with the rejuvenation aspects of the female members of the Amarna royal family. This relationship is even stronger when one considers the hairstyles of some of the women on the birth-bower ostraca: their long hair is bound up in exactly the shape of Nefertiti's crown, with loose tresses falling down on the sides. A similar hairstyle is worn by the Syrian goddess Anat."* In a footnote 145 to her discussion, Arnold added: *"The fact that the sources appear to show the tall flat headdress as a hairstyle leads to a question: Does the peculiar surface of Nefertiti's crown in a relief of the Royal Tomb at Amarna indicate hair? In a brilliant find, the relief was rediscovered by George B. Johnson."*[6]

Noting that the differing opinions of these experienced scholars are based on the unusual form and detail of the headdress worn by the female sphinx of the bracelet plaque, is there perhaps another explanation for these varying interpretations? All the above observations are based on the assumption that the Tiye-sphinx plaque is genuine. Is it possible such a headdress never existed and is simply the combination of other images put together by a modern forger?

A RECONSIDERATION

Is there sufficient evidence to propose that the Tiye-sphinx bracelet plaque is perhaps a modern forgery? The three plaques purchased by Howard Carter are all similar in size and shape. The first two carnelian plaques show well-documented ritual scenes, carved in very small scale with excellent, well-finished craftsmanship. Both show damage and indications of wear. The Tiye plaque, however, is similar only in size and shape. Otherwise the plaque is a dark-colored sard, with rough-cut openwork and poorly incised lines forming the sphinx figure and a clumsily carved cartouche. The patina on the figure is perhaps an indication of modern polishing rather than the result of wear.

The evidence, however, that the sphinx plaque may be a modern fake is not only in the stone and its carving, but in other considerations: (1) Its purchase from a Luxor antiquities dealer and unproven provenance; (2) Its unusual headdress; and (3) Its many similarities to sphinx images in a publication that would have been available to a forger.

Carter considered the original provenance of the two carnelian plaques and the sard sphinx-one to have been a rubbish dump outside the entrance to the Tomb of Amenhotep III. This has been accepted by many scholars because it was, and remains, a logical source of the plaques. There is, however, no evidence, except by association, to support Amen-

Below, Drawing by Joachim Willeitner of Q. Tiye as a striding sphinx, based on a limestone relief at the Temple of Sedeinga in Nubia. She is shown wearing a tall platform-crown quite like the one later favored by Q. Nefertiti, with the ribbon used to secure its headband visible behind the neck.

55

Six of the nine sphinx images by E. Prisse d'Avennes on plate No. II.35 of his Atlas de l'Art Egyptien (Paris, 1868-1878). The one at upper left is his adaptation of the relief on the throne base of a pair-statue of Horemheb & Q. Mutnodjmet, which depicts the Great Wife as a winged female sphinx. For the purpose of his design, Prisse eliminated the cartouche & added a second arm/hand.

hotep's tomb as the source of all three of Carter's purchases.

The design of the Tiye sphinx has unusual inscribed lines on the crown. The supposition that these lines may represent hair is supported only by the plaque itself. There is no other evidence for such a pattern of inscribed lines on a royal headdress or crown. One of the artifacts offered as evidence for a "hair-crown" is the British Museum's birth-bower ostracon, in which a young woman is depicted nursing a child. Her long hair is tied high on her head with a ribbon; this would seem to be more a matter of practicality (keeping her hair out of the child's face) than as the aping of a royal hairstyle.[7]

It now appears that Jusef Hasan, the Luxor antiquities

seller with whom Carter was dealing when he purchased the plaque in 1912, had connections with a skilled forger — or forgers. The still-unknown craftsman's first success apparently came in 1890, when an attractively carved statuette inscribed with the name of Seventeenth Dynasty Queen Tetisheri was purchased from Luxor dealer Mohamed Mohassib for the British Museum by E. Wallis Budge. The Tetisheri figure held an important place in the Museum's Egyptian collection until 1982, when B.M curator W.V. Davies proposed that the statuette was a fake. In 1984 the Museum published Davies's findings and the figure was removed from display.[8]

The statuette supposedly depicting 17th Dynasty Queen Tetisheri, purchased from a Luxor antiquities dealer for the British Museum in 1890 was shown to be a fake some 90 years later, & removed from display in 1984. Photo: Budge, *Egyptian Sculpture in the British Museum* (1914)

In 1982, during preparations for a re-installation of the Metropolitan Museum's Egyptian collection, a re-evaluation of the Thutmose III foreign wives treasure-trove (which Carter had acquired in Luxor for the Museum, after five years of bartering) it was discovered that seventeen of the gold vessels in the assembly were modern fakes.[9]

Thus, Budge's purchase of the forged Tetisheri in 1890 and, beginning in 1914, Carter's purchase of the cleverly forged Thutmose III gold vessels suggest that, during a period of at least twenty-four years, Luxor antiquities dealers, to increase their profits, were paying a talented forger to use patterns of authentic artifacts to produce convincing forgeries. The business philosophy of dealers in the antiquities trade was always buyer beware: *"If you know the piece is fake, good for you. If you don't, good for me."* Business was business. Carter understood this, but apparently believed his long relationship with the dealers offered some protection from being hoodwinked with fakes.[10]

Today, as more Egyptian artifacts with known provenance are available, allowing broader comparative studies of style and technique, mistakes in the early forgeries often become more apparent. The Luxor forger appears to have had a weakness that may be a clue to many pieces of his work, including the Tiye-sphinx plaque: he did not understand the less-obvious small cultural details or the one-dimensional perspective of ancient Egyptian art styles. On the Tiye plaque, he completely misunderstood the significance of the crown; moreover, his workmanship is crude in comparison with jewelry pieces from the Eighteenth Dynasty royal workshops.

The ancient Egyptians seem never to have devised a crown, headdress or hairstyle they could not resist adding embellishments to, making these ever-more extravagant. This can be a trap for a forger. In fabricating the Tetisheri statuette — based on a badly damaged (headless) original, used as his pattern — the Luxor forger created a hairstyle (or wig) never known to have been worn by ancient Egyptian royal women. On the Tiye-sphinx plaque, he obviously copied the

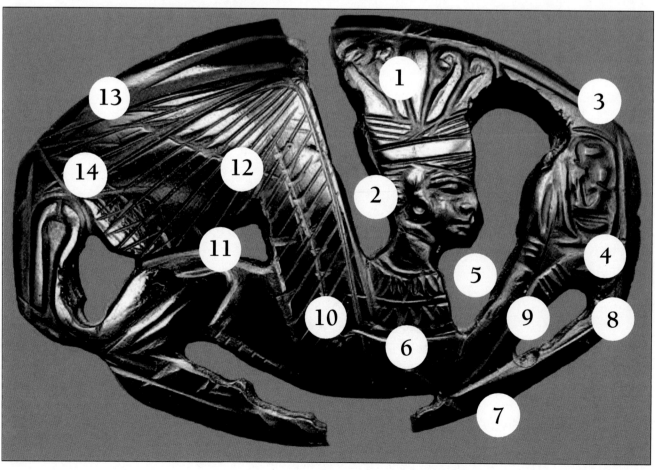

Points of Comparison Between
the Metropolitan Museum of Art
Queen Tiye-Sphinx Bracelet Plaque &
the Prisse d'Avennes Plate II.35 Sphinxes

1. Crown This is the forger's adaptation of the crown worn by Queen Mutnodjmet in the Turin relief and published (in reverse) by E. Prisse d'Avennes. Descriptions proposing that the crown is actually a hairstyle bound by a ribbon are assumptions based only on the supposition that the plaque is genuine. There is no other known evidence that Egyptian King's Wives affected such a hairstyle. All other depictions of this sort of headdress, with or without a floral decoration atop it, indicate it represents a crown and not a hairstyle.

2. Ear and Earring The forger accurately copied the shape and placement of the earring; but, due to the scale of the ear on the plaque, it is summarily rendered as a small lump above the earring.

3. Cartouche The cartouche is a direct, but poorly executed, copied from detail 3 of the Prisse plate, image No. 6 (opposite).

4. Cartouche *Neb* Hieroglyph The forger misunderstood the lack of a line above the *neb* glyph in the Prisse plate No. 5 rendering of "Nebmaatre" and so cut the *neb* as a hollow-bowl shape.

5. Necklace Due to the openwork of the bracelet plaque, the forger was not able to add the pendant necklace seen in the Prisse plate. He did, however, copy the line of the necklace across the throat.

6. Broad-collar Necklace The forger copied the broad collar in the Prisse plate; but, due to the small scale of the plaque, he simplified the design to from three rows to two.

7. Extension of the Arm The forger indicated the bottom of the upper arm with an engraved line extending upwards toward the broad collar (this line occurs only in the Prisse version of the Mutnodjmet-sphinx relief). He accidentally extended the line into the frame of the plaque, indicating the possible use of a file to make the cut.

8. Double Arms Holding Cartouche A variation of the Mutnodjmet sphinx showing both arms occurs only in the Prisse version. The forger combined Plate II.35 details 3 and 8 to complete the plaque design of two hands holding the cartouche.

9. Bracelets These are copied from Prisse Plate II.35 detail 9 (opposite).

10. Wing Base The forger placed the base of the wing at an angle across the body of the sphinx, which appears only in copies of the Mutnodjmet sphinx.

11. Curve of Back Leg The position of the curve of the upper back-leg, that is lower than the curve of the back line on the plaque carving, occurs only in the Prisse plate.

12. Wings The forger simplified the design of the Mutnodjmet sphinx wings, to adapt them to the scale of the plaque.

13. Second Wing The poorly cut second wing on the plaque is a simplified, reduced version of detail 13 on the Prisse Plate II.35.

14. Tail The curve of the tail is copied from the Prisse rendering. The notch at the top of the tail curve has no purpose in the plaque design and may have been a slip of the chisel or the copying of a flaw in the printing of the Prisee edition at hand.

Author's graphic

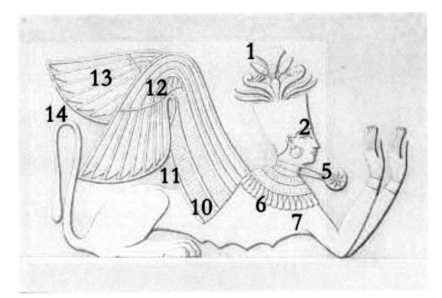

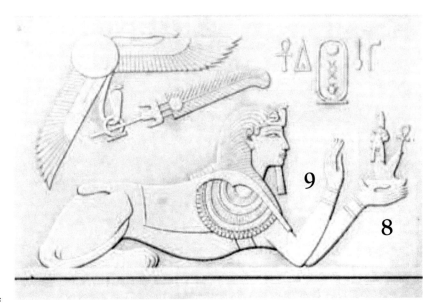

Above, A sard bracelet-plaque from the Tomb of Tutankhamen, showing the quality of workmanship of 18th Dynasty royal jewelers.

Below, Detail of Princess Sitamen, daughter of Amenhotep III & Q. Tiye, from the back panel of a cedarwood chair with gilding from the Tomb of Yuya & Thuyu, in which the royal lady is shown wearing floral embellishments atop her diadem-crown, demonstrating that such were in vogue in the later 18th Dynasty. Whether these were actual greenery or sheet-gold imitations cannot be known. Author's photos

outline of the Mutnodjmet sphinx crown, as seen in a Prisse d'Avennes plate, but then added his own touch: multiple diagonal parallel lines on the crown, that would seem to suggest a hairstyle. These are not supported by any other evidence that such a royal crown or hairstyle ever existed. It is in the details that a forger's work is usually exposed: while the small size of the plaque serves to disguise the poor quality of workmanship, the bit of his own creativity adds weight to the evidence indicating that the Tiye plaque is the work of the Luxor forger.

The Tiye plaque was made to appear to have been created *en suite* with the other two gem-stone bracelet plaques sold to Carter at the same time. But it is sard and is poorly cut with a completely different technique than the carnelian ones. Of the three plaques, however, the Tiye sphinx is the most attractive to the modern eye; and so, in return for the modest cost of the small piece of sard and a few day's labor with contemporary tools, Jusef Hasan increased the value and desirability of the jewelry elements he was selling to the highest bidder.

It is probably no coincidence that erroneously titled *The Tomb of Queen Tîyi* was published by Theodore Davis in 1910, recording his discovery and clearance of KV55 in 1907, thereby making Amenhotep III's Great Wife a celebrity of the day. It was apparently his search for more evidence of the queen that Davis is reported to have briefly examined the vandalized tomb of her husband in 1912 — although there is no known record of this. Carter assumed that Davis's workmen must have discovered and then stolen the easily concealed plaques.[11] He apparently considered that too many years had passed for them to have been carried off during the 1907 clearance of KV55. This opinion was reinforced when he found a piece of a blue-faience plaque during his own excavation of Amenhotep's tomb in 1914.

The sources the forger would have used for the design of the Tiye sphinx originated with the low relief of Great Wife Mutnodjmet — as a left-facing recumbent winged female sphinx with one hand raised to her cartouche — carved on the throne base of a granite seated pair-statue of Horemheb and his queen, now in Turin's Museo Egizio.[12] This Mutnodjmet-as-sphinx image can be traced through three Nineteenth Century publications that indicate it is the probable original pattern used by a modern forger to fabricate a Tiye-sphinx plaque.

A copy of the Mutnodjmet relief was first published by J-F. Champollion le Juene in 1824, as a plate in *Au Musée Royal Egyptien de Turin* (Paris, 1824). Because it is a line engraving, it printed reversed from the original drawing, so that the Mutnodjmet sphinx faces right, as is the case with the two other engraved depictions of this image — and the Tiye-sphinx plaque, as well. The next published image of the sphinx in question is very similar to the Champollion plate and appeared eight years later in Ippolito Rosellini's *Monumenti dell Egitto e dela Nubia* (Pisa, 1832); it differs from the 1824 image only in a simplification of the wing details.

The third version of the Mutnodjmet sphinx — and the "smoking gun" evidence in the case of the Luxor forger — was published in E. Prisse d'Avennes's *Atlas de l'Histoire de l'art Egyptien* (Paris 1868-1878).[13] There, in a plate with a group of nine small sphinx-images from various Egyptian monuments, is a third version of the Mutnodjmet sphinx. The Prisse volume would have been available to forgers in Egypt long before 1912. His image is, again, reversed from the original source, and other changes have been made, as well. The cartouche is removed from this plate, a second hand has been added and the simple lines indicating a broad-collar necklace in the two other publications have rows of beads added. All of these features appearing in the Tiye-sphinx plaque — ex-

Left, Relief depicting Queen Nefertiti wearing her tall blue crown with a headband secured by a red ribbon seen at the nape of her neck. This is also visible on the famous painted bust of the queen in Berlin (above). Bottom left, Two actual gold headbands from the Tomb of Tutankhamen with slots at the ends for the ribbon tie. One was found on the head of the king's mummy, part of a decayed Khat headdress. Author's photos

That netted beadwork was used in the Amarna period to cover crowns & headdresses is evidenced by a relief of Q. Nefertiti's blue crown in the El Amarna Royal Tomb. Author's photo

cept the unusual lines in the crown — can be traced to the Prisse rendering of the Mutnodjmet-sphinx image.

As said the cutting of the opposing slanted lines on the crown is unique, with no known equivalents in ancient Egyptian royal crowns or headdressses. The "floral" top part, more clearly delineated in the Mutnodjmet relief than in the small scale of the plaque, may be equated with the gold plumes represented on the headdresses of Princess Sitamen and other royal ladies of the period.[14] The supposition that the cutting of the headdress of the Tiye-sphinx is meant to represent a hairstyle is probably true. The forger has added this detail to fool the eye and make it appear that his copying of a known image differentiates it from the original, so is not a forgery. Rather, the forger gives himself away by being too clever.

What is the evidence that the inscribed lines on the Tiye sphinx are the forger's invention rather than the representation of a genuine ancient Egyptian royal hairstyle? After all, it has been proposed that Nefertiti's tall blue brown is actually a hairstyle. This began with the 1923 publication of the famous Nefertiti bust by Ludwig Borchardt (following the German discovery of it at El Amarna in 1912), wherein he compares the crown to the tall pompadour hairstyles of the ladies of the French court towards the end of the Eighteenth Century.[15] It is part of the process of scholarship that, once a theory or suggestion enters the literature, it is repeated by subsequent researchers, until it is embedded; and what started out as merely a theory becomes widely accepted as fact.

Is there evidence that the peculiar headdress of Nefertiti is *not* a hairstyle? In an article published in 1991, this author cited three diagnostic features that identify ancient Egyptian crowns:

(1) A Gold Headband and (2) A Tie String or Ribbon. These are visible on many depictions of crowns worn by Egyptian kings and queens; and two actual gold headbands were found in the Tomb of Tutankhamen. One was still *in situ* on the head of that king's mummy, as part of the only *Khat* ever found, although the linen of the headdress was mostly decayed, leaving only bits of cloth on the headband and the chignon "pig tail." The fabric of the *Khat* was attached through eyelets along the top of the gold band, and this has a slot on each end through which a tie was passed to tighten the headdress and hold it in place. This tie might be a simple short string — which could be concealed beneath the headdress, as in the case of the *Khat* — or a decorative ribbon, usually red, which hung down the nape of the wearer's neck from the back of the crown, as seen in numerous relief representations of crowns, and on the aforementioned famous bust of Nefertiti. The headband and ribbon are *always* proof that a royal individual is shown wearing a crown or headdress and not a hairstyle; if the headband or tie are concealed by the material of the headdress (as with the *Khat*), it is *not* proof that what is depicted is a hairstyle, however.

Close examination of the images that were the origination of the winged-sphinx image of Tiye — the line engravings by Champollion and Rosellini, and the Prisse plate

Actual blue beads remain on the small yew-wood head of Q. Tiye in the Egyptian Museum, Berlin. Author's photo

63

— shows that all have a line at the base of the neck, indicating that the headdress represented is a crown and not a hairstyle. The ribbon was left out by the forger, when he decided to change the plaque's crown into a hairstyle; because of the small size of the image of the Mutnodjmet sphinx on the Prisse plate (No. II.35), it is fully possible, even likely, that he did not notice the ribbon detail, in any case.

(3) **The Materials Used in the Construction of Crowns.** This is the most-difficult evidence to categorize, as details of a crown's material are often missing entirely in depictions, or else obscured by stylization. Details on Red Crowns in the reliefs of the White Chapel in the Open Air Museum at Karnak strongly suggest that, at least in these instances, that particular royal headgear was woven, "basket style," of reed material. An image of the White Crown in the Tomb of Nefertari in the Valley of the Queens suggests it was probably made of leather. The small yew-wood head of Queen Tiye in Berlin has remnants of tiny blue-glass beads in staggered (or intersticed) rows, strongly suggesting that the headdress the queen is wearing was covered by such netted beadwork in reality. On a damaged relief in the Royal Tomb at El Amarna, the tall blue crown Queen Nefertiti is shown wearing also has intersticed lines, indicating that it was likewise covered with netted beading.

Is there other evidence that a Luxor forger used a copy of the Prisse d'Avennes book as the inspiration for his forgery? A wooden harp in the Oriental Institute Museum study-collection (OIM 13642), purchased by James H. Breasted from a Luxor antiquities dealer in 1927, is now recognized as a fake. A comparison of a photo of this and the colored depiction by Prisse of a harp player (Plate No. II.70) leaves no doubt that this image was the model for the Luxor forger, when he fabricated the fake harp.[16]

Archaeology is a relatively new discipline and unfortunately, unlike mathematics and physics, not a hard science. Theories and conclusions need to be continuously reexamined, as new evidence and diagnostic tools become available. "A rag, a bone, a hank of hair," a tooth, a CT-scan, a bit of DNA, a hoped-for "smoking gun" can destroy long-held theories and raise new ones. During this process, it sometimes happens that old false assumptions may be replaced by new false assumptions — until, finally, there is a consensus of opinion. This is no discredit to those scholars who came before and attempted to solve puzzles with often-very-limited evidence available to them.

CONCLUSION

It may be sheer coincidence that the Metropolitan Museum of Art Tiye-sphinx bracelet plaque is almost an exact copy of

Above, A wooden harp in the Oriental Institute Museum collection, purchased from a Luxor antiquities dealer in 1927, is now recognized as a fake. Photo courtesy the Oriental Institute Museum *It is highly probable that the forger used Prisse d'Avennes plate No. II.70 (below) as his model, giving credence to the idea that Prisse was also referenced in the fabrication of the Tiye-sphinx plaque.* Plate No. II.70, E. Prisse d'Avennes, *Atlas of Egyptian Art* (Cairo, 1997)

the Prisse d'Avennes engraving of the Turin relief of Queen Mutnodjmet as a sphinx. It may also be a coincidence that a Prisse image was the source for a fake harp at the Oriental Institute Museum. It is certain that an accomplished forger was engaged by Luxor antiquities dealers between at least the years 1890 and 1914, to supply the demand for ancient Egyptian art and artifacts. In 1912 only a relatively few examples of Egyptian royal jewelry were available for comparative study. Even the discovery of the hoard of jewelry in the Tomb of Tutankhamen has not overshadowed the simple charm of a small gemstone plaque supposedly engraved with the well-known Great Wife Tiye in the exotic pose of a winged sphinx. During the many years it has been on display at the Metropolitan Museum, the plaque's provenance has been taken at face value, the anomalous features of the crown sometimes being considered a hairstyle, without the close resemblance to the Prisse d'Avennes sphinx plate ever being mentioned. Reconsideration of the evidence indicates there are only two possibilities for this:

1. Howard Carter was, indeed, correct in his judgment that the plaque is genuine; and so it may be regarded as possibly the prototype for the later Mutnodjmet winged-sphinx image, rather than an amended modern copy of that relief. Although it was seemingly hastily cut and engraved, it does, in fact, represent the figure of Tiye as a winged sphinx, wearing an otherwise unattested hairstyle bound with ribbons and decorated with plumes.

2. The plaque is a modern forgery, purposely fabricated following the publication of *The Tomb of Queen Tîyi* and subsequent undocumented discovery of the Amenhotep III carnelian bracelet-plaques. With those two genuine plaques as bait, a Prisse d'Avennes plate to copy, a small piece of inexpensive sard and a few-days pay for a forger, Luxor antiquities dealer Jusef Hasan increased his profit by a third or more. Carter purchased the plaques as a lot, under pressure from bidding by another would-be buyer. This was ten years before the discovery of the Tomb of Tutankhamen and its fabulous jewelry, a time when the knowledge of ancient Egyptian jewelry styles and craftsmanship was based on a very few comparative examples — chiefly of Middle Kingdom date. In the end Carter did well with his purchase. Today the value of the two genuine plaques far outweighs any value diminished by one of the three not being what it was sold as. Carter/Carnarvon and the MMA received full value for the prices they paid.

Proof of an Amenhotep III/Amenhotep IV "Long Coregency" Found in the Chapel of Vizier Amenhotep-Huy

(Asasif Tomb 28, West Luxor)

**by Francisco Martin Valentin
& Teresa Bedman**

The Vizier Amenhotep-Huy Project was begun in 2009, conducted by the Institute of Studies of Ancient Egypt (IEAE, Madrid, Spain), and has continued annually since that time. The most recent season of excavations was from October 3 to December 15, 2013. An article published in *Kmt* (Vol. 22, No. 2, summer 2011) reported on the first two years of the IEAE work, as well as the provisional conclusions that could be made, in the light of the results obtained until then.[1] In 2013 a preliminary report was published of the excavations carried out in Asasif Tomb 28 from 2009 until 2012.[2] During these years of excavation in the chapel of AT28, it has been possible to prove that the site was used during the Third Intermediate Period to prepare mummies belonging to persons of the high clergy at Karnak, whose bodies were interred in the courtyard of Vizier Amenhotep-Huy. In fact, it has also been possible to confirm the relationship between some of those individuals whose mummified remains were deposited in the chapel during the Twenty-second Dynasty, at the time of Sekhemkhepere Osorkon I (924-889 BC). This conclusion has resulted from the discovery of strips of leather with images representing that king in the presence of a goddess wearing the Red Crown (Neith?).

The 2013 Season Discoveries

It has also been confirmed that AT28 belonged to Amenhotep III's vizier and mayor of Waset (Thebes), Amenhotep-Huy; that work in the chapel was suddenly halted between the years 30 and 35 of the king's reign; and that decoration of the chapel was attacked and destroyed a little time after Amenhotep III's Year 35.

During 2013's AT28 excavation, work was focused on the debris covering the chapel's floor. These excavations began in a mid-level, 0.90+ meters from bedrock. After a month of clearance, when the floor of the chapel had almost been reached (at between 0.40+ and 0.05+ meters depth), there began to appear stone fragments of reliefs which, clearly, had

Opposite, Limestone fragments of Asasif Tomb 28 column AIV.2, with nomen & prenomen cartouches of Amenhotep IV in raised relief. Photo: T. Bedman © IEAE

Above, View of the central corridor of the chapel of AT28 during the 2013 excavations.

Below, Plan showing the stages of excavation in AT28 from 2011-2013.

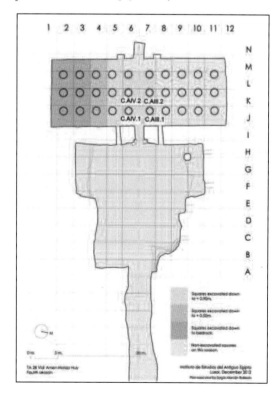

formed part of the original decoration of the chapel and had been attacked, including their inscriptions. All of them were recovered from decoration in the chapel's central hall (in its east-west axis), specifically from the ceiling (architraves), from the two doors on that axis and some of the columns existing in this axis. This destruction can be dated no earlier than after Year 35 of Amenhotep III,[4] since Vizier Amenhotep-Huy was still building monuments and quarrying stone at Gebel el Silsila for Amenhotep III in Year 35.

On November 4, 2013, there appeared in the central corridor of the chapel, at a height of 0.05+ meters above bedrock, a series of limestone shaft-fragments belonging to the chapel's papyriform columns existing in this part of the chapel. These fragments were from the first and second columns in the first row, on the southern half of the tomb colonnade. The discovered fragments contained inscriptions clearly showing the nomen and prenomen cartouches of Amenhotep IV in elegantly cut raised-relief.

Similarly, in the next few days, at the same level of remains, (0.05+ meters above bedrock), were found fragments belonging to the shaft of the second column of the first row in the northern half of the colonnade. These fragments also contained inscriptions showing Amenhotep III's nomen and prenomen cartouches. During the 2010-2011 seasons, several fragments of reliefs belonging to the shaft of another column had been found, the first one of the first row, in the northern half of the colonnade.[5] When the remains of those columns were studied, it was found that they comprised a set (four columns in total) and that they were the only ones which had received decoration on their shafts before construction of the chapel ceased (at an unspecified time, but after Year 35 of the reign of Amenhotep III). These columns belonged to the same row on each side of the central corridor of the chapel.

Texts Found on the Columns
The inscriptions of the four shafts read as follows:

Column AIII.1:
1. Son of Re. He Who appears in the Tjentjat. Lord of the Two Lands 2. Amenhotep Ruler of Waset; 3. King of Upper and Lower Egypt, Ruler of the Nine Bows, Lord of the Crowns; 4. Nebmaatre; 5. Beloved of Ptah...and Sokar

Column AIII.2:
1. Son of Re... He who carries (the Crowns) ...; 2. Amen[hotep Ru-ler of Waset]; 3. [Beloved] of Hathor, who is over the mountain; 4. King of Upper and Lower Egypt, Lord of the Two Lands (He who) joins them; 5.[Neb]maatre; 6. Beloved of Osiris, he who resides in [Ta-Ur] (This/Abydos)

Column AIV.1:
1. Son of Re. One who is in peace, over the Maat; 2. Amenhotep

Reconstruction of the chapel in the Tomb of Vizier Amenhotep-Huy (Asasif Tomb 28), with door-jamb reliefs & column inscriptions indicated.

Drawing by A. de La Asuncion & D. Garcia. © IEAE

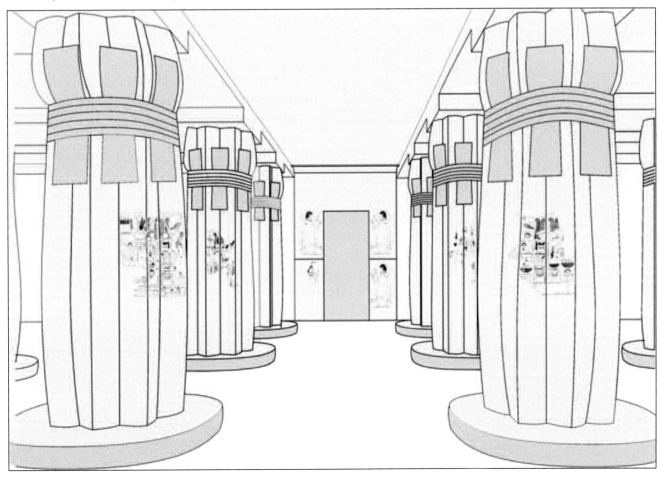

Above, Limestone fragments from Asasif Tomb 28 column AIII.2, with nomen & prenomen cartouches of Amenhotep III. Photo: T. Bedman

Opposite, Limestone fragments of Asasif Tomb 28 column AIII.1, with the nomen & prenomen cartouches of Amenhotep III in raised relief. Photo: F. Martin Valentin © IEAE

Netjer Heqa Waset, [Great] in his [Lifetime]; 3. Beloved of Hathor, who resides in...; 4. King of Upper and Lower Egypt, Lord of the Rites, Son of Amen; 5. Neferkheperure Waenre; 6. [Beloved] of Atum, Lord of the Two Lands and Iuni (Hermonthis)

Column AIV.2:

1. Son of Re. He who unites the Two Crowns of Re; 2. Amenhotep Netjer Heqa Waset, Great in his Lifetime; 3. Beloved of Osiris, Lord of Abydos; 4. King of Upper and Lower Egypt, Lord of the Two Lands, Ruler of Ipet Isut (Karnak); 5. Neferkheperure Waenre; 6. [Beloved] of Amen-Re who resides in (Set)-Djeseret (the necropolis of Waset/Thebes)

Up until now Vizier Amenhotep-Huy is only attested until Amenhotep III's Year 35, at which time he disappears and is presumed to have died. These column fragments represent the first and only known documented association of this individual with Amenhotep IV, with some very significant chronological implications.

The Chronological Accuracy of the Inscription of Column AIII.1

The most important inscription of these four we have discov-

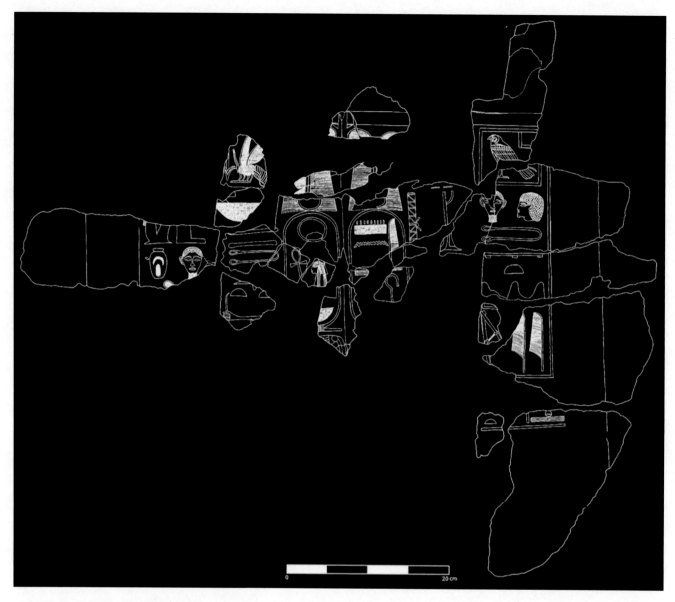

Above, Full inscriptions from column AIII.2. Drawing: Fernando Baéz © IEAE *Below, Reconstruction of the column AIII.2 text.*

ered is that of the AIII.1 column. It is possible read in it the following: *"Son of Re. He Who appears in the Tjentjat."*[6] In itself this text is quite explicit, because it refers to a specific time of the First *Sed*-Festival of Amenhotep III, in Year 30 of his reign. We know that this "appearance" of the king was the moment when — in the presence of courtiers and other officials of the Two Lands — the king, regenerated, received in the *Tjentjat* (Pavilion of Appearances) the crowns of Egypt, as well as the homage of his courtiers. From this moment, the king was ready to resume again his sacred functions.[7]

The ceremony of Amenhotep III's "Appearance in the *Tjentjat*" is fully described and documented as having occured during the king's First *Sed*-Festival. This event is exactly dated to Amenhotep III's Year 30, second month of the third season (*Shemu*), day 27, and is depicted in the Tomb of Kheruef (TT192).[8] That relief scene shows Amenhotep III seated on his throne, wearing the Double Crown, receiving the homage of courtiers and high dignitaries. In front of the *Tjentjat* is a depiction of several royal daughters. It is inscribed: *"Introduction of the great royal children (msw wrw n[swt]) [in the presence of His Majesty]. In their hands, 'nem-set' vessels of gold and 'senbet' vessels of electrum, in order to perform the rituals in the Jubilee. Causing them to be present, next to the steps of the throne in the presence of the King, when in the Tjentjat."*[9]

The last text column, inscribed behind this representation, says: *"The introduction of the wives in the presence of the King to perform the rituals in the Jubilee, when in the Tjentjat."*[10]

It is clear that these three inscriptions — one on column AIII.1 in the Tomb of Vizier Amenhotep-Huy, and other two in the Tomb of Kheruef — all refer to the same ceremony, performed at the same time (a ritual moment).

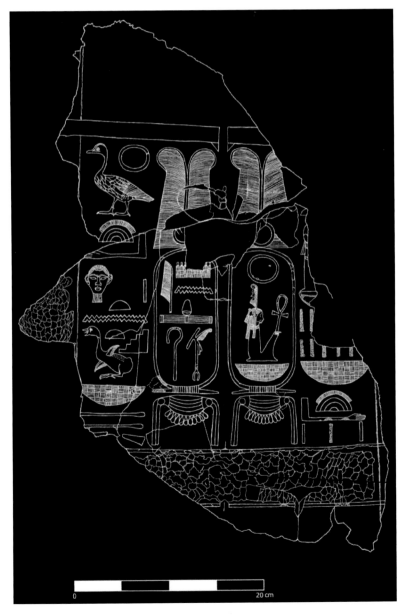

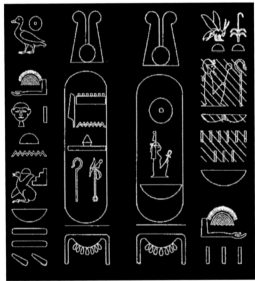

Left, The full inscriptions of Asasif Tomb 28 column AIII.1 fragments. Drawing: Fernando Baéz © IEAE

Above, Reconstruction of the column AIII.1 texts.

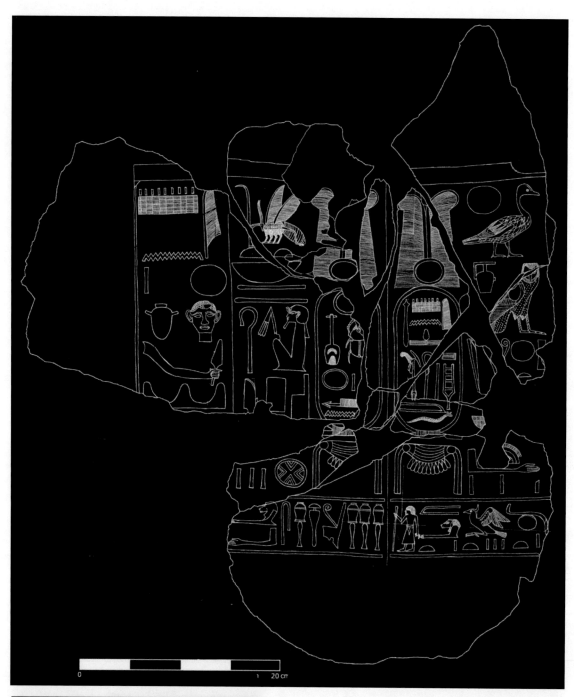

The full inscription of Asasif Tomb 28A column AIV.2 fragments. Drawing Fernando Baéz © IEAE

Below left, Reconstruction of the column AIV.2 texts.

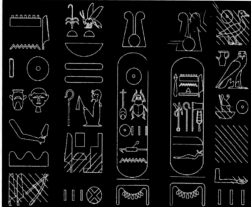

Characteristics & Meanings
of the T28A Discovery

The set of texts collected from the shafts of the four T28A columns constitute what is called a "unicum." That is, a written archaeological document, without parallel among remains known to belong to the reigns of Amenhotep III and Amenhotep IV. There is absolute certainty about their continuity, without interruption or any lapse of time, during the preparation of the decoration of the tomb chapel of the Vizier Amenhotep-Huy.

From our archaeological observations, it is obvious that teams of workers assigned to the excavation and decoration of the tomb of the vizier were active in a continuous

Limestone fragments of Asasif Tomb 28 column AIV.1 with prenomen cartouche of Neferkheperure Amenhotep IV in raised relief. Photo: F. Martin Valentin © IEAE

mode, from sometime prior to Year 30 of Amenhotep III's reign, up to when the work was suddenly interrupted and stopped between Year 30 and Year 35, or shortly after that year. The decoration of the chapel was never resumed after the interruption, so it cannot be thought that these column-texts have different dates of execution. Thus, the texts referring to Amenhotep IV are not in any way posterior to Amenhotep III. Therefore, they are emphatic evidence that the decorative plans for the tomb included the mention of the two crowned kings, both, at same time, Sons of Re and rulers of Upper and Lower Egypt.

As evidenced by these AT28 contemporary inscriptions,

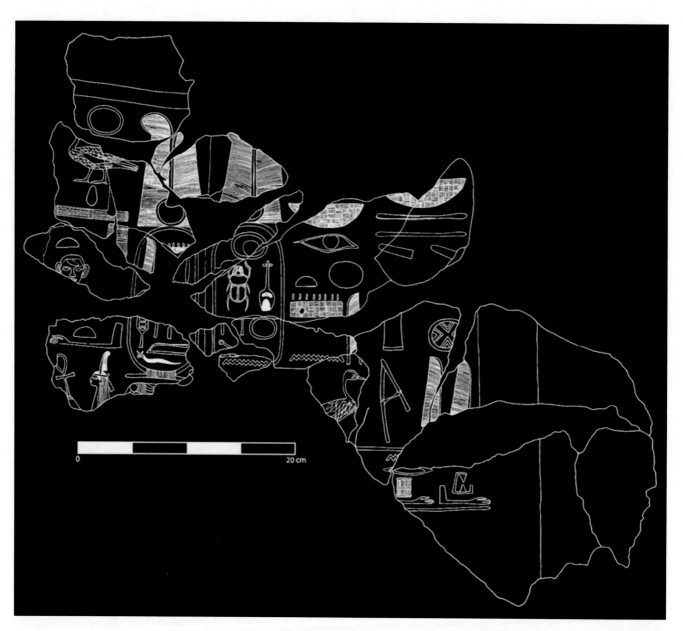

Above, The full inscription of AT28 column AIV.1 fragments. Drawing Fernando Baéz © IEAE

Below, Reconstruction of the column AIV.1 texts.

Amenhoteps III and IV were, at the time of Amenhotep III's First Jubilee, simultaneously kings of Upper and Lower Egypt.

A New Light on the So-called "Long Coregency"

Consideration of a "Long Coregency" between the sovereigns has been largely rejected to date, chiefly because it was difficult to understand how it would have been possible for two courts to coexist in "parallel," each with different viziers and separate administrative and religious organizations. But what is now being proposed is a reconsideration of a historical phenomenon represented by the joint rule for more than ten years of father and son, during a period of transformation by Amenhotep III, when he was consumed by his *Heb-Sed* preparations, by virtue of which, he became a new deified being, the "resplendent Aten." Thus, both kings represented a religious and political fiction, by which, ultimately, only one ruler (Amenhotep IV) would exist, albeit, alongside his newly divine father — who henceforth would be the god Aten-Tjehen Nebmaatre, and never more King Amenhotep Ruler of Waset — still living, however.

In the Theban necropolis are several private tombs dated in the reign of Amenhotep III: TT numbers 8, 46, 47, 48, 54, 57, 58, 78, 89, 90, 91, 102, 107, 116, 118, 126, 139, 161, 181, 192, 201, 226, 253, 257, 294, 295, 333, 334, 383, 402, A.24 and C.1, and now Asasif Tomb 28: thirty-three, altogether. Those Theban tombs dating to the reign of Amenhotep IV are TT numbers: 40, 55, 181, 188-192, and now in Asasif Tomb 28: a total of six. None of them — except in the case of the Tomb 28, after the new discovery — have the names of the two kings, father and son, in the same space, as in the chapel of the Tomb of Vizier Amenhotep-Huy.

A good test of what is said here is that all the known examples in other tombs of the Theban necropolis — wherein can be found inscriptions mentioning the father and son — are always dated after Year 30 of Amenhotep III; and there Amenhotep IV is proclaimed as king of Upper and Lower Egypt, Amenhotep Netjer Heqa Waset, with his father present only as Nebmaatre.[11]

In the case of Kheruef's TT192, both sovereigns are represented as kings of Upper and Lower Egypt, but are sufficiently separated in their representations on the walls of the tomb, thus cited by scholars opposed to the so-called "Long Coregency" as evidence that Amenhotep III was already dead when represented on the south wall in the tomb entrance-corridor, his son worshipping him there.[12]

We can understand, therefore, without difficulty the scheme developed to transform the reigning king, Amenhotep III, into an independent god, with his own theology. To become the god Atum-Re in the form of the Aten, Amenhotep III needed, alongside him, another king to facilitate the cult of this new deity. Thus, he necessarily required that his heir practice this new formulation of political-religious power in Egypt.

The solar cycle of Heliopolis provided the *dramatis personae* for the roles that each one of the royal family would perform in this sort of "religious mystery play." Amenhotep III would be the god Atum-Re, who would deliver his kingdom on earth to his son, the god Shu — in this case, Amenhotep IV. The goddess Tefnut, wife of Shu, would be Nefertiti, spouse of the new co-ruler. Amenhotep III's Great Wife Tiye would play the role of the divine Hathor, the heavenly cow, a divinity very compatible with the sun.[13]

In view of this evidence, we argue that really there was a chronological overlapping of Amenhotep III/Nebmaatre and Amenhotep IV/Neferkheperure, first, as kings, and then in a

coexistence, after the First Jubilee of Year 30: one, as pharaoh, and the other, as a living divinity, at least from Year 30 of Amenhotep III until the time of his death, commonly agreed in the year 38/39 of his reign.[14] Thus, there was a definite "coregency" between the kings, at least during the decade from Year 30 to Year 39, with Amenhotep IV then occupying the throne of Egypt alone after Amenhotep III had, indeed, died.

Conclusions

For many years Egyptology specialists have studied and discussed the possibility of the existence of a coregency between Amenhotep III and his son Amenhotep IV, without having clarified the case and leaving much unresolved, either in favor of or against the matter.[15] From the moment that Pendlebury[16] defended the existence of a coregency between the two sovereigns, based on the first proposal to this effect made by Norman de Garis Davies, the controversy has been a constant one, with the specialists taking strongly opposing positions.

The recent relief-fragment discoveries in Asasif Tomb 28 represent, we believe, the definite evidence for proving a coregency between Amenhotep III and Amenhotep IV, given that we now have documents dated exactly at the beginning of the First *Heb-Sed* of Amenhotep III, in Year 30 of his reign, thus marking the beginning of the so-called "Theban period" of Amenhotep IV: the start of the crisis which would lead to the rupture resulting in Akhetaten. It is, therefore, a period whose research is a priority for understanding the world of Akhetaten and the Amarna "revolution" in its true dimension.

Opposite, The Tomb of Khereuf (TT192) raised-relief depiction of Amenhotep III (accompanied by Hathor & Q.Tiye) seated in the Tjentjat kiosk during his First Heb-Sed. Photo adapted from Plate 25 of *The Tomb of Kheruef, Theban Tomb 192*, the Epigraphic Survey, Oriental Institute, Univ. of Chicago, 1980

Above left, Text in TT192 which firmly dates the time of Amenhotep III's appearance in the Tjendjat during his First Heb-Sed to Year 30, second month of the third season, day 26. Adapted from Plate 28 *of The Tomb of Kheruef, Theban Tomb 192* by the Epigrapic Survey, Oriental Institute, Univ. of Chicago, 1980.

Above, Daughters & wives offering to Amenhotep III in the Heb-Sed Tjendjat, as depicted in TT192 (Tomb of Khereuf). Photo: T. Bedman © ISAE

Circumstantial Evidence
for an AmenhotepIII/Amenhotep IV Coregency

by Dennis C. Forbes

The possibiity of a coregency between Nebmaatre Amenhotep III and his son/successor, Neferkheperure Amenhotep IV, has been heatedly debated at least since 1933, when it was first proposed by Ludwig Borchardt. The arguments in favor of such a joint rule, for a period of from two to twelve years, has depended by and large on several examples of what can be styled circumstanial evidence. This essay presents some dozen of these, in light of the recent discovery (2013) in Asasif Tomb 28 of two sets of those rulers' prenomen and nomen cartouches in the exact same context (see preceeding essay).

Of the examples, perhaps the strongest — or at least most difficult to refute by coregency naysayers — is a small pigmented-limestone raised-relief stela from the house of Panhesy at El Amarna and now in the British Museum, which depicts a decidedly corpulent Amenhotep III seated (or, more acurately, slouched) beside Great Royal Wife Tiye, with a heavily loaded table of offerings in front of them and the Aten disk overhead, the hand of one of its fourteen rays extending an *ankh* (life) to the king. Cartouches at the top of the stela identify the royal pair and the god, although the king is identified only by his Nebmaatre prenomen, repeated twice, instead of his Amenhotep nomen. The Aten's name is in its late form, suggesting that the stela was carved after Akhenaten's Year 9.

A good portion of Tiye's figure is lost, only her lower face profile, part of a Nubian-style wig, her lower torso and red-pigmented legs remaining. She is seated on a garland-draped armless chair and her sandaled feet rest on a low footstool or cushion, right hand languidly draping her thigh.

The figure of Amenhotep is largely intact, most of the original pigmentation remaining. He wears the *Khepresh* crown and a large broad-collar. His pleated garment would seem to be sheer (similar to the one he wears in a Metropolitan Museum statuette), his sagging breast and distended abdomen visible through the folds. The king's sandals also rest

Above, Relief scene in the El Amarna Tomb of Huya depicting seated Amenhotep III (l.), Q. Tiye & their standing daughter, Baketaten, facing one another under the rays of the Aten, very likely recording the visit of the king to Akhetaten.

Adapted after Davis, *Rock-Cut Tombs of El Amarna* III (1905)

Right, Talatat painted sunk-relief in the collection of the Metropolitan Museum of Art almost certainly depicting a thick-necked Amenhotep III wearing the she-byu collar favored by him during the final decade of his reign. Author's photo

Opposite, A plaster head (probably cast from a near-life-size statue), found in the workshop of sculptor Thutmose at El Amarna & today in the Egyptian Museum, Berlin. It is thought to depict Amenhotep III.

Photo: A. Dodson

on a foot support, just lower than Tiye's. His right arm lies along his right thigh, the hand hanging limp beyond the knee, paralleling the position of his spouse's right hand.

Anti-cogregency scholars have argued that the Pan-hesy stela is a posthumous depiction of the king, a cult object used in the worship of the deceased Nebmaatre. This seems highly unlikely, inasmuch as Tiye was definitely living well into Akhenaten's residency at Akhetaten (which began in Year 8 of his reign), and it would be very odd to depict her casually intimate with a dead husband in what appears to be a domestic setting. Rather, the stela most probably was carved on the occasion of the deified Nebmaatre's visit to El Amarna, which would seem to be recorded in another context.

This would be a relief scene (drawing above, after Norman Davies) on a lintel in the El Amarna Tomb of Huya, steward of Great Wife Tiye at Akhetaten. Balancing a companion scene of seated Akhenaten and Nefertiti greeting four of their daughters, the composition in question shows seated Tiye and her standing daughter, Baketaten, facing a seated Amenhotep III (although both of his identifying cartouches have been erased), the Aten shining on the grouping, *ankhs* being extended to both the king and his spouse. While this almost certainly records the occasion of the visit of Nebmaatre to Akhetaten, scholars debunking a coregency have ar-

Adaptation of a 19th Century drawing by Auguste Mariette of the large rock-cut private stela in Aswan depicting father/son royal sculptors Bek (on left) & Min making offerings to their respective king-patrons, Amenhotep IV (Akhenaten, erased) & Amenhotep III. This was obviously carved during the Amarna period, inasmuch as the physiques of both sculptors are in the exaggerated style of the reign of Akhenaten.

gued that the king is deceased in the scene, as evidenced by his separation from Tiye and Baketaten. Rather it seems wholly unlikely that mother's and daughter's hands are raised in adoration of of Amenhotep's ghost, but rather in greeting to him, fully alive, after his arrival at Akhetaten, for a visit to his coregent and other family members. Because the scene is in the tomb of Tiye's employee, it is highly probable that she is set apart from her husband in order to indicate her prominence and importance.

Another evidence of Amenhotep III's presence at Akhetaten is a pigmented sunk-relief *talatat* in the collection of the Metropolitan Museum that would seem to come from a scene with the king represented wearing the *shebyu* collar that was part of the regalia he affected following his deifica-

tion as a moon-deity, Nebmaatre, in Year 30, during his first *Heb-Sed*. That this depicts Amenhotep III rather than Akhenaten is further evidenced by the shortness and thickness of the neck, rather than the long, thin, arching neck that the latter king is typically shown with in El Amarna reliefs.

A fourth evidence of Amenhotep III's presence at Akhetaten is a plaster head found in the workshop of the sculptor Thutmose there and today in the collection of the Berlin Egyptian Museum (AM 21299). Although always included along with the numerous plaster "mask" studies found at the same site, this under-life-size representation of a chubby-faced, thick-necked king (judging from the indicated headband) is a cast of a stone statue-head in the round. That it is almost always identified as representing Amenhotep III

While little of Amenhotep III's Third Pylon has sur-vived, one relief scene preserved on the lower part of the north wing (at left) contains a controversial scene which may hold a clue to the coregency of Amenhotep III & his successor. The senior king (wearing his re-galia seen after his self-deification in Year 30) is shown aboard the divine barque of Amen-Re during the Opet Nile voyage, offering to the god in his shrine (opposite, bottom). Behind Amenhotep III is the "ghost" figure of another offering king (shown on a smaller scale & wearing the Khepresh, below) whose image was re-placed by an offering table carved in now-vanished plaster. Those opposed to a coregency argue that the junior king is Tutankhamen, subsequently erased by Horemheb. A more logical explanation is that the sec-ond king is Amenhotep IV (possibly "hidden" by his own agents, or else obliterated by post-Amarna revi-sionists). Author's photos

later in life is probably correct (since it clearly doesn't depict any others of the kingly personalities of the time: Akhenaten, Neferneferuaten, Smenkhkare, Meritaten or Tutankhaten). But why a study of the sculpted head of Nebmaatre Amenhotep III in the Thutmose workshop, if not to create his likeness(es) for display in the Aten capital, on the occasion of the elder king's state visit there?

Perhaps a depiction of Amenhotep III together with his coregent at that time is an unfinished stela from El Amarna and now in the Berlin Egyptian Museum collection, which shows two kings facing one another, one seated and holding a goblet, the other standing and pouring wine into the other's drinking vessel. The seated king, wearing the *Nemes* royal head-covering, is shown to a slightly larger scale, suggesting his senority. The standing king wears the tallish version of the *Khepresh* crown favored by Akhenaten. Some scholars have interpreted the anonymous pair as Akhenaten (seated) and his putative coregent, Smenkhkare; while others

would prefer them to be Akhenaten attended by his more likely female coregent, Neferneferuaten (Nefertiti). But an Amenhotep III/Akhenaten identification is equally plausible.

Amenhoteps III and IV are represented mutually on a private monument at Aswan of father/son royal sculptors Min and Bek. Unfortunately this open-air relief, carved on a boulder near the Old Cataract Hotel, has been greatly damaged by drainage pollution, but was drawn by Auguste Mariette in the Nineteenth Century. Min, who was probably responsible for the several colossi of Amenhotep III that decorated his memorial temple, is shown offering to a representation of such a seated colossus. Balancing this is a representation of son Bek, likewise offering to an erased depiction of Amenhotep IV (his cartouches also hacked out in antiquity), under the protective rays of the Aten. This private joint-memorial was most likely carved late in the prospective Amenhotep III/VI coregency, as both father and son sculptors are shown with physiques in the exaggerated Amarna style.

Another circumstantial evidence for an Amenhotep III/Amenhotep IV simultaneous rule can be found on the mostly gone Third Pylon at Karnak. On the right-hand (northern) wing is a sunk-relief depiction of Amenhotep III standing aboard a sacred barque, offering to a deity shrine. Immediately behind the king is a somewhat-smaller figure of a standing king (wearing the *Khepresh* crown), also originally in sunk relief, but then cut back and mostly erased, the area subsequently recarved with an offering table. The identity of this phantom second king has been debated, some commentators favoring Tutankhamen, depicted in the post-Amarna style affected by that king's artists. But then, why the erasure? The act of agents of Horemheb (who tended to favor usur-

Opposite, Reassembled blocks from the southern wing of the Third Pylon at Karnak, on display in the Open Air Museum there. A colossal Amenhotep IV is shown (in the art style of his father's reign) in a traditional pose of smitting the enemies of Egypt. It seems highly unlikely that the king, who was busy fomenting a religious revolution, would have gone to the considerable effort — following his father's demise — of decorating the Amen-Re temple gateway in a manner & role he was rejecting. Author's photo

Above, Sandstone block from a Karnak-area Temple of Re-Horakhty, dismantled in antiquity, depicting Neferkheperure Amenhotep IV in the style of the latter part of the reign of Amenhotep III (thick neck, snub nose), offering to a deity, probably Re-Horakhty.
Photo: W.R. Johnson

Above, A sandstone block found at Karnak & probably also from the vanished Temple of Re-Horakhty (today in Berlin) shows that deity & Amenhotep IV Neferkheperure in the raised-relief style of his father (thick neck, snub nose). Above the king's Khepresh is an early version of the Aten disk, with pendant uraei & ankhs. Photo: A. Dodson

pation of Tutankhamen's images) or the early Ramessides?

It seems more reasonable that the second king depicted was not a later addition to the pylon scene (Tutankhamen), but rather represented Neferkheperure Amenhotep IV in the early years of the coregency with his father, when his personal style was evolving from that of Amenhotep III's artists towards the radical royal-depictions of the first decade-plus of the Amarna period. The squattish *Khepresh* is of the sort favored by Amenhotep III, and the smaller scale of the figure would have been appropriate to the junior status of Neferkheperure in the joint-rule arrangement. Of course, any convenient public representation of the "heretic" would have been eliminated in the post-Amarna rewrite.

But Neferkheperure was also depicted on the Third Pylon in a scale that would have been all but impossible to obliterate. On the southern (left) wing of the gateway, the king is shown, monumentally in deep sunk-relief, in the tra-

Below, Another sandstone block from Karnak (& also in Berlin today) shows Amenhotep IV in a further development of his new Aten iconography: the now-pot-bellied, heavy-jawed king wearing the Khat is shown twice (accompanied by his name in cartouches) censing the Aten disk with long rays ending in hands. Archival photo

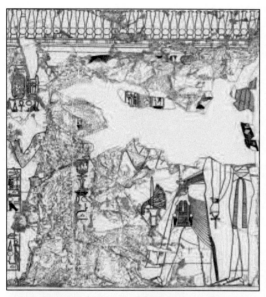

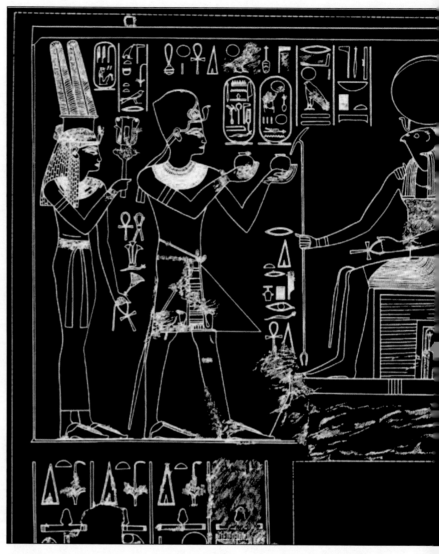

ditional act of smiting foreign foes, as represented today by a section of dismantled Third Pylon blocks reassembled and displayed in the Karnak Open Air Museum. It is highly improbable — if he was consumed with defining and refining perimeters of his new deity, following the death of his predecessor — that Neferkheperure would have expended the considerable time and expense to have himself portrayed on a grand scale in a kingly role of the sort he was definitely turning his back on. It is morely likely that co-ruler Amenhotep III allotted decoration of that half of the Third Pylon to his son and ultimate successor.

Three individual sandstone blocks from Karnak-area monuments dismantled in antiquity also are evidence that Neferkheperure Amenhotep IV was represented early on in the style of the last part of Amenhotep III's reign. One of these, from a demolished Temple of Re-Horakhty, shows him in raised relief with a thick neck and snub nose, offering to a deity (probably the sun god).

Two others were found in the Tenth Pylon as filler. One, now in the Berlin Egyptian Museum collection, proba-

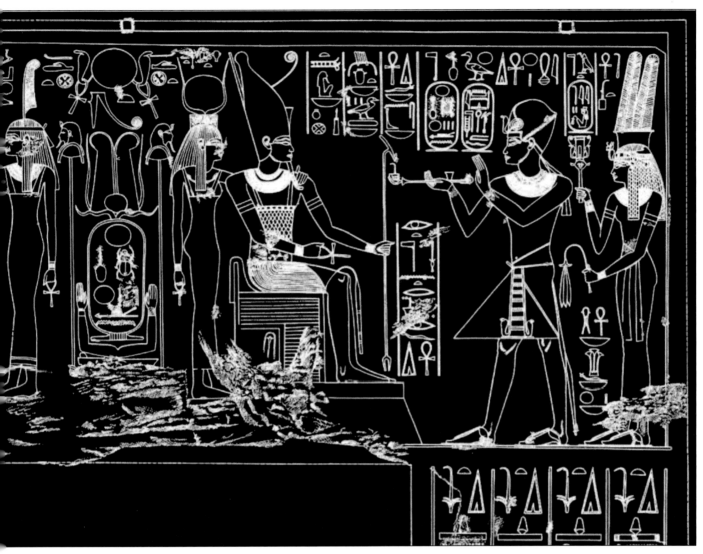

Above, Depiction (adapted from an Epigrapic Survey drawing) of a lintel in TT192 (the Tomb of Kheruef) at West Luxor with an elegant double-scene relief of Neferkheperure Amenhotep IV (accompanied by Q. Tiye) offering to Re-Horakhty & Maat (l.) & Amen-Re & Hathor, the young king identified by his cartouches. Decoration of TT192 dates to Amenhotep III's First & Third Heb-Seds. An Epigraphic Survey photo (opposite, bottom) shows the righthand vignette of Amenhotep IV & Tiye in detail.

Another Epigraphic Survey drawing (opposite, top) from the same tomb shows Amenhotep IV twice, back-to back (both images hacked out), offering to Re-Horakhty (unseen on left) & Nebmaatre (Amenhotep III) accompanied by Q. Tiye. Those who deny a coregency between father & son would have Nebmaatre deceased in this scene (although Tiye, clasping his wrist, is undoubtedly living!).

93

Two private tombs in the Theban necropolis on the Luxor west bank are the final circumstantial evidences for an AIII/AIV long coregency. One, TT192, is the Tomb of Kheruef, steward of Great Wife Tiye, and is famous for its elegant relief depictions of the various events of Nebmaatre Amenhotep's First and Third *Heb-Sed* celebrations. But it is also noteworthy for its inclusion of four images and accompaning cartouches of Neferkheperure Amenhotep IV, shown in the art-style of his father, strongly suggesting that he was co-ruler at the time of the First *Heb-Sed*. On a lintel the junior king is depicted twice (both times accompanied by his mother, Tiye), in one instance offering to Amen-Re and Hathor, in the other to Re-Horakhty and Maat. In a larger scene, Neferkheperure is seen back to back (both images hacked out), on the left offering to Re-Horakhty and on the right to Nebmaatre (who is accompanied by royal spouse Tiye). Coregency naysayers would have Nebmaatre deceased in this instance, despite the fact that the obviously still-living Tiye is shown clasping her husband's wrist. Neferkheperure would not be offering to a ghost in this instance (nor even to a statue), but rather to the living deity Nebmaatre.

The second tomb, TT55, is that of Vizier Ramose, and is unique in that it depicts Neferkheperure Amenhotep IV in the elegant raised-relief style of the third Amenhotep, shown on a large scale enthroned within a pavilion and accompanied by the goddess Maat; and in a parallel scene is the first instance of a Window of Appearances depiction of the same king, now Akhenaten, accompanied by his Great Wife, Nefertiti, both under the protective descending rays of the Aten. The raised-relief carving is in the radical style seen at the Karnak Aten temple and, later, at El Amarna. Thus, in TT55, it is likely that Neferkheperure Amenhotep/Akhenaten is shown early in the coregency and again perhaps at the beginning of his sole reign.

One or even a couple of these cited examples might be dismissed out of hand as lacking definitive proof of anything; but so many (over a dozen) examples surely are arguments that an Amenhotep III/Amenhotep IV coregency is not only likely but rather very probable, even without the newly discovered "smoking gun" in Asasif Tomb 28.

Chips Off Old Statues

Carving the Amenhotep IV Colossi of Karnak

by Arielle P. Kozloff

The colossal sandstone statues made for Amenhotep IV before he became Akhenaten are nearly legendary. Remains of around thirty were found at Karnak in the 1920s, and in subsequent excavations.[1] When intact, they reached some six meters (twenty feet) in height. Today they exist as fragments, mainly heads, faces and busts. It seems that the statues stood in the Osiride pose with massive back pillars, arms crossed against the chest holding the crook and flail. The legs of two of the more complete ones are together rather than in stride. The other largely complete figure is often referred to as nude, sexless or female and its right leg is slightly advanced.

In the decades since they were discovered, these ungainly statues have dominated the modern image of this king, intriguing and puzzling scholars and amateurs alike. Their bizarre physical features — abnormally long chin, attenuated fingers, sunken chest and wide hips — have inspired wide-ranging speculation about Amenhotep IV/Akhenaten's medical issues, two of the most popular diagnoses being acromegaly and Marfan's syndrome, both associated with psychological disabilities.

How closely the huge figures represent the king's actual physical features, however, is not known. Amenhotep IV's colossi are not scientific records, but works of art. The degree to which they can be taken as true likenesses on which scientific statements can be based is called into question by his later portraits, such as the sublime yellow-stone seated figure in the Louvre (N831 = AF 109), which shows him paunchy but hardly misshapen. No one has yet explained a disease which might cause striking deformities in a young man, but effect a miraculous self-cure in middle age.

To complicate matters more, the colossi are not original to the reign of Amenhotep IV, but were usurped from a previous king and completely revamped. That this has gone nearly unnoticed until relatively recently is understandable for several reasons. First, when on exhibition the statues are

Opposite, Comparative profiles of an Amenhotep IV sandstone colossus from Karnak with the quartzite life-size standing statue of Amenhotep III, found in the Luxor Cachette. Graphic by Steven Probert

97

Above, The Louvre's yellow-quartzite statue of Akhenaten in the later style of his reign, showing him paunchy but not misshapen. Right, JE 49529, the most intact of the Amenhotep IV Karnak colossi, today displayed in the Amarna Gallery of the Cairo Museum (Photo: Kmt/Forbes), *has the anomaly of two navels, detail below*

(Author's photo)

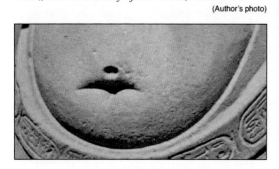

so tall the most idiosyncratic features — the faces and torsos — are well above eye level, too distant to be easily seen. And second, most Egyptologists are interested in language, history and field archaeology. Few, like Rita Freed of the Museum of Fine Arts, Boston, are intrigued by the surface details of stone sculptures, such as tool marks, degrees of polish and traces of decoration.

After examining Cairo's statues in the 1990s, as they lay in Cairo's restoration lab, Freed published a few of her observations, including several remarks about areas of the statues which had undergone secondary carving.[2] For example, JE 49529 bears two navels of entirely different shapes. From a distance the higher navel, a mere cylindrical hole, looks like a simple defect in the stone. But Freed was clear that it is indeed a purposely carved navel.

Freed's revelations struck this author as remarkable. After discussing her work with her and learning that she had no time to pursue the subject further, I proceeded to seek answers to the obvious questions. If these statues were recut, whose were they originally? Where did they stand?

In 2008, under the aegis of Dr. Zahi Hawass, his assistant, Dr. Janice Kamrin, and director of the Cairo Museum, Dr. Waafa el Sedak, I was given full access to the statues in the Cairo and Luxor museums. By that time the Cairo examples had been conserved, reassembled and installed in Room 3 of the Museum's ground floor, in such a way as to recreate their original height. The Museum provided me with a movable electric lift, so that I could study and photograph each statue from just inches away. Among the Cairo and Luxor statues, I found close to eighty points of evidence of recarving. Only a few can be summarized here; they are grouped according to general characteristics I have observed on re-cut statuary from the New Kingdom through Ptolemaic times.[3]

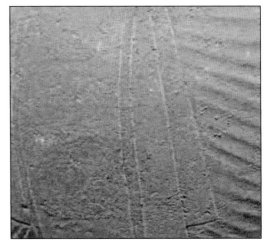

Above & top, Two very different carving styles are apparent on JE 49529: the delicate rendering of the shendyt *kilt & the coarse angularity of the rest of the statue. Below, The elegant pleats of the same* shendyt *kilt disappearing behind dozens of crude chisel marks.*
Author's photos

Two Radically Different Styles on the Same Statue
One remarkable feature is visible on JE 49529 from a distance: the work of two different sculptors resulting in two different styles of carving. One is characterized by the shallow, graceful, sweeping pleats of the *shendyt* kilt and the other by the coarse angularity of carving on the rest of the statue, for example, the sloppy, deep, butchery of the hieroglyphic signs in the cartouches on the belt. That the vulgar style is carved on top of the more delicate one is obvious on the proper left hip, where the elegant, beautifully carved kilt pleats gradually disappear under a flat-planed area pocked with dozens of crude chisel strokes. The pleats gradually reappear behind this flattened area.

It is important to remember throughout this discussion that in antiquity all of the secondary changes were well

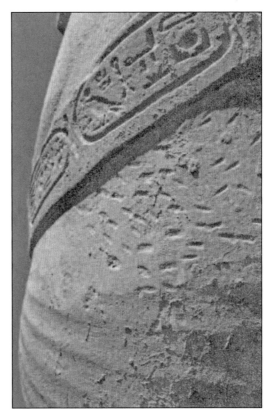

The Amenhotep IV cartouche of the belt of JE 49529 runs past the break at the back of the hip, indicating the belt had been recarved after damage to the statue. Below, The Khat *headcovering of JE 49529 (below) terminates well above the shoulders, rather than draping somewhat lower, as seen in a fragmentary Akhenaten ushabti in the collection of the Metropolitan Museum (bottom).* Author's photos

camouflaged with plaster, gesso and paint.[4] The differences in style are apparent now that almost all of the surface decoration has vanished.

Carving Extends Past Area of Damage

This characteristic and the next deal with work done to the statue after it had been damaged. On JE 49529's *shendyt* belt, the last Amenhotep IV cartouche runs past the break at the back of the hip. This means that the belt was recarved after damage had occurred.

Damage Losses Require Compromise in the Proportions of Attributes

JE 49529 wears a Double Crown on top of a *Khat* headcovering, which has a shape somewhat similar to the striped *nemes* headcloth, except that it lacks lappets in the front and is bag-shaped at the back. On representations of Amenhotep IV/Akhenaten as well as Nefertiti, the *Khat* normally drapes onto the shoulders. On this statue the sack shape terminates well above the shoulders. In fact, it finishes at about chin level, where the neck broke apparently when the statue toppled.[5]

A great deal of stone in the area of the neck was lost. If this statue was wearing a *Nemes* headcloth under its Double Crown, like many of the other statues in this group (for example JE 98915) enough stone would have remained at the back of the head to salvage this abbreviated *Khat* and chisel away the *Nemes* lappets.

The bust (R47) currently on view in the Luxor Museum appears to have originally worn a *Nemes* headcloth, which was in process of being chiseled and filed down; but the process was stopped midway and the remains of the lappets are quite visible.

Strange Gaps and Quick Fixes

On JE 49529 the remaining right arm juts out awkwardly from a sunken chest. A close view from underneath reveals that a great deal of stone was roughly hacked away, leaving sharp angles on the flesh and quite a large a gap between the arms and torso.[6] Where the hands cross each other, a thickness of stone (formerly part of the corpulent torso) connects them to the sunken chest, a good strategic move to anchor the weight of the arms and attributes at a central point. In Roman sculpture this brace for a heavy sculptural element is called a strut. Struts are completely out of the norm for Osiride statues, and are rare in Egyptian art in general.

The sculptor hid the brace by incorporating it into the wrists and hands, camouflaging it by lengthening the statue's fingers. This is where he got into trouble. The third phalanges (finger segments closest to the hand) became disproportionately long for the size of the hand, so he cut finger nails into

Detail of one arm of JE 49529, showing that it juts out from the torso in a manner not seen in Osiride statues, & suggesting a considerable amount of stone was cut away in the recarving of the Amenhotep IV colossus. **Author's photo**

Fingernails mistakenly cut into the 3rd phalanges of the right hand of the JE 49529 colossus. Author's photo

Above, The exaggerated thickness of the jewelry elements of the colossi (JE 49529, above) resulted from the sculpture's original corpulent arms being cut back to conform to Amenhotep IV's image. Author's photo

Left, A typical Osiride colossus, of Rameses II in the Ramesseum. Photo: Kmt/Forbes

The bust fragment of colossus R47 (in the Luxor Museum) shows a confusion over details, with the recarved left hand being given a new thumb without the original thumb being removed (inset). The bust also demonstrates some uncertainy in the tentative recarving of the Nemes headcovering. **Authors photos**

The rectangular protrusion on the torso of JE 49529 (inset) is probaby to be interpreted as a pendant which would have been flush with the original surface of the statue, so shows how much stone was cut away in the recarving. A similar pendant (but its original gilding gone today) is to be seen on the Amenhotep III statue from the Luxor Cachette. Author's photos

the knuckles. Again this was done hastily and summarily with the chisel, but would have been enhanced with paint. These redesigned fingers appear nearly normal from the side, unless the viewer notices that the original middle and first phalanges (the finger tips) are still in place, neatly curled against the body grasping the crook and flail. The fists, wrists and arms were too beefy for the new king's image, so their exterior surfaces were shaved down. This left the backs of the hands paper thin, nearly on a plane with the surfaces of the attributes they hold. This is impossible to see from the normal observer's height and distance, and in antiquity was easily hidden under paint.

Reducing the size of the wrists and arms left abnormally thick jewelry — armlets and wrist bands. Resizing these elements involved nothing more than sawing flat their outer faces. Traces of rough saw-marks are evident on the faces of all of the wrist bands and armlets worn by this group of statues.[7]

The edges of many of these adornments show two stages of carving, as seen on an armlet on the proper right arm of Luxor bust R47. The outermost centimeter has a nicely finished edge, perhaps the thickness of the original armlet. The two centimeters closest to the surface of the arm, however, are roughly cut, suggesting the amount of stone hacked away during the process of trimming down the arms.

Colossus fragment TR 29.2.49 (above) demonstrates the extent to which the uraeus is cut back and the Nemes bites into the skull. A detail of JE 99065 (below) shows how the eyebrow has been reworked & the sides of the nose have been shaved down to make it appear longer. Author's photos

Confusion Over Details

The fist of Luxor bust R47 is not as thin as JE 49529's. It preserves some flesh around the attributes, but the proper left hand was cut deeply into the slimmed-down chest, and with it a new thumb. The original thumb was not removed, however, so the left hand appears to have two thumbs or else to be holding some undefined object. Confusion over the identification of details is a typical result of recarving.

On the front of JE 49529 is a roughly cut, rectangular protrusion of stone crudely inscribed with the king's name.[8] It is about the same thickness as the width of the gap between the statue's arms and its chest. Therefore it equals the amount of flesh carved away from the original statue's torso. Such a protuberance, apparently unique to this reign, has neither a tradition in Egyptian art nor any recognizable *raison d'être*. Because it is similar in size and shape to the chunky armlets and wristlets described above, it must have been read by viewers as a pectoral, and the supporting chain or necklace could easily have been painted on. Amenhotep III's life-size red-quartzite statue from the Luxor Cachette originally wore a pectoral at about this height.[9]

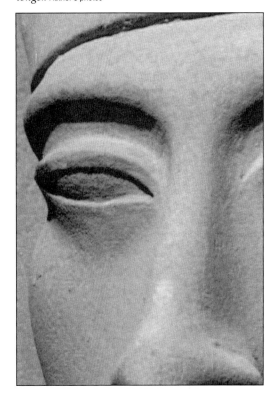

Left, The red-quartzite statue of a statue of Amenhotep III, from late in his reign, found in the Luxor Temple Cachette & today in the Luxor Museum. Author's photo

Above, Possible configuration of a colossal Osiride statue of Amenhotep III before re-cutting. Kmt Graphic

The Ultimate Plastic Surgery:
Lengthening a Short, Round Face

Amenhotep IV's face is unusually long and is emphasized by his attenuated chin. Forming such a shape out of what could only have been a much shorter, rounder face required tremendous ingenuity. The sculptor undertook the following procedures, as seen on Cairo TR 29.5.49.1:

1) He moved the root of the nose higher, making it longer from top to tip by gouging the area above the inside corners of the eyes leaving an unnatural ridge; 2) he shaved down the sides of the nose to make it appear longer; and 3) he re-carved the top of the beard, so that it no longer overlapped the chin but started underneath it. The first few horizontal bands of the former beard turned into a narrow chin the width of the root of the original beard.

Above & below, Graphics by Steven Probert merging JE 49529 and Luxor Museum's red-quartzite statue of Amenhotep III.

The fronts of many of the headdresses show signs of having been cut back to accommodate a resized face. This is most obvious on the sides of the uraei close to where they attach to the headdress. Luxor J 53 shows rough hacking at least a centimeter in depth at the uraeus's base.[10] The brow band also bites into the skull — which is common among

these statues — rather than resting neatly against it, as is normal in unrecut statues.[11]

Variations in Polish Where There Should Be None
The surface textures on the nose and the cheeks of JE 49529 (for one) vary enormously and have developed different patinas, for example, a blue/gray tinge on the top and sides of the nose and a brown tinge on the cheeks. This results from using two grades of sanding, possibly to cover smaller chisel marks on the nose and heavier ones on the cheeks and sides of the face. This never (I hesitate to use the word) happened in traditional Egyptian royal portraiture. Differences in polish between the eyebrow and the face or the eyeball and the skin are common, but not between two areas on the same skin surface, unless the portrait has been recut.

Structures That Are Shadows of Their Former Selves
It is clear that these portraits once had eyebrows, but what remains of an eyebrow today on most of them has the appearance of a mountain ridge that has been bull-dozed nearly flat, as on Cairo's JE 99065. In some cases a bit of the ridge remains at one edge or another, but the structure is murky and ill-defined.[12] This is out of character for Egyptian portraits, unless recut.

The treatment of nipples of these statues varies greatly. Some are nearly completely erased, while others retain more of their original shape. Variations can be found on the same statue. Cairo JE 99065's right nipple is hardly visible, while the left retains more of its original shape.

Whose Statues Were They Originally?
Putting back all the stone that was cut away results in a corpulent Osiride-type figure with a high cylindrical navel wearing a beautifully carved *shendyt* kilt, a pectoral at mid-torso, armlets, bracelets and a *Nemes* topped off with a Double Crown, something like a cross between the Osiride portraits of Amenhotep III found by Hourig Sourouzian and her team at Amenhotep III's grand memorial temple at Kom el Hettan — of which two heads are in the British Museum — and the red-quartzite statue of Amenhotep III from the Luxor Cachette.

The exquisite mastery of the *shendyt* pleats on JE 49529 is typical of the high point of Amenhotep III's greatest artists, while the coarseness of the later carving is typical of the rough-and-ready style of Amenhotep IV/ Akhenaten. This is not to say that sculptural masterpieces were absent from the latter's reign, of course, but much of the art from the Amarna period is characterized by a sketchy, hurried style.

JE 55938, the other largely intact Karnak colossus in the Egyptian Museum, right, is unique among the Amenhotep IV colossi for being nude, sexless & possibly female; & also for its leg-forward stance.

Photo: Kmt/Forbes

Amenhotep III commissioned dozens of series of large to super-colossal images of himself in brown quartzite, red granite and black granodiorite. A series in sandstone is to be expected, considering the amount of this rock quarried late in his reign. The series discussed here is the only one in any material yet known for Amenhotep IV/Akhenaten. As a group, therefore, they fit within the normal scale of Amenhotep III's oeuvre and are outside his son's usual commission.

Overlapping photos of JE 49529 and Luxor's red-quartzite statue of Amenhotep III show how easily a portrait of Amenhotep III could have been recut into one of Amenhotep IV.

It took exceptional skill and ingenuity to morph the statues of the father into images of the son. Compromises were made, inconsistencies arose and a great deal of superficial makeup must have been applied. The results were the best that could be achieved, considering the challenges; but, in the end, these statues are not likely to provide reliable evidence for the assessment of Amenhotep IV's health and possible medical conditions.

The Female Statue

The aforementioned JE 55938 may have originated as a portrait not of a king but of a queen. Aside from its appearing nude and rather feminine, the tiny head is badly out of proportion with the body. This statue seems to have been conceived without a false beard, but one was slotted in at a later time. There is no sign of a kilt or belt.

At Tell Basta stands a 9.2 meter (thirty-foot) tall statue probably of Great Wife Tiye — or another queen of of Amenhotep III — against a back slab later inscribed for Osorkon. Notable, especially, is the huge mass of wig (typical of Queen Tiye) and the extremely thick neck and body. Removing all of the wig, shaving down the sides of the neck (leaving enough in front to slot in a beard), abrading the front of the chest, and erasing the drapery would result in a statue resembling JE 55938. Since there was no beard from which to carve a chin, the same effect was achieved simply by cutting down the sides of the face to lengthen its proportions vertically.

Chisel marks between the legs of JE 55938 show that a mass of stone (the pleats of a gown?) was removed from that area. These tool marks could easily have been masked with gesso and paint. More egregious hacking under the arms was well hidden by virtue of its height and location. Evidence of costume where it hugged the body closely were simply abraded and smoothed away.

Tell el Basta colossal statue of Great Wife Tiye, re-inscribed for a queen of Osorkon. Author's photo

110

Where Did the Statues Stand?

As said, the existing fragments represent about thirty original colossal sandstone statues, a number that would fit very well into Amenhotep III's Sun Court at Luxor Temple. To the postmodern eye, this clean elegant space framed by its spare columns is beautiful as it is; but Amenhotep III had a *horror vacui*. His habit was to commission sets or series of statues of himself, of Sekhmet, of seated or standing deities and of recumbent divine animals, and to place them in rows within his architectural spaces or along grand processional avenues. It is impossible to believe that he left Luxor's Sun Court devoid of sculpture other than the few individual pieces found buried there in 1989. In fact, it is most likely that he created a mirror image of the sun court at Kom el Hettan, with each column fronted by an Osiride-type statue flanked by Sekhmet statues against the walls and accompanied by a myriad of other statues, as well. It would have been just like him.

Statues of Osiride form would have been appropriate at Luxor temple, not because of a funerary association, but because this was the sacred spot of Osiris's mother, Ipet; and, on the east bank of the Nile, the god represented the regeneration that comes with the dawn. Early in Amenhotep IV's reign, however, like most of Egypt's gods, Osiris fell out of favor, but especially because he traditionally represented darkness and night, the opposite of the Sun Disk, the Aten.

Amenhotep IV made a speech which may refer to a disaster involving these very statues. The king spoke of temples falling into ruin saying that divine statues "cease one after another," as if a series of statues had toppled sequentially. Top-heavy statues holding large attributes and standing on narrow legs and feet would have been among the first to fall in a catastrophic event such as an earthquake — or perhaps even an uncharacteristically high inundation. Even if these particular statues had not fallen and been damaged, considering the new king's vendetta against Osiris, they were vulnerable to his hammers; and a great deal of the recarving, especially the slimming down of belly and arms may have aimed less at erasing Amenhotep III's image and more at reducing the Osirian physique.

The sequence of events in the ancient history of these statues is not known. It is clear from the above evidence that some carving happened after the statues fell and broke; but, after the resculpting had been completed and the statues were at their final installation site, their massive back pillars were forcibly removed, as evidenced by the large amounts of chips found nearby. This may have been either opportunistic quarrying to repurpose the sandstone or rough revision to make the statues fit their new location or both.

It has always seemed odd that Amenhotep III had no sandstone statuary other than minor fragments found by Sourouzian at Kom el Hettan. She reminded me, however, of Mohammed Ali's Nineteenth Century search through the Nile Valley for sandstone to be made into cannon balls, and suggested that any obvious sandstone statuary at Kom el Hettan

Below, How colossi Osiride statues of Amenhotep III might have been positioned in the Sun Court of Luxor Temple. Kmt Graphic

would have been easily victimized. A colossal sandstone head of Amenhotep III recut for Ramesses II was sold at Christie's New York in December 2007,[13] and likely more evidence of sandstone statuary will be found for Amenhotep III as time goes on. Many granodiorite statues original to Amenhotep III were recut by Ramesses II and stand in Luxor temple's precinct today. Much more of his art production may be stuffed inside the two wings of Luxor Temple's first pylon, a pair of huge interior spaces built by Rameses II and still awaiting investigation and exploration.

Same Statues, Different King

by W. Raymond Johnson

Arielle Kozloff's preceding essay on Amenhotep IV's famous sandstone colossi from East Karnak highlights some significant details of reworking/revision of the statues, and her excellent photographs a real service to the study of these statues. But her statement that the statues *"were usurped from a previous king"* — and in particular were originally Amenhotep III colossi — is not possible.

There are many reasons for this. The areas of reworking are completely valid and, yes, suggest that the statues were originally more traditional in their proportions. But they are far more likely to have been statues of Amenhotep IV in his early, more traditional style, a possibility that Kozloff doesn't even mention. Nor does she refer to the discussion of the material by Lise Manniche, who back in 2010 published a tremendously useful catalogue of all the known Karnak colossi (*The Akhenaten Colossi at Karnak*, AUC Press, 2010) and who discusses Kozloff's hypothesis and finds it unlikely (see Manniche, 97-102). Kozloff includes the book in her endnotes but does not discuss Manniche's findings or conclusions.

Reliefs of Amenhotep IV from his first temple at Karnak, the Re-Horakhty temple, are executed in the traditional Thutmosid-style of relief carving that he favored until his third regnal year. There are many large blocks from that temple visible in the ruins of the Tenth Pylon at Karnak, where they were reused by Horemheb, showing traditional raised- and sunk-relief decoration. The named figures of Amenhotep IV with their thick necks and snub noses look nothing like Akhenaten's later portraits, but do look very much like his father, Amenhotep III. This would be expected if the two kings did indeed rule together (which I believe they did), in the manner of Thutmose III being depicted with the features of the senior Hatshepsut during their coregency (discussed by Dimitri Laboury in his *La Statuaire de Thoutmosis III: Essai d'interprétation d'un portrait royal dans son contexte histortorique Leodiensia* 5, Liege, 1998).

Opposite, Amenhotep IV colossi in the Cairo Museum.
Author's photo

Above, Block from a demolished Re-Horakhty temple at Karnak with raised-relief depiction of a thick-necked, snub-nosed Amenhotep IV (partial cartouche & epithet in text column) in the Thutmosid style of Amenhotep III. Author's photo

Below, Ostracon recut trial-sketch of Amenhotep IV, adapting a traditional jaw to an underslung one of the Akhenaten radical style after Year 3.

Adapted from *Karnak 7*, 1982

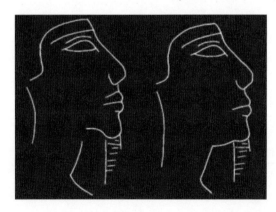

There are several little-known granodiorite and limestone statue-fragments of Amenhotep IV in the traditional Thutmosid style that have been excavated from North Karnak over the years. The most recent were found there in the area of the Treasury of Thutmose I in the 1980s and 1990s by Helen and Jean Jacquet, for the Institut Francais d'Archéologie Orientale (IFAO) (published by Helen Jacquet-Gordon in *Karnak-Nord VIII, Le Trésor de Thoutmosis Ier, Statues, Stèles et Blocs Réutilisés*, FIFAO 39, 1999).

Overlying the treasury remains was debris from the Horemheb-period demolition of Akhenaten's temple and palace complex immediately to the east, which contained *talatat* fragments, blue-painted pottery and statue fragments — even at least one sandstone colossus-fragment. Two statue fragments (catalogue nos. 20 and 21, pages 53-55, a granodiorite shoulder fragment and a limestone chest fragment) preserve the name of the Aten without cartouches that firmly date the statues to the same time as the Re-Horakhty temple, when the Aten's name had not yet received the cartouches of a king (which eventually happened in Year 3).

Earlier, in 1943, Alexandre Varille found an even larger section of a royal arm, preserved from shoulder to elbow, also inscribed with the names of the Aten without cartouches (Varille, *Karnak I*, FIFAO XIX, 1943, plate 64 F, inv. 1726) that must have been part of a statue of Amenhotep IV in the traditional style.

When Amenhotep IV started using his innovative, smaller *talatat* blocks for the quick construction of the Aten-temple structures at Karnak from Year 3, the sunk-relief decoration of many of these blocks shows a continuation of the traditional style that shortly evolved into Amenhotep IV/ Akhenaten's famous exaggerated style. Some of these blocks and groups are published in *The Akhenaten Temple Project, Volume I: The Initial Discoveries* (Ray Winfield Smith and Donald B. Redford, Aris and Phillips, 1976, plates 1-10), where one can see more traditional sunk-relief figures beginning their evolution into the new style. A wonderful limestone ostracon/trial piece found at Karnak in the early 1980s beautifully illustrates this transitional period. It preserves a practice carving of a head of Akhenaten with a full, square jaw represented in the traditional way, which was then modified into the underslung jaw that we associate with Amenhotep IV/Akhenaten's later art (Claude Traunecker, "Un portrait d' Aménophis IV sur un ostracon de Karnak," *Karnak 7*, 1982: 303-306).

It seems that the colossal statues of the king, designed for and set up along the southern interior wall of the great jubilee-court of the new Gempaaten temple (east of Karnak) also experienced an evolution of style. Rita Freed has remarked that *"some of the king's ideas must have evolved as the colossi were carved, since many show corrections in the area of the eyes, the headgear, and the navel"* (*Pharaohs of the Sun: Akhenaten, Nefertiti and Tutankhamun* exhibition catalogue, Museum of Fine Arts, Boston, 1999, 113).

The areas of reworking on the figures suggest that the statues were the king's own, started in a more traditional Thutmosid style, and subsequently modified to Amenhotep IV's new, exaggerated style. One can sympathize with the artists who were instructed to make these increasingly radical changes, and who might have made mistakes requiring correction by the master sculptor, perhaps even the king himself.

The odd details brought up by Kozloff and Freed are easily explained. Some represent the transition from the old style to the new, like the traditional, round navels recarved into the crescent-shaped navels that undoubtedly more reflected Amenhotep IV's own particular navel-shape. The chisel marks that "flaw" the surface of some of the statues indicate plaster infilling of areas that had been cut too deeply — such chisel cuts are the standard way Egyptian artists created a rough surface to which the plaster could adhere, in both relief work and sculpture. Paint traces on the colossi attest to the complete painting of the statues, which would have hidden these plaster repairs. In many cases the plaster has fallen away, creating — to us — a disparity of "smooth" and "crude" surfaces. But they are actually evidence of a painstaking process by which the sculptures were adjusted, perhaps several times, until the king — or the official in

Statue fragment of an arm from North Karnak, the name of the Aten carved without cartouches, dating it to before Year 3 of Amenhotep IV. Karnak I, 1943

117

The quartet of shu feathers atop four of the Amenhotep IV colossi heads is too large to have been recut from any known crown, so are unique to Amenhotep IV. Author's photo

"The pectoral of the Amenhotep III quartzite statue in the Luxor Museum is located on the king's chest, while the raised area of the Amenhotep IV colossus with the Aten cartouches is located considerably below the chest, at the top of the stomach, not the same area at all."

charge — was satisfied.

The iconography of the figures is also an important clue; and Kozloff is correct when she points out that they bear no relationship to the actual, physical appearance of the king. The new style introduced by Amenhotep IV by his Year 3 intentionally exaggerates his male and female characteristics and explicitly identifies him as the sun god's firstborn, Shu, who is both male and female. In the new reliefs and sculpture, Nefertiti, who is often shown with Akhenaten's face at this time, takes on the role of Shu's twin sister/wife Tefnut, Amenhotep IV/Shu's female equivalent. Queen Tiye assumes the costume, crown and aspect of the sun god's consort, Hathor. And Amenhotep III, of course, adopts the trappings and identification of the sun god himself.

While many of the Amenhotep IV colossi wear Double Crowns atop *Nemes* or *Khat* headdresses — and represent the creator god Atum with Amenhotep IV's features — at least four of the sandstone colossi wear four, large ostrich (*shu*) feathers atop the *Nemes* that further identify the king as the god Shu. This four-feathered crown and the explicit iconographic identification of the king with Shu is exclusive to Amenhotep IV, and was never utilized by any other ruler, including Amenhotep III. The feathers are too large to have been cut down from any known crown and can only be original to an Amenhotep IV statue.

It is also probable that the "nude" colossus with the Double Crown that has no genitalia, male or female, is not female at all, but an extraordinary representation of the sexless creator-god Atum, and original to Amenhotep IV (see Manniche's discussion, *Akhenaten Colossi of Karnak*, 93-102).

It should also be mentioned that, while Kozloff ascribes to the consecutive-reign model where Amenhotep IV/Akhenaten ruled only after Amenhotep III's death, in the long-coregency model — where the two kings ruled for up to eleven years — it is unlikely that the junior king would be reusing any statuary of the senior coregent. There is no evidence that Akhenaten ever appropriated any of his father's statues.

There are a number of errors in the Kozloff essay, such as the reference to the raised *"rectangular protrusion of stone crudely inscribed with the king's name."* The raised areas, as well as the bracelets and sides of the belts, all preserve the names of the Aten in cartouches, not the king's name. The latter is preserved on the belt buckle only .

Note also that the pectoral of the Amenhotep III quartzite statue in the Luxor Museum is located on the king's chest, while the raised area of the Amenhotep IV colossus

(JE 49529) with the Aten's cartouches, is located considerably below the chest, at the top of the stomach, not the same area at all.

Regarding the Luxor Temple Amenhotep III court, the lack of pharaonic statues in the court is due to the late Third Century AD Diocletianic remodeling of that part of the temple for the Imperial Cult. All pharaonic sculpture was removed from the court and adjacent king's chamber and were either taken elsewhere or ritually buried. The Luxor Temple statue cachette of buried sculptures on the western side of the court, discovered in 1989, was part of this late-Roman program. (The American Research Center in Egypt is preparing a volume of essays on the Roman interventions at Luxor Temple, *The Art of Maintaining an Empire: Roman Wall Paintings in Luxor Temple*, Yale University Press, forthcoming.) Also, the cult of Osiris's mother, Ipet, was celebrated at Karnak in a complex next to Khonsu Temple on the western side, not at Luxor Temple.

While I may take issue with some of her conclusions, Kozloff's observations and documentation of the recarved and adjusted areas on the colossi are a major contribution to the study of the period. In many ways the changes Kozloff and others have noted on these enigmatic colossi are representative of the mercurial, ever-changing theological and artistic programs of Akhenaten throughout his seventeen-year reign. It may be impossible to ever really pin down and understand this king and his constantly changing programs, but it certainly is fun to try!

Inscribed Cartouches on the Shoulders of Amenhotep IV/Akhenaten Statues

Ancient Egyptian kings rarely display cartouches on their shoulders or chests, and Amenhotep IV/Akhenaten is the first attested king to do so. While royal officials utilized inscribed names on their statues to associate themselves with the ruler under whom they served, Amenhotep IV/Akhenaten utilized the device to show his special relationship to his god, the Aten. By inscribing the name of the deity on the shoulders, arms and chests of Akhenaten's statues, before and after the names were enclosed with royal cartouches, the king was indicating his role as a servant of the god, just as his officials were servants of the king. With this device Akhenaten was also emphasizing the unique, royal nature of the god Aten, his divine coregent. Nefertiti is also depicted with the cartouches of the Aten on her body, another indication of her own special relationship to the Aten.

Painted reliefs of Akhenaten and Nefertiti on Karnak *talatat* blocks show that the Aten cartouches are not "tattoos," but are often the only carved part of painted gold-jewelry, such as bracelets, armlets and collars; when the paint is washed away the carved Aten names "float" on the royal couple's bodies. The Aten cartouches on the arms, chests and bodies of the Amenhotep IV sandstone colossi from East Karnak, and the later statuary from El Amarna (like the MMA 21.9.3 Akhenaten torso in indurated limestone) with inscribed cartouches were also painted and may have been part of jewelry now washed away.

When royal cartouches occur in the Ramesside period on the shoulders of the king it usually indicates something quite different, in many cases that the statue is of an earlier king that has been appropriated by the king whose name is inscribed. WRJ

Smiting the Enemy in the Reign of Akhenaten

A Family Affair

by Earl L. Ertman

The earliest illustration in ancient Egypt of an individual smiting foes is found in Tomb 100 at Hierakonpolis.[1] On its painted walls, an individual without symbols to identify status, rank or nationality, is poised to strike three smaller foes. This vignette is an inconspicuous detail in a much larger painting. It is not until the so-called Narmer Palette,[2] on which we see King Narmer about to strike down Egypt's enemies that this subject is solidified into a national symbol of dominance over other regions and peoples. Later, on a small ivory label for a pair of sandals of King Den,[3] this pose is repeated and associated with actions of the king and his army against Asiatics in the east. Typically the mace-wielding king was poised to bash or slash and destroy the enemy, who was usually placed kneeling in front of him. The scenes of Thutmose III on the temple walls at Karnak[4] illustrate the might of the king, and therefore Egypt, during the New Kingdom.

The present evidence points to the fact that in the Amen Temple at Karnak, early in his reign, Amenhotep IV continued this tradition of the king smiting enemies, initially without modification, and then with some changes. On a monumental scale, the partial figure of the fourth King Amenhotep may be seen on a reconstructed portion of the Third Pylon facade now in the Karnak Open Air Museum, with similarities to the smiting scene of Thutmose III on the Seventh Pylon.

This subject is also found on *talatat* blocks from a dismantled Aten temple at Karnak. A scene on block No. 3198[5] depicts Amenhotep IV wearing the Red Crown under the rays of the Aten, his body tall and thin, as he is about to strike at least two captives, one bearded, the other beardless, perhaps representing northern and southern foes. The published photograph of this block is not sharp enough to determine whether the two cartouches on the upper right contain inscriptions. The two cartouches behind the king on the left appear to be blank, but that may be due to salts on the sur-

Opposite, Detail of Amenhotep IV smiting the enemies of Egypt on a reconstructed portion of the southern wing of the Third Pylon at Karnak, now displayed in the Open Air Museum there. Photo: Kmt/Forbes

Above, Traditional smiting scene of Thutmose III on the 7th Pylon at Karnak. Below, The reconstructed section of the Karnak 3rd Pylon, with Amenhotep IV smiting foes. Photos: Kmt/Forbes

face of the block. Another *talatat* example (no number given) of the king with elongated proportions and wearing the tall White Crown, shows his raised right arm containing a weapon, about to strike a foe.[6] In this case the Aten shines down on the king's actions. Two blank and empty cartouches are seemingly incomplete at the top right of the scene. The foe and much of the lower part of this scene is lost.

On a *talatat* (No. 0202 05114) illustrated by Donald B. Redford,[7] we have one of the earliest deviations from the standard king's smiting pose since its inception. This partial scene includes Queen Nefertiti placed behind the king. She holds a straight object in her raised right hand. One wonders whether this object is a weapon or a scepter. On her head are the double plumes of her headdress. This illustration is quite small, but the one small and two large cartouches appear to be blank.

Not only is the queen's presence behind the king in a smiting pose a deviation from the norm, but Nefertiti alone smiting an enemy is unprecedented. Redford lists two *talatat* from Karnak that show such a smiting pose, but illustrates only one.[8] On this block Nefertiti smites the enemy in three separate pavilions or enclosures. In the left scene she wears

Left, Talatat *No. 3198 from Karnak showing Amen-hotep IV in the Red Crown smiting two foes, northern & southern.* Adapted from *Kêmi* 20, Fig. 2

Below, Detail of a talatat from Hermopolis & formerly in a private American collection, depicting a royal-barque kiosk with Khepresh-crowned Akhenaten smit-ing a standing foe, accompanied by figures of Nefertiti & a single princess After Cooney (1965), Pl. 50

her unique tall flat-top crown. In the center and right scenes, she wears double plumes. A fourth pavilion is too damaged to determine its contents. It was one thing to include the queen in a smiting scene behind the king, but quite another to have her smiting enemies (albeit females) herself. The de-piction of this action by Nefertiti is much more significant than at first realized. Yes, the queen is shown performing an action earlier reserved for the king alone, but this action is of paramount importance, inasmuch as it represents the domination, subjugation and embodiment of Egypt over all

Talatat *from Hermopolis, now in the collection of the Museum of Fine Arts, Boston, which depicts a royal barque of Nefertiti with an aft kiosk showing the queen (above) in her tall platform crown under the rays of the Aten smiting a female foe. The paired steering poles have the queen's effigy as finials.* After Cooney (1965), Pl. 51a

foreigners (enemies) of the Two Lands by the ruler performing the action. While Akhenaten is at times shown larger than Nefertiti on *talatat*, signifying his greater importance, Nefertiti performs as the supreme ruler in those instances where she stands alone smiting enemies, a position she apparently filled during the lifetime and following the death of her husband.

From the surviving evidence none of the royal daughters were included in the smiting scenes in the Aten temple at Karnak. While Nefertiti is present in at least one instance where Amenhotep IV performs this action, it appears that it was only after the move to the new capital at Akhetaten, or after Year 5 of his reign, that a daughter is included in a smiting scene, positioned beside or behind Nefertiti. As new research is published, this thesis will either be supported or will have to be modified.

Later — the elapsed time has not yet been established — at Amarna, separate scenes of Akhenaten and Nefertiti smiting the enemy show these rulers accompanied by a child, undoubtedly the eldest daughter, Meritaten. This addition extends the "typical" smiting scene even further. Some might see the addition of a child as inconsequential, but it has great significance when a compositional arrangement is altered after more than a millennia of continuous use.

A limestone *talatat* from Amarna shows Akhenaten — symbolically representing Egypt — slaying enemies, accompanied by both Nefertiti and a daughter. This block was formerly in the Norbert Schimmel collection (now Metropolitan Museum 1985.328.15).[9] Here, on the side of a kiosk at the prow of a royal barque, Akhenaten brandishes a blade rather than a mace. What is the significance of this action occurring in the presence of a female and a child? For the answer we can only speculate.

A related *talatat* now in Boston (Museum of Fine Arts 63.521) shows Nefertiti in a bow kiosk of a royal barque in a smiting pose. The late John Cooney commented on this fragmentary scene, saying, *"It is uncertain if Nefertiti was followed by a princess, but in the lower left of the relief is what appears to be a curved blade possibly held by a princess. This too would be unique, but one is forced to conclude that anything is possible in the iconography of the Amarna Period."*[10] If this is in fact accurate, that a young princess held a weapon in the scene, the implications are astounding, since it would imply that all members of the royal family of Akhenaten — not just the queen — but a child (and a female at that) possessed the might to vanquish the foes of Egypt. I doubt that a blade-wielding child was pictured here. In a related smiting scene (Boston 63.260),[11] on a bow kiosk on an adjacent *talatat*, a female smites a foe.[12] Not enough of this particular scene remains, however, to determine if any figure was placed behind the monarch in this instance.

Recently Dutch excavations at Sakkara, sponsored by the Leiden Museum of Antiquities and Leiden University, discovered the Tomb of Meryneith, a high priest of the Aten in the reign of Akhenaten.[13] An effaced relief-fragment from this tomb shows a child included in at least one smiting scene, and probably several others, as well. An epigraphic drawing of this fragment[14] reveals not only the main scene but the remains of the partial register that was directly above it.

In a forward kiosk of a royal barque is a damaged scene showing the king, with a raised right arm, grasping a foe (probably by the hair) with his left hand. Rays descend diagonally from the Aten disk placed at the top center of this scene (within the kiosk). The lines of the kilt of the person performing the action indicates this is King Akhenaten. A child, apparently nude, stands behind the king and observes the event. If such is an accurate analysis of the scene's content, this may be the earliest known instance where a princess accompanies her father rather than her mother. In later years of the reign, of course, when Meritaten served as consort, she, as an adult, followed the king. The scale of the individual behind Akhenaten in the scene in question argues against this figure portraying Nefertiti, who is never shown this much smaller than her husband, and without regalia denoting her rank, even when she is behind him.

A kiosk at the bow of the same royal vessel depicts a similar, but even more damaged, scene. Just two diagonal rays of the Aten are visible within the kiosk. At the left of these the king's raised arm holds a weapon high above his head, poised to strike a foe. One cannot be certain whether two lines near the base and towards the bow end of the kiosk

Drawing of a damaged relief in the recently discovered Tomb of Meryneith at Sakkara, depicting a royal barque with fore & aft kiosks bearing scenes of Akhenaten smiting enemies accompanied by a princess. In the partial register above that scene are two representations of the barque kiosks before installation on the vessel, possibly under construction. A seated workman visible directly above the barque mast would seem to be adoring one kiosk's smiting scene.

Adapted from image provided by Drs. Maarten Raven & Rene Van Walsem, courtesy of the Leiden Expedition in the New Kingdom necropolis at Sakkara

relate to the ruler or the foe, but the forward leg of the king would be expected there. A diagonal dotted line (denoting a damaged area) towards the stern may relate to the kilt of the ruler. If this is not the case, no other solution seems evident. The lines behind the king may be part of the torso and arms of a child, closely repeating the form and arrangement seen in the forward kiosk.

The presence of a child behind figures of the king in a smiting pose at this supposed early time in Akhenaten's reign — around Year 5 — is surprising, as well as previously unknown from surviving *talatat* scenes at Karnak.[15]

Scenes of Nefertiti smiting a foe, in the Karnak *talatat*,[16] also show her alone. It would be unusual to have representations of the king in one kiosk and the queen in the other on the same vessel, since scenes preserved from the Amarna *talatat* indicate that Akhenaten and Nefertiti had separate royal barques with curtains (?) on the sides of their repective kiosks depicting them smiting the enemy. For that reason, the barque in the scene in question must belong to the king, whose image, possibly on fabric panels, decorated the sides of both forward and aft kiosks.[17]

In the register directly above the mast of the royal barque are two flanking male figures, one squatting, one seated, who were initially thought to be working on the structure between them; but, after review, the gesture of the seated workman on the right may signify that he is praising an image of the king smiting a foe, which is attached to the side of a kiosk under construction.

The smaller size of the foe in this scene compares well with the prisoner in the bow kiosk of the king's barque in the complete register below, in terms of the placement of an arm and the angle of the foe's kilt. To the left of the king's figure is a foot and ankle, not that of the king himself, since it is shown in a vertical standing position. A curved solid line behind this foot extends to the ground, indicating a dress like those worn by Amarna ladies. The loosely pendant hand to the left of the solid curved line undoubtedly belongs to this female, probably Nefertiti. Firmly drawn lines of unknown shapes take up the remainder of the space within the kiosk enclosure. The dotted lines to the left side of this kiosk could indicate the contour of a small person.

The right or bow side of the left kiosk depicted in this upper register in Meryneith's tomb seems to show a foe with limp arms and the forward leg of a smiting king. A diagonal solid line and dotted lines (indicating damage in the epigraphic rendering) may indicate his rear leg. Following this are two smaller vertically placed legs and feet and a dotted line in front of them suggesting the dress of a female, the dotted line descending to and touching the ground. This is not the garment of the king, but of the person standing next to or immediately behind him. The remainder of the scene is difficult to determine with any certainty. The solid vertical line may be the shin and foot of another person, possibly a child, as no garment seems present. The combination of solid and dotted lines at the far left of this kiosk do not readily reveal, however, what was originally depicted.

Both "enclosures" seen in the fragmentary top register could be kiosks under construction, prior to their placement on the royal barqe being towed in the lower register, except that the scenes in these kiosks are different from those of the barque kiosks. Therefore, the kiosks under construction must be intended for yet another royal vessel of the king, also under construction. We thus for the first time can see the bases for a ship's kiosks, which when in place on board are not visible above the vessel's gunwales. This scene is from a shipbuilding workshop which undoubtedly was the responsibility of the tomb owner, Meryneith, who portrayed these and other activities under his charge. The kiosks in both registers were purposely effaced because of their subject matter, Akhenaten and family members.

What reason could there be for the addition of Nefertiti to a ritual scene that previously depicted only the king? And why do later scenes include both the queen and a princess? John Baines discussed the inclusion of family members in scenes during Akhenaten's reign (but not specifically smiting scenes), indicating, "*Instead of this vision of a corporeal descent from god to king, Akhenaten offered one of the royal family, all of them dwelling on earth and in that sense 'human' rather than divine.... That family included himself, his queen, Nefertiti, and a variable number of their daughters.... The group of king, queen and daughters was presented as a family communicating within itself under the sun disk's protection. The function of these reliefs remains controversial, but they are probably the nearest Akhenaten's iconography approached to something that could be worshipped by the nonroyal.*"[18] This may be what is occurring in the fragmentary upper register from the Tomb of Meryneith, where a workman seems to offer praise towards the kiosk scene containing the king's image.

Maarten Raven (in a personal communication) has indicated that no certain dates can presently be assigned to the Tomb of Meryneith; but the relief under discussion here was decorated in the first of three phases of construction and decoration of the tomb, which consisted of "*three chapels and the adjoining west portico of the courtyard. Since it mentions the deceased as 'steward of the Aten temple' (doubtless the Memphite temple) and Beate Gesslar-Lohr argued that this temple did not exist yet in Year 5, we would be tempted to date this phase (which includes the ship scene) immediately after Year 5. This would probably predate the scenes from Amarna/Hermopolis.*"[19] I agree with Raven's assessment that the ship scene we are considering was undoubtedly created before similar subjects at Akhetaten, and after the abandonment of Waset (Thebes).

Did the change in form of the traditional smiting scene during the reign of Akhenaten by the inclusion of Nefertiti and a daughter affect the form and arrangement of smiting scenes by later kings? Indirectly, the answer is yes, but only in so far as the image of the female depicted behind the king now is that of a goddess rather than a queen. There is an exceptional incidence of Tutankhamen being accompanied in a smiting scene by his queen, Ankhesenamen, on a thin gold-foil strip, which also includes the presence of the courtier Ay, who would succeed the young king.[20]

I was of the opinion that the composition of Akhenaten's smiting scenes, especially those depicted in association with kiosks, may have been imitated by the artists of later rulers. A surviving relief of a royal barque from the reign of Rameses III[21] is strikingly similar to examples from Akhenaten's reign. Not only is the king shown smiting an enemy within a kiosk, with a female figure behind him (in this instance a goddess rather than a queen), but also the streamers which flutter in the breeze from the forward and aft supports of the kiosk would seem to be copied directly from those shown in scenes during the reign of Akhenaten. The same might be said for a relief in the Temple of Khonsu at Karnak, dating to the reign of Priest-King Herihor,[22] who ruled Upper Egypt at the beginning of the Twenty-first Dynasty. Two

Above, Drawing of gold-foil fragment depicting Q. Ankhesenamen attending a smiting Tutankhamen, with Ay looking on. After Davis, *Harmhabi* (1912), 128, fig. 4

Below, Rameses III in kiosk smiting-scene, accompanied by a goddess. After Epigraphic Survey (1954), Pl. 88

kiosks are shown, with H-P Herihor in each in the role of a king smiting enemies. In both instances a goddess stands behind the priest-king, in the position occupied by Nefertiti in the Amarna-era kiosk scenes. In the case of one of these Herihor kiosks, streamers flutter from the aft support of the kiosk, just as they had in the Akhenaten examples. These similarities surely cannot have been coincidental.

My belief that some *talatat* blocks were available and were copied in later reigns was wrong, however. Raymond Johnson of the Epigraphic Survey has convinced me that copying from *talatat* was not the case; rather, the inclusion of streamers attached to the kiosks, as well as a female figure behind the smiting king, was due to the later artists imitating scenes of the Opet Festival river procession from the Colonnade Hall of Luxor Temple, dating from the time of Tutankhamen, rather than inspiration provided by stray *talatat* blocks.[23] Johnson's explanation for the continued use of these details is undoubtedly correct.

To summarize, in most smiting scenes, the king and the enemy make up the total composition. During the reign of Akhenaten, smiting scenes changed to include a figure of Queen Nefertiti, standing behind the king. Later the king is shown accompanied by Nefertiti and a child, most likely eldest daughter Meritaten. And Nefertiti is also shown smiting an enemy (female) on her own. These alterations to the traditional smiting composition add elements not present previously.

Akhenaten and Nefertiti are seen smiting enemies in *talatat* reliefs from the dismantled Aten temple at Karnak. In some of these instances, the queen is in a subordinate position behind her husband. After Year 5, outside of Karnak, a child was added to smiting compositions, most often placed behind the queen. This unique grouping never occurred again in subsequent reigns, as far as this researcher can determine. Obviously no later queen enjoyed the same status vis-à-vis the king as Nefertiti with Akhenaten. Thus, other queens are never shown smiting enemies, or even shown accompanying the king on the occasion of a smiting. An exception to the latter situation is in the reign of Tutankhamen, when Queen Ankhesenamen — retaining a little of the prestige of her mother — was occasionally placed behind her husband in smiting scenes; she is never shown smiting per se, although in two such scenes she mimics Tutankhamen's actions by brandishing a blade while standing behind him.[24]

When Tutankhamen's smiting scenes on the kiosks of the royal barques in the Opet Festival reliefs of Luxor Temple were copied for later kings, the position of the queen was retained, but a goddess was substituted for a wife. Then this placement of a female of any rank disappears, leaving no trace of the brief change to the traditional smiting composition which was introduced under Akhenaten.

A relief in the Khonsu temple at Karnak depicts Priest-King Herihor in a kiosk smiting foes while the goddess Mut looks on. After Epigraphic Survey (1979), Pl. 20

131

Nefertiti's Final Secret

Did Cairo Receive a Modern Forgery in Exchange for the Bust of the Queen?

by Rolf Krauss

In November 1912 the Egyptologist Hermann Ranke and three architects started the third season of excavations at the site of El Amarna in Middle Egypt, on behalf of the German Oriental Society (DOG). These were formally under the direction of Ludwig Borchardt, head of the Imperial German Institute for Egyptian Archaeology, who physically joined the team on December 6, 1912 — and it happened that the expedition discovered the now-famous painted-limestone bust of Nefertiti on that same day. He left El Amarna for Cairo ten days later, returning again in mid-January, for the division of finds.

Following an invitation by Borchardt, Gustave Lefébvre, inspector of Antiquities for Middle Egypt, arrived at El Amarna on January 20, 1913, to effect the division of the 1912 season's finds. Before setting out Lefébvre contacted Gaston Maspero, the head of the Egyptian Antiquities Service, for instructions.

The negotiations between Lefébvre and Borchardt resulted in splitting the finds into two unequal groups. The list of objects for Cairo was headed by a small painted stela; the corresponding first item in the Berlin column was the bust of Nefertiti, not described as such, however. Ten further objects for Cairo and more than twenty-five for Berlin were specified. About 400 lesser objects, likewise allocated to Berlin, were not listed in detail. The original document was kept in the archives of Cairo and a copy subsequently went to Berlin.[1]

By coincidence, the DOG's secretary, Bruno Güterbock, visited the El Amarna excavations for a week, January 17–24, and was a witness to the division, which he described in a letter written in 1924.[2] According to Güterbock, Borchardt and Lefébvre decided on the allocation of the finds using photographs; and Lefébvre signed the protocol after he had inspected the magazine where the originals *"stood already packed into crates, but open and without lids. Had he wished to do so, he could have taken out any individual object which he might have liked to examine more closely."* Güterbock

Opposite, Painted-limestone household stela depicting the Amarna Royal Family, found by the German Oriental Society at El Amarna in 1912 & today in the Egyptian Museum, Cairo, JE 44863. Photo from L. Brochardt, Porträts der Königin Nofretete (Leipzig, 1923), Pl. 1

does not intimate that Lefébvre asked for one single object to be removed from its crate. In later years Lefébvre did not dare to admit that he had not been interested in seeing the originals. For the benefit of those who would read and accept it, Borchardt wrote in the official diary of the expedition: *"Then he [Lefébvre] looked at the finds in the bureau; there the excavation journals were put at his disposition. With special care, he viewed the objects in hard stone: stelae, the colourful queen [= bust of Nefertiti], the statues and heads of the princesses, the queen and the king."*

Borchardt admitted at least once, if obliquely, that Lefébvre did not really examine the bust itself. In the 1920s he confided to the art critic Julius Meier-Graefe: *"the gents in Cairo [read: from Cairo] were just too slack to look into the box. Had they cared, they could have had the queen."*[3] In a letter written in 1918, to one of his superiors in the German Foreign Ministry, Borchardt ascribed the outcome of the division as resulting from Lefébvre's amiability and other handicaps: *"Mr. Lefébvre, who had put both objects as equivalent on the preliminary list, amiably condescended to take the altar stela for Cairo considering my remark that Berlin already owns such a family scene as depicted on the altar stela."*[4] Here, Borchardt is referring to the Royal Family scene on the stela Berlin 14145, which was acquired in 1898.[5]

According to Borchardt it was Lefébvre who placed the painted stela and the bust as counterparts on a preliminary list. The situation remains unclear, however. In his letter of 1924, Güterbock praised *"Borchardt's clever move of putting the painted stela on the list as second to the bust in beauty. Thus he could count on Maspero's great interest for the genre of depictions to which the painted stela belonged, and which was not represented in Cairo by an example as good as the one in Berlin."*

In his letter to the Foreign Ministry, Borchardt remarked on Lefébvre's choice of the stela: *"By training, he is a scholar of inscriptions and papyri and presumably it was thus his lesser ability to judge works of art which prevented him from justly recognizing the value of the object in question. And finally, my skills in negotiating may have prevailed over his."* These remarks made sense to somebody who was unaware that Lefébvre had not seen the bust itself and that the photo shown to him had been chosen by Borchardt, meaning *"that it was not possible to recognize the full beauty of the bust."*[6] Instead of admitting that he had led Lefébvre astray, Borchardt denounced him as being aesthetically handicapped.

Lefébvre also disregarded Maspero's telegraphed instructions to divide the finds into two exactly equal halves. Borchardt honestly noted that *"the telegraphic order appeared to him — as he himself told me — too severe."* Did Lefébvre simply disobey Maspero's plain order? To divide finds strictly,

The bust of Queen Nefertiti found by the DOG at El Amarna in 1913. *Damage to the bust reveals that it is carved of limestone & coated with a thin layer of gypsum plaster, which was then painted.*

Photo: Greg Reeder

Opposite, The bust of Nefertiti soon after its discovery: l. to r., Hermann Ranke, Paul Hollander & unidentified reis. Photo: Albert-Ludwig-University, Freiberg

Above, Ludwig Borchardt in the 1920s. Below, Gustave Lefébvre in old age. Archival photos

into two exactly equal halves had already been the law, at least on paper.[7] Earlier in 1912 Lord Kitchener, Great Britain's proconsul in Egypt, had reprimanded Maspero for his too-generous handling of divisions and demanded a strict division into two equal parts in future. It is possible that Maspero, personally affronted and angered, complied with Kitchener's directive superficially, but tried to thwart it in practice. He would thus have had a henchman in his protegé Lefébvre, who might have nonchalantly and politely conceded far more than half of the DOG's 1912-13 El Amarna finds to Berlin, precisely because of Kitchener's overbearing behavior.

The outbreak of the Great War in 1914 may have delayed any inquiries about the bust of Nefertiti, as it had been made known by Borchardt in 1913 — in a cropped photo,[8] presumably the same one he had shown to Lefébvre. The first one who wanted to see the original was Jean Capart of the Egyptian Department of the Royal Museum of Arts in Brussels, who visited Berlin in November 1920, and asked Heinrich Schäfer, director of the Egyptian Museum, about the object, which he could not find in the exhibition.[9]

But it took four more years until Maspero's successor, Pierre Lacau, became completely aware of the bust and its importance. He rejected the assessment of Lefébvre and Borchardt that the painted stela was second in beauty to the bust: *"Isn't it clear that the bust is by far the more important piece and that the division being vitiated by an obvious error ought to be revised?"*[10] Lacau approached Borchardt and asked him to arrange the return of the bust. Borchardt explained to Lacau that he himself had never owned the bust and that it was James Simon who owned it in 1913, as holder of the concession to excavate at El Amarna; Simon had since donated the bust to the Egyptian Museum in Berlin. When Lacau realized that Borchardt would not cooperate, he denied him a concession for a new excavation.[11]

The resulting stalemate lasted until 1929. When Borchardt turned sixty-five (on October 5, 1928), he did not retire immediately, but acted as director of the German Institute until March 1929. His successor Hermann Junker held the office from October 1929.[12] Presumably Lacau had waited for the arrival of Junker, who later proved indeed to favor Nefertiti's return to Egypt. Lacau traveled to Berlin in the last week of October 1929. He first suggested trading the painted stela for the bust of Nefertiti, *"adding objects which would even out the difference in value."* Schäfer talked Lacau out of this proposal, by indicating that Berlin had already *"owned a corresponding object for decades."* However, Schäfer did concede to Lacau that *"it cannot be well denied that the equal status of the bust and stela as established by Lefébvre and Borchardt was*

Berlin Stela 14145. Made of limestone, it is 13 cm. h., 39 cm. w. & 3.8 cm. d. Acquired in 1898, its exact provenance is unknown, although probably El Amarna. It almost certainly was part of a household shrine dedicated to the Royal Family, who are depicted in an intimate domestic scene. Gypsum plaster on the stela's backside suggests this was used to attach the slab to a wall niche in a private home. Photo: Bildarchiv PK Berlin

mistaken." Yet years earlier, in an article intended for the visitors of the Amarna exhibition of 1913/14 in Berlin, Schäfer had words of high praise for the painted stela: *"there is nothing of its kind among the Amarna reliefs as far as preservation and artistic interest is concerned."*[13]

The last one to insist on the great value of the stela was Otto Rubensohn, in his defence of Borchardt against Feder's critique: *"Lefébvre decided in favour of the better lot; all connoisseurs are unanimous in this respect."*[14] If only Rubensohn knew what his friend Borchardt had written to the Foreign Ministry: *"A juxtaposition of the bust, which we got as object no 1, and the coloured altar stela, which Cairo got as no 1, clearly shows that it is only on paper that the division can be described as 'à moitié exacte'."* Could he possibly have been implying that the painted stela which went to Cairo was the more valuable object and that he did everything he could to bring the less important piece to Berlin?

When, in 1923, Borchardt found himself compelled by Schäfer to publish the Nefertiti bust, he also dealt with the

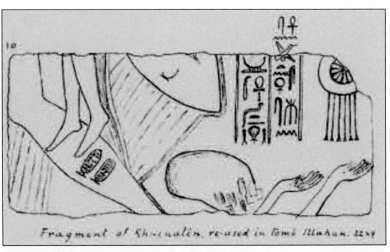

Fragment of Khuenaten, re-used in tomb Illahun. 22×9

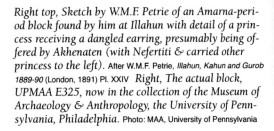

Right top, Sketch by W.M.F. Petrie of an Amarna-period block found by him at Illahun with detail of a princess receiving a dangled earring, presumably being offered by Akhenaten (with Nefertiti & carried other princess to the left). After W.M.F. Petrie, Illahun, Kahun and Gurob 1889-90 (London, 1891) Pl. XXIV *Right, The actual block, UPMAA E325, now in the collection of the Museum of Archaeology & Anthropology, the University of Pennsylvania, Philadelphia.* Photo: MAA, University of Pennsylvania

painted stela. He dedicated twenty-four pages of the brochure he produced to the painted stela, and a mere fourteen pages to the bust. He compared the painted Cairo stela and the stela in Berlin at length. The two reliefs are easily described — on the painted one, the king hands an earring to princess Meritaten; on the other in Berlin, he kisses the same princess; in both, Nefertiti and two younger princesses are present. Borchardt acknowledged that *"in detail the differences between the two depictions are not exactly significant,"* but he still maintained that he regarded the painted stela as aesthetically the more valuable object.[15] Alluding to the palm branch as a symbol of triumph and victory, Borchardt asserted that *"the palm undeniably is due to the master of the Cairo stela, and not to the master of the Berlin relief."* Borchardt's judgment contrasts markedly with the more recent evaluation of the Berlin relief by the late British Egyptologist Cyril Aldred, who viewed it as *"the most celebrated of its kind, and surely no more appealing domestic conversation piece has survived from antiquity."*[16]

Borchardt described the symmetrical structure of the painted stela as an *"almost architectural equilateral coordination."* Being both Egyptologist and architect, he was entitled to pronounce a qualified judgment. Yet, in our time, the art historian Whitney Davis did not agree with Borchardt's evaluation: *"It is not as effective as the Berlin relief, perhaps because of a lack of subtlety in the use of concentric arrangement; the circularity of the composition does not harmonize with the square setting of the stela. The composition lacks moderating structural forces, such as we see on the Berlin relief."* [17]

Yet Borchardt held that the artist of the Berlin relief was *"less fortunate with regard to the structure of the whole, by contrast to the other who was able to create a more unified group which he placed close to the frame."* Egyptologist Gerhard Fecht pointed out that the qualities seen by Borchardt pertain to a certain class of modern pictures, rather than to ancient Egyptian reliefs: *"King and Queen are seated much too closely to the frame thus undoing the (relatively) isolating Egyptian depiction of the two main figures. The result is a modern uniform genre picture."* [18]

Borchardt recognized a motif shared by the painted stela and a relief block found by William Flinders Petrie in 1899/90 at Illahun. [19] The Illahun block preserves part of the figure of Nefertiti carrying a princess. Before the queen stands another princess receiving an earring, undoubtedly from the king. The princess holds her hands differently on the block and on the stela. Borchardt explained that, in comparison to the painted stela, there is more space between the princess and the king on the Illahun relief and, therefore, the artist of the Illahun relief chose a space-filling posture for the hands. Otherwise the posture on the painted stela is used in reliefs when an object such as a vessel or a bouquet is grasped with both hands. The posture on the Illahun relief is used when receiving an object such as, for example a collar, and thus the posture on the painted stela seems to be iconographically exceptional.

Fecht recognized that two motifs are shared by the painted stela and the Window of Appearances scene in the Tomb of Ay at El Amarna. One motif is the standing princess

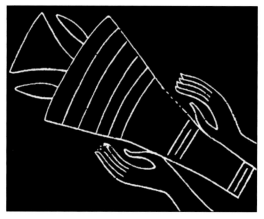

The position of the hands of the princess receiving the dangled earring in JE 44865 (detail at left) is iconographically exceptional, inasmuch as this is the conventional hand position in Amarna reliefs of persons who are lifting objects in presentation, as illustrated above in details of scenes from the private rock-cut tombs at El Amarna.

Another anomaly in the representation of the JE 44865 princess is the apparent un-Egyptian neck-choker of multiple rings that she wears, which is otherwise unknown in ancient Egypt.

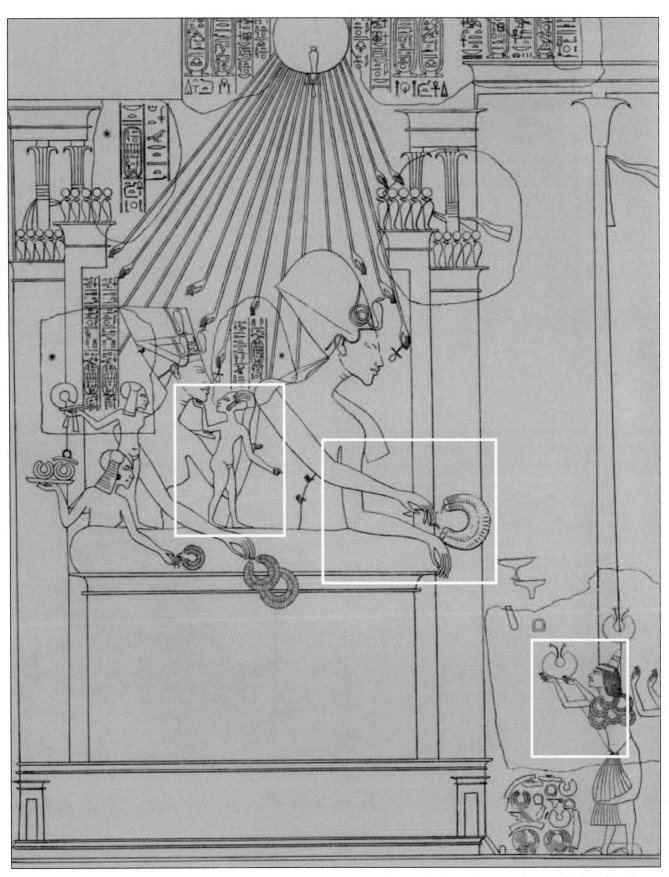

The Window of Appearances scene in the Tomb of Ay at El Amarna offers interesting correspondences with JE 44865: the figure of a princess touching Nefertiti's chin; collars awarded by the king — using his right hand; the conventional hand-positions of recipient Ay.

who turns her head and touches the queen under the chin. The other motif is the bestowing of golden collars by the king, which is quite common in Amarna art. As a rule tomb owners are depicted as the recipients of the collars, as in the Tomb of Ay for example. On the painted stela, the golden collars which await presentation to the princesses seem to be somewhat out of place, inasmuch as the royal daughters are never shown wearing such collars, just handling them.

Borchardt discovered what he considered an apparent blunder in the Berlin relief: *"On the altar stela in Cairo each line fits. By contrast the author of the Berlin relief quite often made a mistake. He got the proportions of the royal heads massively wrong: They are too large by a quarter."*

Let us check this assertion by superimposing both reliefs, adjusted to the same scale, determined by the bodies of the seated royal figures. Borchardt's assertion is clearly correct. Nevertheless, today Borchardt would have to reverse his evaluation, because it is now known that Amarna royal figures are generally "top heavy." Thus it was the artist of the painted stela who chose the "wrong proportions" (in terms of Amarna style), when he drew naturally sized heads.

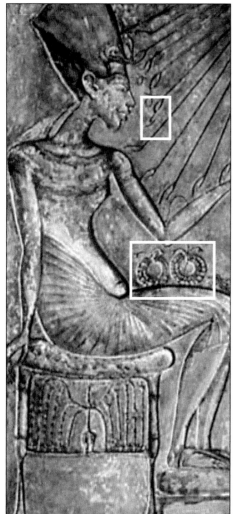

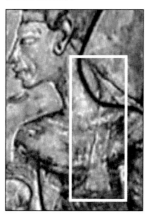

The seated king supporting himself with one arm in JE44865 is known from other Amarna reliefs (e.g., one in the British Museum, BM 24431, seen at right, where the king gestures with his right hand), except that the arching of the elbow differs from all the other examples. Two other anomalies are the presence of the was *glyph being offered to the king by the Aten ray & the collars on his lap, of a type the princesses are never shown wearing. Also, there are no other examples of a streamer hanging onto the breast of the queen (or king) as seen in JE 44865 (detail below).*

Superimposition of the rescaled figures of JE 44865 onto Berlin stela 14145, suggesting that the latter very well may have served as the pictorial basis of the Cairo stela. The over-sized heads of the king & queen on 14145 are typical of proportions in Amarna art, whereas the correctly proportioned ones of 44865 are anomalies. Author's graphic

In general it can be concluded — from the superposition — that the figures of king and queen have been copied directly from one relief and used as a pictorial basis for the other. Either the Berlin relief is copied from the painted stela or vice versa. Certain details are to be found on both reliefs, but as mirror images. On the Berlin stela, it is the queen's crown that is clasped by the hand of a ray of the Aten. On the painted stela, the corresponding ray clasps the king's crown. Similarly on the Berlin stela, the queen's sash covers the right side of the *sema*-hieroglyph, whereas it covers the left side on the painted stela.

Given this inversion one can argue either way. However, a decision is possible on the basis of those details which are iconographically correct on one stela, but wrong on the other. One such example is the disproportionally large heads. Another example of a wrong detail on the painted stela is that the king seems to be left-handed, insofar as he offers the princess an earring with his left hand. There are no other examples in Amarna art where the king gives something with his left hand. Certainly, even where the king's figure is oriented facing to the right — as it is on the painted stela — he nevertheless uses his right hand, as is the case in the Tomb of Ay Window of Appearances scene, where the rightward-looking king bestows with his right hand.

A similar detail of interest is how the king supports himself with his right hand on the Cairo stela. Borchardt cited other Amarna reliefs that depict the king supporting himself in a similar fashion. As an example he chose London BM 24431, the fragment of a stela, where — according to Borchardt — the artist was less successful in the rendering of this position.[20] But on the Cairo stela, the arch of the king's elbow goes the wrong way; and, in all the other examples, the arch of the elbow corresponds to the model of the London relief. It seems to follow that these iconographic mistakes came about when a copy of the Berlin relief was made, and the position and posture of the king's arms and hands were modified.

In fact there are other modifications which likewise went wrong. On the painted stela, the king's footstool and its cushion are much higher than are the queen's. But whenever the seated figures of king and queen are of standard size, the queen's footstool is higher. If the king's feet rest on a higher footstool, with the figures of king and queen nevertheless seated at the same height, it follows that the king's legs are shorter than the queen's. If the king's legs are shorter, it follows that the queen is taller than the king — which contradicts a convention that knows no exceptions. Borchardt noticed that the streamers on the queen's crown are *"treated with more freedom than those of the king."*[21] The streamers may not flutter as in the Berlin relief, but there is no other instance of a streamer hanging over the shoulder onto the breast of the queen (or king), as on the painted stela.

The motif of the *was*-hieroglyph offered by a sun ray to Akhenaten, as a sign for prosperity, is quite common in the early monuments from Waset (Thebes). Later it went out of use, finally being proscribed because of its resemblance to the name of the Theban province — which had become anathema, together with the gods of the cult center of Amen-Re. At El Amarna, there seems to be but one example of a *was*-glyph offered by a sun ray, namely a stela from the royal tomb.[22] The stela can be dated as one of the earliest objects created at El Amarna, because it uses Epithet I of the Aten, whereas the painted stela uses Epithet VI. The ordering and numbering of the epithets of the Aten are known through the work of Jurij Perepelkin.[23] Thus the *was*-glyph on the painted stela constitutes an anachronism.

An apparently un-Egyptian detail on the painted stela

The inscriptions on the frame of stela JE 44865 repeat the same error four times (indicated opposite), where the stock epithet of Akhenaten, "living in Truth" is not correctly written. It is in each instance written as above right, whereas it should be written as either middle right or bottom right. That an ancient artisan might have made a mistake once is not uncommon (in fact, is seen in the Tomb of Mahu at El Amarna), but the same error repeated four times on the same small object is highly suspicious.

Also note the sockets for what is presumed to have been for a pair of "wing doors" to the stela, otherwise not known in ancient Egypt, but for one later New Kingdom example.

is the neck jewelery adorning the princess Meritaten — a *"high tight neck adornment,"* according to Borchardt's description. This seems to consist of a set of neck rings or perhaps chokers. Single chokers and neck rings are known from Pharaonic times, but not from the Amarna period.[24] Whatever the artist who created this stela had in mind — a set of neck rings or chokers — it does not seem to be known from ancient Egypt, nor from any neighboring countries during the Amarna period.

The painted stela also lends itself to quite different subjective evaluations, of which one example in particular might interest the reader. Schäfer was inspired by *"the podgy body of the small child, the little one sitting on her mother's lap."*[25] By contrast Fecht reckoned that *"the profile view of the sitting princess in her dumpiness — reminiscences of modern pictures impose themselves — is non Egyptian."*[26] The present author asserts that the sitting princess (Ankhesenpaaten) is the "most ugliest" little toad he has ever seen — be it modern or ancient.[27]

But, returning to strictly objective criteria, what should one make of the fact that the inscription of the painted stela repeats exactly the same mistake four times? The two cartouche names of Akhenaten are repeated twice on the stela frame. Thus four times we read "living in truth," the stock epithet of Akhenaten. "Truth" is not correctly written. "Truth" can be written in various ways, but not as on the painted stela. The same error is found in Mahu's tomb at El Amarna. In other words all four times the hieroglyphic writing of "truth" is wrong. Are we entitled to read, individually and separately, four times: "no truth," or "wrong," or perhaps "fake"? It would seem far-fetched to propose that some jester forged the painted stela and put in the sand for the excavators to find!

Against this obvious conclusion, Borchardt could have objected that the painted stela has a patina: *"By oxidization what is blue has developed into a darker, greenish hue; as in similar cases, the yellow ground might have darkened."*[28] Together with all the finds of 1912-1913, the stela was temporarily exhibited in Berlin.[29] At that time there would have been an opportunity to analyse the paint and to determine the kind of oxidization. Later Borchardt gave a good reason why he did not undertake such an analysis: *"The object is someone else's property and therefore I did not feel entitled to take even minute samples for an analysis when by the kindness of Monsieur Maspero it was entrusted to my custody and exhibited during the winter 1913/14 in Berlin. It is to be hoped that the administration of the museum in Cairo will test the stele at some time in the future."*[30]

Together with the other objects which had been exhibited in Berlin, the painted stela entered Cairo Museum in

Author's graphics

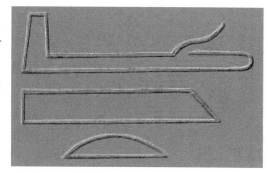

WRONG "Truth" as inscribed on JE 44685

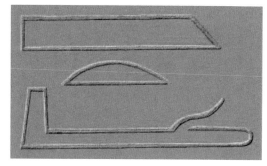

CORRECT

CORRECT

145

spring of 1914. It took almost 100 years until the stela was at least preliminarily tested.[31] Of these tests only one has been described in detail: *"The darker background color in the photograph [that accompanies the report] was originally thought to be surface weathering, but UV testing shows that it is a type of surface preparation for the stela and is original."* Is this to be understood that the stela was created with a patina?

In the early 1980s, the present author — with a Cairo Museum restorer nearby — had the opportunity to examine JE 44865 outside its case, aided by a high-resolution magnifying glass fixed to an arm lamp. A few years earlier, nitrocellulose lacquer had been applied to the stela; and this had

Reconstruction by Borchardt of how Cairo stela JE 44865 may have been anciently displayed in the house where it was found at El Amarna. Bilderatlas zur Religionsgeschichte 2-5 (Leipzig, 1924), Fig. 12

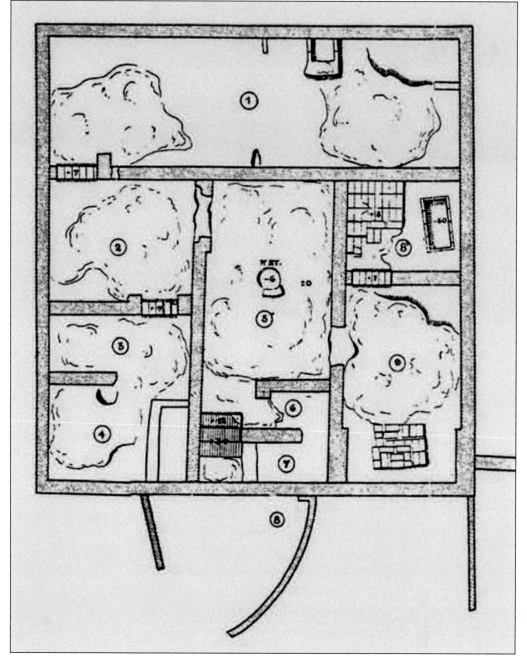

The plan of Q 47.16, the El Amarna house where stela JE 44865 was found, as recorded by Borchardt & H. Ricke (*Die Wohnhäuser in Tell el-Amarna* [Berlin, 1980] Plan 45).

over time developed a brownish hue. The paint layer appeared to be rather soft, especially in the more deeply cut signs like sun disks and *t*-hieroglyphs. It seems possible that the pigments were actually kneaded into a matrix of beeswax.[32] Thus it could be that the "greenish" oxidization is simulated, perhaps by a mixture of blue and yellow pigment. Materials like red and yellow ochre — used by the ancient Egyptians — would have been available in Cairo at the time. Furthermore, the excavation of the Thutmose compound yielded finds of red and blue pigments.[33] The pigments and binding agents actually used in painting the stela could be determined by a full-scale analysis.

The painted stela thus looks like a forgery modeled upon the Berlin relief. Regardless of who the forger was, the painted stela offered Borchardt an object that he could praise as counterpart to the bust of Nefertiti. At the same time, it assured that he had an object that he could decline to take as part of Berlin's share (with a good reason). The stela thus served Borchardt's purposes; and, therefore, the suspicion is justified that he might perhaps be the one who is behind the deception. But is it admissible to suspect Borchardt of forgery?

In fact Adolf Erman, Borchardt's Egyptology teacher, reported one instance when Borchardt faked an ancient object. In 1887-88 Borchardt had a part-time job under Erman, who was in charge of the Egyptian Museum in Berlin.[34] At that time Borchardt studied architecture at the Technical University Berlin; Erman gave him private lessons in Egyptology. He must have also taken private lessons in Assyriology, because — in his first scholarly work — he published and explained the layout of a building and the accompanying texts on a cuneiform tablet.[35]

Erman was also responsible for the Assyriologists employed in the Egyptian Department. He recalled, *"that Borchardt tried to find out how the Babylonian scribes produced the cuneiform signs. Soon he found out how cuneiform could be reproduced in a very simple fashion. The script which he produced was impeccable, and thus he made a clay tablet which was completely akin to the authentic ones with the exception that it contained logarithms in cuneiform numbers. Borchardt put the tablet into a box with genuine tablets which were studied by the Assyriologist [Felix]Peiser. The latter and a colleague were enthusiastic when they deciphered the tablet and Peiser intended to publish it immediately. Who knows what might have happened, had Borchardt not confessed that the tablet was of his own making? Thus the affair had no other consequences besides that the unpleasant task fell to me to calm down Peiser who had every right to be provoked."*[36]

Presumably Borchardt hit upon the idea of a logarithmic tablet early in 1888, when Erman bought an Old Babylonian tablet containing square numbers.[37] The idea of preparing a tablet with logarithms was very original — and to date Assyriologists know of only one such tablet.[38] Another original idea of his seems to have been outfitting the Cairo stela with sockets, as if it had had doors like a Medieval triptych or winged altar. No other relief with fixtures for a door has ever been found at El Amarna. There is one stela of New Kingdom date in the Cleveland Museum with door sockets.[39] This stela has no provenance and was bought in 1920, when Borchardt's winged-door stela had been on exhibition in Cairo for several years.[40]

The bust of Nefertiti was excavated on December 6,

1912. Some days may have passed between the conception of the desperate idea how it could be won for Berlin, and the decision of how to execute the plan. Borchardt returned to Cairo on December 17 and came back to El Amarna on January 16, 1913. He seems to have stayed in Cairo during the interim.[41] The painted stela was found on January 11, 1913. On that day the excavation foreman, Ahmad el Senussi, and his workmen cleared house 47.12; at the same time and some 200 metres away, foreman Abulhassan and his crew finished work on house Q 47.16. Abulhassan — or rather one of his workmen — unearthed the painted stela behind the house. The stela lay below a mere twenty centimeters of sand.[42]

Had the forger hidden the painted stela behind Q 47.16 without telling a confidant where to look, the object might easily have remained buried in the sand. The forger required an accomplice and Abulhassan must come to mind; and the architect who supervised him, as well. The forger had to reckon with the possibility that Egyptologist Ranke would recognize the fake. Instead, Ranke praised the relief when he entered a description of it into the expedition diary. He noticed the similarity to the Berlin Royal Family stela and stated that *"the artistic execution of the object is definitely superior to that of the Berlin relief."*[43] If we bear in mind that such fulsome praise of the stela came to a halt soon after it was decided that Nefertiti would stay in Berlin, we could guess that Ranke was bowing to Borchardt's opinion, and therefore may have been a confidant.

More than a month elapsed between the discovery of the bust and the finding of the stela, providing enough time to carve and paint the relief. There are no indications as to who the forging sculptor might have been. It is just possible that he was able to make use of a plaster cast of the Berlin relief. According to the catalogues of the Berlin plaster-cast department, casts of the Berlin relief have been sold since 1924. But the respective master-form received a number, according to which it ought to have been made between 1912 and 1914. Thus, we lack firm proof that the master-form existed by December 1912. Nevertheless, the possibility remains that, in that month, a cast of the Berlin relief was ordered and used as the physical model for the painted stela. At that period it took seven to eight days for a post parcel to get from Berlin to Cairo.

Borchardt conceived the painted stela to be an object which would be revered for ages. According to him, already at El Amarna it had been *"the object of daily reverent worship. But a happy coincidence and above all the high and subtle craftmanship of the artisan who created it, assured to it the continuous devout admiration of later generations appreciative of art."*[44]

Were Nefertiti & Tutankhaten Coregents?

Exploring a New Option for
the Post-Akhenaten Transition

by Aidan Dodson

Vast amounts of ink have been spilled over the minutiae of the Amarna period, yet many points remain seemingly beyond concensus. Among these is the issue of the coregent — or coregents — whom Akhenaten took to rule alongside him in his last years, and whether one or the other might have continued ruling after his death. That at least one individual was interposed between Akhenaten and Tutankhamen in the late Eighteenth Dynasty succession has been apparent from the early days of Egyptology, when a number of Nineteenth Century travelers recorded a pair of cartouches accompanying a scene in the Tomb of Meryre II (TA2) at El Amarna.[1] Indeed, so interesting were these cartouches that they were cut out by thieves in the 1880s — and have never been seen since! However a number of copies survive, the prenomen clearly reading "Ankhkheperure," while the nomen, with the terminal epithet "Djeserkheperu," was variously copied as "Senkare," "Seheqakare" and "Saakare": from a squeeze made by the Prussian Egyptologist Carl Richard Lepsius in 1845, it can be seen that the crucial second hieroglyph is poorly carved and difficult to interpret.[2] However, fresh examples of the cartouche were found by Flinders Petrie on ring bezels in his 1890 excavations at Gurob and his 1891-92 work at El Amarna, which showed that it should certainly be read as "Smenkhkare."[3] At the same time, Petrie also found a more elaborate version of the Ankhkheperure cartouche, with the epithet "Mery-Neferkheperure" (i.e. "Beloved of Akhenaten," referred to by his prenomen).[4] This was naturally assumed to also belong to Smenkhkare, as during the earlier part of the New Kingdom a "core" prenomen such as "Ankhkheperure" would only be used by one king: at this time epithets were generally an "optional extra" — unlike during the Ramesside Period, when "Setepenre" vs. "Setpenamun" was enough to distinguish Usermaatre Rameses (II) from Usermaatre Rameses (IV).

In Meryre II's tomb, Smenkhkare is accompanied by

Opposite, Gilded-wood ritual figure from the Tomb of Tutankhamen, the very evident breasts of which would suggest that it depicts a female king, not Tutankhamen himself. Photo: Kmt/Forbes

An unfinished tableau in the Tomb of Meryre II (TA2) at El Amarna, showing Smenkhkare & Meryetaten rewarding the tomb owner. The texts were carved, but the figures only sketched out. Parts of the text (the royal cartouches, highlighted here) were cut away and stolen in the 1880s, but are restored after a squeeze made by Lepsius's team & his published copies.

Adapted from Davies, *Rock Tombs of El Amarna II*, pl. xli

a Queen Mery(et)aten, who was universally recognized from the outset as Akhenaten's eldest daughter. His position as son-in-law and coregent and/or successor of Akhenaten accordingly seemed assured, while it was agreed that he had used both a "simple" and a "long" prenomen, the latter linking him with his father-in-law.

However, things became more complicated in 1922, when Howard Carter found in the Tomb of Tutankhamen a piece of a box, which named together Akhenaten, King Ankh-kheprure-mery-Neferkheperure Neferneferuaten-mery Waen-re and Queen Meryetaten.[5] This led to the recognition that the dateline in a graffito in the Tomb of Pairi (TT139) at Luxor[6] should be read as referring to the second-named person, rather

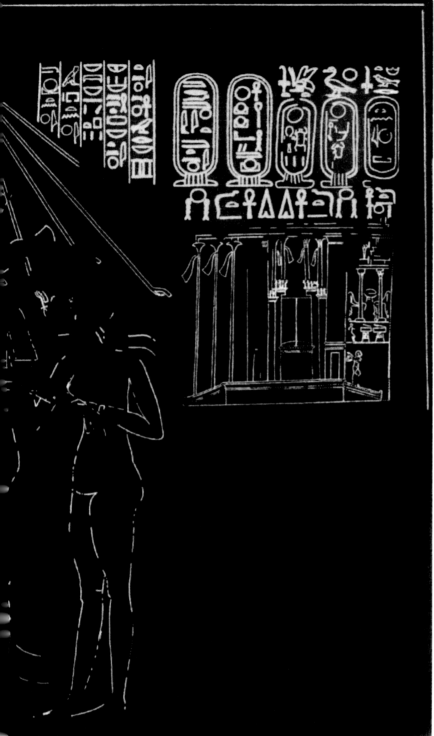

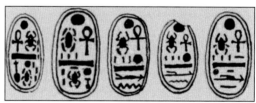

Above top, Ring bezels of Smenkhkare. Above, Ring be-
zels of Neferneferuaten.

Adapted from Petrie, *Tell el Amarna*, pl. xv

than an obscure "Akheperure Neferneferuaten," as had first been posited, or even "Neferkheperure Neferneferuaten" — assumed to be an early form of Akhenaten's name.[7]

    Given the associations with Meryetaten and Akhenaten, it was assumed that Smenkhkare and Neferneferuaten were one and the same, and that a change of nomen had accompanied the switch between the "simple" and "long" prenomina. As to which form came first, there was rather less unanimity; but the general feeling came to be that the "Neferneferuaten" form belonged to a coregency with Akhenaten and the "Smenkhkare" form belonged to an independent rule between the death of Akhenaten and the accession of Tutankhaten. Other Egyptologists, however, denied any independent reign under either name, while others promoted the view that Smenkhkare was the earlier and Neferuneferuaten the later name.[8]

This "single individual" theory remained intact within the first challenge to the consensus in 1974. Then, in the first of a series of papers,[9] English Egyptologist John Harris, then of Copenhagen University in Denmark, noted the existence of versions of the "long" prenomen that seemed to include the feminine t-ending. This could further be linked with a limited number of images — including a gilded-wood ritual statuette found in Tutankhamen's tomb — of a king whose appearance was particularly feminine, even by Amarna art's androgynous standards. These were in some cases juxtaposed with figures of Akhenaten in distinctly affectionate poses that had led to a suspicion of a homosexual relationship between Akhenaten and Smenkhkare.[10]

Harris's conclusion was that Neferneferuaten (and thus Smenkhkare) was actually a woman, and none other than Nefertiti — who had in any case borne the cognomen Neferneferuaten since Year 5. Her exceptional status while still queen-consort was put forward as a possible step towards this ultimate pharaonic status. It was additionally suggested that after Akhenaten's death she, the former Nefertiti, had changed her name once again to Smenkhkare, to mark her status as an independent ruler.

Against these pieces of evidence could be stacked various other evidence. First there was Smenkhkare's possession of a wife (Meryetaten) in TA2; then there were differences between the queenly and kingly orthographies of the name Neferneferuaten, plus the existence of a queenly ushabti of Nefertiti. In addition there was the existence of the body of a young Amarna period (male) king in KV55 in the Valley of the Kings, which many simply could not accept as being that of Akhenaten.[11] Attempts to explain some of this away through sheer obfuscation[12] or to posit that Meryetaten might have become the nominal spouse of her mother were always distinctly unconvincing.

A middle way was, however, proposed by Rolf Krauss of the Egyptian Museum, Berlin, in 1978, in which he suggested that while Smenkhkare/Neferneferuaten was a man, his wife, Meryetaten, might have ruled briefly with the feminized prenomen "Ankhetkheperure" between Akhenaten's death and her husband's accession.[13] Ten years later in 1988, James P. Allen, then of the Metropolitan Museum of Art and now of Brown University, published a paper in which he proposed cutting the Gordian Knot by separating Smenkhkare from Neferneferuaten,

Graffito from the Tomb of Pairi (TT139), dated to Year 3 of Neferneferuaten, showing that the cult of Amen was once again permitted by then.

Adapted from Gardiner, *JEA* 14 (1928), pl. v-vi

recognizing that the "simple" and "extended" versions of the Ankhkheperure cartouche could, after all, have belonged to different kings. A key observation was that there were no occasions where the "long" version of the prenomen occurred alongside the nomen Smenkhkare, nor the "short" version with the name Neferneferuaten. There was by no means universal acceptance of this, the present writer arguing against the proposal as late as 2003.[14]

However, in 1998, French Egyptologist Marc Gabolde pointed out that a number of cartouches of Neferneferuaten that had been read as using the epithet "Mery-Akhenaten" actually bore the epithet "akhet-en-hi-es" — "effective for her husband." The correctness of these readings by Gabolde was confirmed beyond any doubt by exhaustive reassessments of the palimpsest inscriptions inside the canopic coffinettes ultimately used for Tutankhamen, which had long been known to have been usurped from Neferneferuaten: wherever the epithet could be detected, it was indeed "akhet-en-hi-es."[15]

The femininity of Neferneferuaten having been proved beyond doubt, what other name might she have borne before becoming a king? And did (the male) Smenkhkare precede or succeed her? This latter issue is significant when trying to work out their possible origins. As already noted, the majority of scholars (whether accepting one or two kings, of whatever sex) have lent towards the conclusion that the Smenkhkare titulary is the later of the two. However, this conclusion is by no means definitive; and a good case can be made for Smenkhkare being, in fact the earlier of the two rulers.

First, there is a jar from KV62 that bears the joint names of both Akhenaten and Smenkhkare.[16] While this can of course be explained away as a mere "memorial," it can be used to reinforce other data. Second, if the Smenkhkare sketch in the tomb of Meryre II was placed on the wall after the death of Akhenaten, this has to be dated half a decade or more[17] after any other known decoration in an El Amarna tomb.[18] If work continued on decorating El Amarna private tombs after Akhenaten's death, why do we have no depictions — even initial sketches — of Neferneferuaten or Tutankhaten in any of them?

It would thus seem more likely that the Smenkhkare/Meryetaten depiction was executed shortly after the completion of the explicitly dated Year 12 "durbar" scene on the adjacent wall — and thus securely within the reign of Akhenaten. Indeed, the placement of the Smenkhkare scene within weeks of the laying out of the "durbar" scene is suggested by the tableaux's position in the tomb — directly above the sloping passage to the substructure. Until the artists had adorned the whole righthand side of the chamber and gotten out of the way, the builders could not make progress in cutting the long corridor and chamber in which Meryre II intended for his mummy to be laid.

Third, when confronted by the respective prenomina of

Unfinished stela in Berlin, dedicated by Pay, which shows two naked Amarna kings in an affectionate pose. This was long cited as evidence for a homosexual relationship between Akhenaten & Smenkhkare. The shape of the breasts of the lefthand figure makes it clear, however, that it is meant to depict a female — almost certainly Neferneferuaten. However, the presence of only three cartouches indicates that she was not yet a full king when the stela was carved, in spite of wearing the Blue Crown. Such "quasi-kingly" status is later found among some of the high priests of Amen during the Twenty-first Dynasty. Author's photo

Smenkhkare and Neferneferuaten, one feels rather uncomfortable with the simple "Ankhkheperure" following after the more elaborate "Ankhkheperure + epithet."[19] As already noted, the use of the same core cartouche-name by two successive pharaohs is unusual prior to the late New Kingdom; but, when it is, one finds epithets added to the previously used core to distinguish the "new" owner — not the other way round.[20]

A fourth consideration — which must, however, be used with care — concerns the aforementioned graffito of Year 3 of Neferneferuaten in the Tomb of Pairi. It contains three mentions of the "Estate of Ankhkheperure" and its Amen temple. All mentions lack the epithet that is to be found in the Neferneferuaten-prenomen in the first line. Since all known examples of the prenomen of Neferneferuaten include an epithet, the implication seems to be that the simple "Ankhkheperure" refers to Smenkhkare, who must therefore have preceded Neferneferuaten.

Accordingly, taking all the evidence together, it would seem most probable that Smenkhkare was appointed coregent with Akhenaten some time around the latter's thirteenth regnal year and married to Meryetaten. Whether this marriage produced offspring is unclear, although at twelve/thirteen she would have been just about old enough to bear children. Potentially theirs are two girls, Meryetaten-tasherit and Ankhesenpaaten-tasherit, known from Amarna blocks found at Ashmunein.[21] It is clear that at least one of these girls was a granddaughter of (presumably) Nefertiti[22]; but there is no real evidence for the general assumption that they were the offspring of Meryetaten and Ankhesenpaaten by their own father, Akhenaten — or, indeed, that the latter impregnated any of his daughters.[23] Far more reasonable would be the view that Meryetaten-tasherit and Ankhesenpaaten-tasherit were the children of Smenkhkare and Meryetaten, named after their mother and aunt.

Concerning Smenkhkare's origins, there is very little to go on. Under normal circumstances one would expect a coregent to be the eldest son of the senior king, the heir presumptive. Thus, one could take the view that Smenkhkare was Akhenaten's elder son, perhaps a year older or younger than his sister-wife, Meryetaten. However, in Year 13/14 he would only have been aged twelve or so, and perhaps a little young for elevation to joint rule. In any event, however, a good case can be made for Smenkhkare's skeletal remains having survived,[24] which are those of an adult of at least twenty years of age. If these bones are indeed Smenkhkare's, he cannot have been a son of Akhenaten. Since the latter had a son in the person of Tutankhaten,[25] the question becomes why someone other than Akhenaten's son was elevated to kingship ahead of Tutankhaten, who would, by all appearances, have been the heir to the throne.

The answer may well lie in the identity of the person who followed Smenkhkare in the coregency. The very fact that Smenkhkare was succeeded as coregent by a woman suggests that Akhenaten's motivation for appointing a coruler in the first place may have been something other than the usual concept of elevating the crown-prince to the throne to guarantee the succession and/or allow him an "apprenticeship" under his father. Rather, one wonders whether circumstances had come to demand that Akhenaten needed to have someone to share the burden of rule. Perhaps his own health was breaking down —

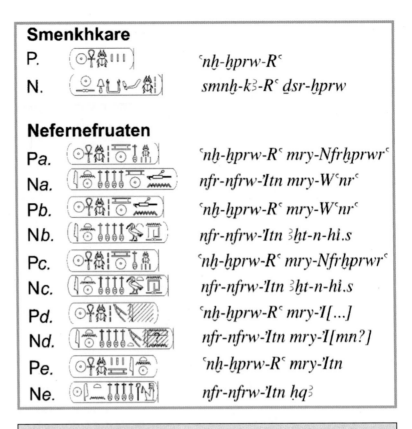

Smenkhkare

P. ꜥnḫ-ḫprw-Rꜥ

N. smnḫ-kꜣ-Rꜥ ḏsr-ḫprw

Nefernefruaten

Pa. ꜥnḫ-ḫprw-Rꜥ mry-Nfrḫprwrꜥ

Na. nfr-nfrw-'Itn mry-Wꜥnrꜥ

Pb. ꜥnḫ-ḫprw-Rꜥ mry-Wꜥnrꜥ

Nb. nfr-nfrw-'Itn ꜣḫt-n-ḥỉ.s

Pc. ꜥnḫ-ḫprw-Rꜥ mry-Nfrḫprwrꜥ

Nc. nfr-nfrw-'Itn ꜣḫt-n-ḥỉ.s

Pd. ꜥnḫ-ḫprw-Rꜥ mry-'I[...]

Nd. nfr-nfrw-'Itn mry-'I[mn?]

Pe. ꜥnḫ-ḫprw-Rꜥ mry-'Itn

Ne. nfr-nfrw-'Itn ḥqꜣ

Above, Known variants of the cartouche names of Smenkhkare & Neferneferuaten. Author's graphic *Below, Restored cartouches of Akhenaten & Smenkhkare on a jar from the Tomb of Tutankhamen (in the Cairo Museum).* Author's graphic after Loeben, *Amarna Letters* 3 (1994), fig. 5

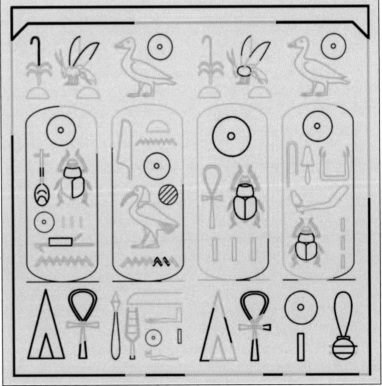

or he feared the plague that some have suggested was brought to Egypt by those attending the "durbar" and may have caused the death of Meketaten and Dowager Great Wife Tiye, both of whom died soon afterwards — and feared for the continuation of his religious revolution if he died leaving just the five-year-old Tutankhaten. With an anointed coregent in place there would be an adult in a position to ensure continuity — and become Tutankhaten's co-ruler and guardian in turn, if need be.

This reasoning rules out James Allen's recent candidate for King Neferneferuaten's earlier identity: Princess Neferneferuaten-tasherit, fourth daughter of Akhenaten,[26] who would have been hardly older than Tutankhaten himself (or even younger). Meryetaten, the eldest daughter and now dowager-queen of Smenkhkare, has also been put forward as a possibility.[27] However, her candidacy seems fatally undermined by the existence of the aforementioned box fragment from Tutankhamen's tomb, which gives the names and titles of Akhenaten, Neferneferuaten and Meryetaten as clearly separate individuals.[28]

This of course leaves the option of Nefertiti, whose role even as queen has long been seen as having many pharaonic traits,[29] had used the name "Neferneferuaten" since her husband's Year 5. She is now known to have still been using the title of Kings Great Wife in Year 16,[30] but the stela on p. 156 would indicate that a women — presumably the future King Neferneferuaten — was wearing a pharaonic crown while not yet an actual king. It thus seems to the writer all but certain that on Smenkhkare's demise, perhaps around Year 14 of Akhenaten, Nefertiti assumed near-kingly titles, becoming King Neferneferuaten during the last year of her husband's life.

The status of Meryetaten in the later setup is intriguing, given her mention as a King's Great Wife after her parents on the KV62 box fragment. Does this relate to her status as the widow of Smenkhkare, as "wife" of her father — or, perhaps, even of her mother as well? It is clear that the title of "Great Wife" was not simply a designation of the king's senior sexual partner. Rather, she had key ritual roles,[31] and it was to have someone capable of fulfilling these latter functions that probably lay behind our cases of a father "espousing" his daughters. Rameses II did this after the deaths of his Great Wives, and perhaps Akhenaten did so after Nefertiti had given up her "Great Wifely" duties to become a pharaoh.

The remaining key question is whether Neferneferuaten remained in office after Akhenaten's death. For this the crucial document is, of course, the TT139 graffito, dated as it is to a Year 3; but from what point did Neferneferuaten count her reign? Was it from her appointment as coregent, or from the death of Akhenaten? The former has generally been assumed, particularly in light of the view that she was followed, rather than preceded, by Smenkhkare. However, given her anomalous status as a female king — by her names explicitly dependent on her husband — is this likely? Indeed, if the Year 3 is to be counted from Akhenaten's death, is it of Neferneferuaten alone, or might it have been shared with the young Tutankhaten, just as Hatshepsut had shared the regnal years of Thutmose III? Such a counting would be consistent with the jar docket from El Amarna that has "Year 1" written over "Year 17."[32] This has always been an obstacle to any view that has Neferneferuaten beginning to count her years during Akhenaten's lifetime, yet also having a period of rule after his death (although, as it is now known that Neferneferuaten only became a full king during Akhenaten's last year, this may not necessarily be an issue,

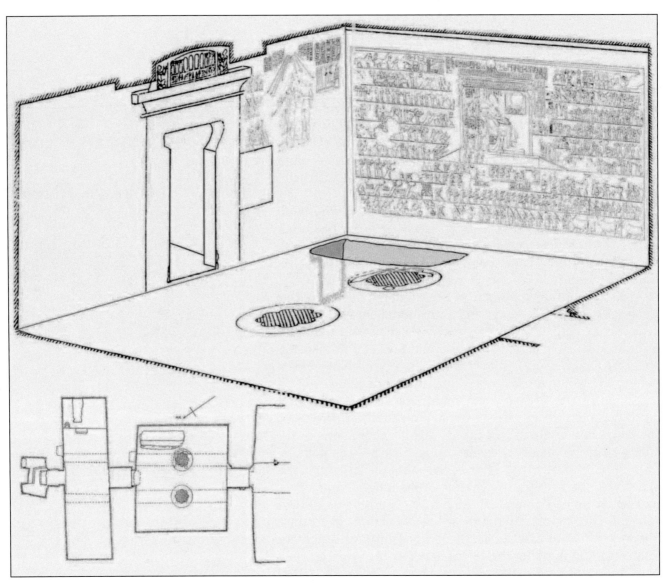

Locations of the "durbar" & Smenkhkare tableaux in the El Amarna Tomb of Meryre II. This shows how the latter was clearly part of the same decorative scheme as the "durbar," with its carving interrupted by the need to begin work on the entrance to the substructure directly below.

Author's graphic, after Davies, *Rock Tombs* II, pls. xxvii, xxxvii, xli

as any independent "Year 1" of hers would have corresponded in whole or part to his Year 17).

If she began the count simultaneously with Tutankhaten on Akhenaten's death, this would work nicely on many levels. Indirect support for this reconstruction may derive from a letter[33] found at El Amarna from Hittite king Suppiliumash to a king "Khuriya" of Egypt on the latter's accession. At this time, the normal way of referring to a pharaoh was by his prenomen; and his overseas correspondents followed this convention, albeit transcribed into Akkadian. So Thutmose III (Menkheperre) appeared as "Manakhpiya," Amenhotep III (Nebmaatre) as "Nibmuariya," Akhenaten (Neferkheperure) as "Napkhuriya" and Tutankhamen (Nebkheperure) as "Nibkhuriya." Thus, Suppiliumash was writing to a king whose prenomen was clearly "X-kheperure," but with the first element omitted.

Four kings fit this pattern: Akhenaten, Smenkhkare, Neferneferuaten and Tutankhamen. The second can be ruled out, as Smenkhkare seems never to have reigned alone, as is demanded by the contents of the letter. Arguments can be made for Akhenaten being the recipient, but the letter has a tone that suggests that not all was well with Egypt-Hittite relations. This

Table of the proposed configuration of the reigns around the end of the reign of Akhenaten & indicating probable uses of regnal years by each ruler.

fits better with the aftermath of the Great Syrian Campaign, which took place well after Akhenaten's accession, and in which the Hittites had begun to undermine Egyptian authority in north Syria. The letter was thus most likely written to Akhenaten's direct successor(s). Its address to the Hittite king's "brother" would seemingly suggest that the intended addressee was not the female Neferneferuaten; but, on the other hand, diplomacy may have deemed her to be technically male — and certainly "Khuria" could be taken as a contraction of "Ankhkheperure," the Hittite ear conflating the two kh-sounds at the beginning of the name. Or perhaps the existence of two kings may have led to a confusion in Hatti that led to the use of a neutral "Khuriya" that could fit both rulers?

As we have suggested, Akhenaten's motivation for elevating Nefertiti to kingship may have included a desire to guarantee the continuity of the Atenist revolution. That he would have been sadly disappointed is clear from the content of the TT139 graffito, which comprises a prayer to Amen written for Pawah, himself a priest of that god. It is also unclear what precisely Neferneferuaten was calling herself at this time. Although damaged, there seems insufficient space at the end of her prenomen to include the expected "mery-Neferkheperure," while the traces at the end of the nomen may — or may not — contain "Waenre." It could thus have been a simple "mery(et)aten" — or conceivably even "mery(et)amen"! In favor of the former for the prenomen is its presence of the name "Ankhkheperure-meryaten" on three gold sequins, accompanied by the nomen "Neferneferuaten-heqa."[34] Both fit well with Neferneferuaten distancing herself from her late husband after his death and a decision to seek reconciliation with the status quo.

Thus we have a seemingly incongruous scenario of Akhenaten's wife and apparent fellow prime-mover of the Atenist revolution overseeing its dismantlement and a return to orthodoxy — or at least a more pantheist view in which Amen was once again acceptable. However, it is clear that, for at least some traditionalists, the former Nefertiti's position was not tolerable. This is demonstrated by the fact that Neferneferuaten was not buried as a king: much of her funerary equipment, including such key pieces as the canopic coffinettes, was taken out of storage and used a few years later for the interment of Tutankhamen.

One might thus see that soon after Year 3, Neferneferuaten either died or was removed from power, delivering the young Tutankhaten into the hands of new associates, whose approach to the return to orthodoxy was more radical. It would be at this point that the king and Great Wife Ankhesenpaaten had their names changed to Tutankhamen and Ankhesenamen, and that the events were set in motion for the formal counter-reformation.

A fragmentary stela, apparently from El Amarna, depicting Tutankhaten offering to Amen & Mut, thereby marking the end of the Aten's exclusivity & the beginning of the road back to orthodoxy. This piece, in Berlin, was severely damaged during World War II.

After Erman, ZÄS 38 (1900), 113

Seats of Power

The Thrones of Tutankhamen

"Beneath one of the couches was the State Throne of Tutankhamen, probably one of the most beautiful objects of art ever discovered."

by Marianne Eaton-Krauss

This first mention in print of Tutankhamen's gold throne appeared in an article which announced the finding of the tomb in the edition of *The Times of London* of November 30, 1922. A popular account of the "marvellous discovery," published in the *Illustrated London News* little more than a week later, on December 9, 1922, alloted pride of place to the throne — the "first ever discovered" — in a preliminary survey of the tomb's contents. Shortly thereafter Howard Carter entered his detailed, sober description of the throne under Obj. No. 91 in the card catalogue of the items removed during the clearance.

Three more chairs from the tomb merit the description "throne," by virtue of their texts and decoration. Along with four chairs, eleven stools, twelve footstools, six beds and more than fifty boxes, they represent the most important, as well as the best-preserved group of furniture to have survived antiquity virtually intact.

Howard Carter would have glimpsed Tutankhamen's cedar throne (Obj. No. 87), lying on its side next to the gold throne, on his initial inspection of the contents in the tomb's Antechamber. This room, at the bottom of the entrance corridor, provided access to the remaining three chambers in the tomb. The objects arrayed against the far wall — on top of, underneath and in front of the three large gilded "ritual couches" — included five footstools, eight stools and all but one of the chairs, as well as the gold and cedar thrones. The two remaining thrones — the child's (Obj. No. 349) and the inlaid ebony one (Obj. No. 351) — were found with two stools, seven footstools, and the remains of a wickerwork chair and stool in the Annexe, the last chamber to be emptied of its "treasure."

The child's throne is the most modest in design and

Opposite, Detail of the backrest of the elaborately inlaid gold throne (Obj. No. 91) found in KV62. It depicts a casually seated king, identified as Tutankhamen, wearing an elaborate Atef Crown & attended by a queen (named as Ankhesenamen) in a Nubian-style wig with a Hathor headdress atop a modius. Photo: G.B. Johnson

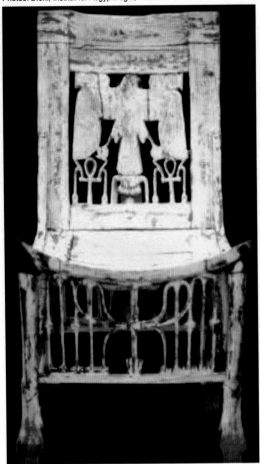

Three views of the child's throne (Obj. No. 349) found in the KV62 Annex. Howard Carter was of the opinion that it came from the "royal nursery." Of the Tutankhamen thrones, it is the simplest in design & workmanship. Made of wood painted white, the openwork backrest displays the motif of a falcon with opened wings.

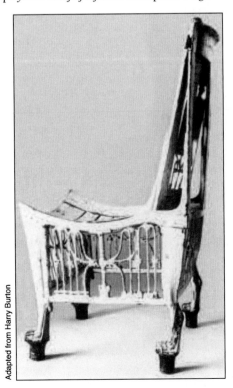

Adapted from Harry Burton

workmanship of the thrones from the tomb. The nearly square seat measures only about 33 cm. on a side. When Carter published the first photographs and description of it, he relegated this child's throne to the "royal nursery." I have cited the inscriptions which call the king Tutankhamen as evidence that he was still a boy when his name was changed from Tutankhaten, as he was called at his accession, and therefore even younger when he became king.[1] (The name, which means "Living Image of Aten," unequivocally associated the bearer intimately with Akhenaten's sun god and would have been inappropriate for anyone other than a prince.) E.F. Wente and J.E. Harris, who believe Tutankhamen was in his mid-twenties when he died and thus a teenager a decade earlier when he came to the throne, suggest that the child's throne was not made for him but for a child of his.[2] There is no parallel in support of this idea; and, furthermore, other child-sized objects — in particular, a little flail (Obj. No. 269e), which is inscribed with the name Tutankhaten — certainly cannot have been made for any child other than the king himself.

The child's throne shares four diagnostic features with the cedar throne. The design of both includes lion legs on ribbed "drums," a curved and inclined backrest decorated with openwork, a double-coved seat frame (i.e., curved on all four sides) and openwork "grilles" filling the space between the seat and the stretchers.

The earliest seats (and beds) preserved from Egypt have bull legs. During the Old Kingdom, lion legs slowly supplanted them, initially in the design of furniture made for royalty. Egyptian craftsmen were not only keen observers of the flora and fauna surrounding them, they were also respectful of nature. They shaped the left-rear leg of a piece of furniture like the left hindleg of a bull or lion, and the other legs accordingly, right down to the careful replication of the characteristic spur and rudimentary claw in the case of feline forelegs. A three-legged stool with animal legs from Tutankhamen's tomb, Obj. No. 412, provides substantiation of the adage "the exception proves the rule." It has only three legs, and they are canine. Dog legs are very rare in Egyptian furniture. The motif the designer chose to decorate this stool's seat may well have influenced his choice of dog legs: the openwork depicts two bagged lions, bound head to foot. Hounds accompany the pharaoh in depictions of him hunting lions and desert game from his chariot, as well as in scenes showing him in battle against Egypt's foreign foes.[3]

The ribbed "drums" that are carved in one with the lion paws or bull hooves imitate palm fiber or reeds wrapped around the bottom of a chair leg to protect it from dirt and damage. Stretchers were introduced to increase the sturdiness of straight-legged furniture; respect for nature inhibited craftsmen from using them in the design of animal-legged stools and chairs, until shortly before Tutankhaten's accession.

The seats of the earliest stools and chairs were flat; sometimes they sloped slightly downwards towards the back. Double-coved seat frames were first used for stools at the beginning of the New Kingdom. Bed frames, too, were sometimes coved. Specialists have conjectured that coving might have been introduced to Egypt from the Near East, but I believe it is more likely that seat (and bed) frames sagging under the weight of the owner suggested the curved shape. Chairs with double-coved seats are documented from the Amarna period onwards. The seat frame was filled with wooden slats, as in the construction of the child's and cedar thrones from Tutankhamen's tomb, or with webbing of palm fiber or linen cord.

The first lion-legged chairs that have curved and inclined backrests date to the Middle Kingdom.[4] There are only three examples of such backrests that are embellished with openwork: the cedar throne and the child's throne from Tutankhamen's tomb and an armchair in Cairo, which comes from the tomb of Amenhotep III's parents-in-law in the Valley of the Kings (KV46).[5] An openwork panel is also set into the flat, perpendicular backrest of a lion-legged chair from the burial of Senenmut's parents, now in the Metropolitan Museum of Art, New York.[6] The dominant element in the openwork design of the child's throne — a falcon with unfolded wings — is apotropaic, like the motifs in the openwork of the chair in New York and the one from KV46: amuletic hieroglyphic signs and figures of the household gods Bes and

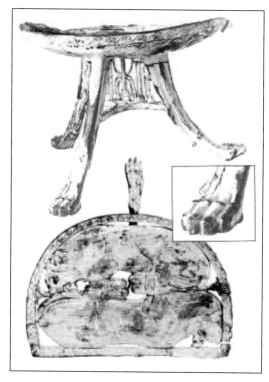

Above, Three-legged stool (Obj. No. 412) from the KV62 Annex, with bound lions on the seat & unusual canine legs. Below, a lion-legged small stool (Obj. No. 78) from the KV62 Antechamber. Openwork grilles on the four sides are the Unification of the Two Lands motif. Photos adapted from Harry Burton

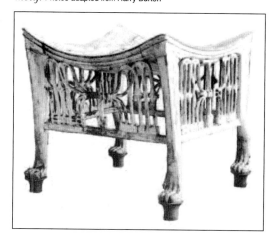

Right, Tutankhamen's cedar throne (Obj. No. 91) from the KV62 Antechamber & its accompanying cedar-wood footstool (Obj. No. 90), decorated on its top surface by Egypt's bound traditional foes. Opposite, Detail of the decoration of the backrest, which is dominated by the kneeling figure of the god Heh, who offers an endless reign to the king, symbolized by the notched palm-ribs he holds. Flanking the god — who is crowned by a sun disk with uraei & has a large ankh pendant from one arm — are panels with the king's cartouches & larger serekhs surmounted by Horus falcons. Decorative openwork grilles depicting the Unification of the Two lands once filled the spaces between the seat & stretchers on all four sides of the throne; but these are missing, except for the sema-glyph. At top of the throne back is a sheet-gold winged sun-disk.

Photos adapted from Kodansha, Ltd © 1978

Below. A backview of the cedar throne.

Adapted from Harry Burton

Taweret. This kind of decoration is typical for the private, domestic rooms of the home, rather than for the more public areas, and is especially appropriate for bedroom furnishings, where it should protect the owner when most vulnerable, during the hours of sleep. The white painting of the child's throne and the minimal use of gold (only the claws of the lion paws and the drums below are gilt) are consistent with non-official use, in the private apartments of a palace.

By contrast, the elements combined in the openwork decoration of the cedar throne are not apotropaic. The kneeling figure of the god Heh refers to the function of the backrest it decorates, for this demigod is closely associated with erect posture as manifest in the *djed*-pillar as the backbone of Osiris. Heh proffers an endless reign, symbolized by the notched palm ribs in his hands, to Tutankhamen, immanent

166

in his names inscribed in the flanking *serekhs* and in the smaller cartouches.

Once decorative openwork "grilles" filled the space between the seat and the stretchers on all four sides of the cedar throne, as they still do in the child's throne. They are also intact in two lion-legged stools from the tomb (Obj. Nos. 78 and 467). But those of the gold throne are missing, as are those of the cedar throne, and they are damaged in the inlaid ebony throne. The motif shared by all these grilles is the unification of Egypt, expressed by the heraldic plants of Upper and Lower Egypt, the water lily and papyrus, knotted around the *sema*-hieroglyph which reads "to unite." Many commentators have followed Carter and Mace in supposing that tomb robbers after precious metal made off with the grilles that are missing from the cedar and gold thrones. But some Egyptologists have dissented from this idea, pointing out that once a tomb robber held a grille in his hands, he would have realized that it was made of gilded wood, not solid gold. And why should a robber go to the trouble to wrench away the grille from between the legs at the back of the gold throne but leave the conspicuous gilded-lion protomes at the front untouched?

In fact, only one seat found in the tomb preserves unequivocal evidence for a robbery in antiquity, the stool with flared legs (Obj. No. 142b+149). Recent studies of this type of stool err in supposing that the Tomb of Tutankhamen did not contain one.[7] In fact, every type of stool in use during the later Eighteenth Dynasty is represented in the treasure. The legs of flared legs stools, which were customarily decorated with grooves, were not made on a lathe but rather produced by hand turning.

The culprit who destroyed Tutankhamen's flared-leg stool tore the legs out of the seat frame to get at the thick gold bands encircling the top of each, and he ripped the thin gold sheeting from the flared sections, leaving behind only some of the tiny nails that once held it in place. Three legs of this stool were found with their stretchers under one of the ritual couches in the Antechamber; the fourth leg and the seat were shoved down behind the chariot wheels leaning aganst the opposite wall. The findspots suggest a surrepticious attempt to hide evidence; perhaps the thief was a member of the burial party.

Another theory proposed to account for the missing grilles of the gold and cedar thrones suggests that when King Ay made the arrangements for Tutankhamen's burial, he ordered the removal of the grilles to deny his predecessor's claim to rule Egypt. But such action is at odds with the official policy of Ay's reign, which endeavored to associate him closely with Tutankhamen.[8] Nor can it be reconciled with

Ay's role in the wall paintings of the tomb, which show him in the pious act of a priest performing the Opening of the Mouth ceremony on Tutankhamen's mummy, essential for his continued existence in the Hereafter.

I suspect that most damage to the grilles of the thrones occurred when they were in use, or, at the latest, during their transport to the tomb. Rather than replace or repair the missing and damaged parts, those responsible for stocking the tomb removed the remaining stems and stalks for appearances' sake, but not the undamaged *sema*-signs, which were in any case securely attached by tenons to the stretchers below and seat frame above. Perhaps these *sema*-elements were even considered sufficient to express the symbolic message of the complete design.

The remains of the grilles of the cedar throne present an anomaly. The bases from which the missing plants sprang are still attached to the stretchers. At the left both exemplify the bases appropriate for papyrus plants. In other words the *sema*-hieroglyph on the left side was flanked not by the papyrus and the lily, but by the papyrus alone. On the right the single preserved base belongs to the Upper Egyptian lily, while the grilles at the front and the back both showed the papyrus at the king's left and the lily to the right, so that the entire left side of the throne cited the north and the right the south. Because the cardinal points played an important role in the consciousness of the Egyptians, this arrangement implies that when Tutankhamen sat on the cedar throne, it was placed so that he faced eastwards. Perhaps it was even intended for one particular place in the palace at Mennufer (Memphis), where the court resided when the "Restoration Decree" that institutionalized the re-endowment of the cults for the traditional gods in the aftermath of Akhenaten's "heresy" was promulated.

There is no reason whatsoever to suppose that the cedar throne was used at Tutankhamen's coronation, as has been suggested. According to the representations in relief and painting, the appropriate throne in that context was the so-called block throne. The texts inscribed on the front of the backrest and those across the headrail and down the stiles and center brace behind include Tutankhamen's complete titulary and a number of epithets associating him with Mennufer (Memphis) and Iunu (Heliopolis). A cabinet (Obj. No. 403) and a chest (Obj. No. 585), which are also made of cedar and likewise embellished with gilt, are similarly inscribed. The more extensive texts of the cabinet parallel passages in the "Restoration Decree," whose complete text is preserved on the monumental stela CG 34183 from Karnak Temple.[9] This leads me to propose that this suite of furniture could have been ordered in connection with the restoration.

A cedar footstool (Obj. No. 88) lay overturned underneath the cedar throne. Since the footstool is made of the same material as the throne and was found with it, Carter's idea that they belonged together is quite plausible. The sunk-relief decoration on the top of the footstool depicts nine bound foreigners, who embody Egypt's traditional nine foes.[10] Subjected enemies are also featured in the decoration of four more footstools from the tomb (Obj. Nos. 30, 90, 378 and 511). The visual message is made explicit in the texts of the cedar footstool: *"all foreign lands are under the feet of this perfect god* (i.e., Pharaoh)." A variant of the text which describes foreign countries as under the king's sandals is found on a footstool inlaid with ivory, ebony, calcite and faience (Obj. No. 378). These materials, its technique and the patterns used in its decoration associate the footstool with the inlaid ebony throne (Obj. No. 351), next to which Carter found it in the Annexe. This throne is an imitation folding chair. Carter called it the king's "ecclesiastical throne," because it reminded him of the kind of chair used by bishops since the Middle Ages. There is, however, no reason to suppose that Tutankhamen used it in a specifically religious context. "Inlaid ebony throne" — which refers to the material of the chair and the technique of its decoration — is an appropriate descriptive name for this imitation folding chair from the tomb.

Specialists have found it difficult to respond objectively to the design of the inlaid ebony throne. For Hollis Baker it is a masterpiece of craftsmanship; for Danish historian of furniture Ole Wanscher, who devoted a book to the history of the folding stool,[11] its design is a clumsy and ultimately unsuccessful pastiche of incompatible elements. William Stevenson Smith — for many years responsible for the Egyptian collection in the Museum of Fine Arts, Boston — thought it exemplified the "disastrous" consequences of "Syrian" influence on Egyptian taste.[12]

The earliest evidence from Egypt for folding stools dates to the later Middle Kingdom. (Two examples — Obj. Nos. 139 and 140 — were found in Tutankhamen's tomb.) Perhaps the design was introduced at that time from the Near East. All the comparative evidence suggests, however, that the imitation folding chair was a fancy invented by an Egyptian craftsman in the later Eighteenth Dynasty. Only the ebony and ivory used in the manufacture of Tutankhamen's imitation folding chair are undeniably non-Egyptian in origin. In statuary and in scenes in tombs, only men are depicted using folding stools. The same applies to the imitation folding chair which makes its initial appearance in a painting fragment, now in the British Museum, from a Theban tomb datable to Amenhotep III's reign. The context is not preserved. Rameses II is the only king shown using an imitation folding chair;

Opposite, Full view of the KV62 heavily inlaid ebony throne (Obj. No. 351) & its footstool (Obj. No. 378) — with depictions of Egypt's traditional nine foes. Carter called this seat an "ecclesiastical throne," since it reminded him of a bishop's chair, although there is nothing to suggest that Tutankhamen used it in a purely religious context. Photo adapted from Kodshanda Ltd. © 1978

Details of the heavily inlaid ebony throne. Right, The back is exceptionally ornate & has been suggested to reflect the "disastrous" consequences of Syrian influence on Egyptian taste. Photo: Diehl, Institut fur Aegyptologie und Koptologie, Westfalische Wilhelms-Universitat, Meunster

The deeply covered seat of the throne (below) imitates a piebald cowhide with a rectangular panel in the center suggesting a cushion of animal skins.

Photo adapted from Burton

Bottom, One of the richly inlaid goose-headed legs of the throne, of a type known from folding stools, including one from KV62 (Obj. No. 83). Author's photo

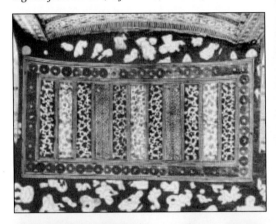

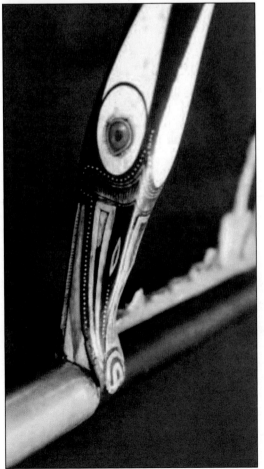

in all other reliefs and paintings non-royal men sit on them.[13] The only actual preserved example comes from Tutankhamen's tomb.

Goose-headed legs are often found in the design of preserved folding stools from Egypt. Here the goose heads are richly inlaid with ivory, and there is a panel made of bark decorated with a pattern of lily petals and "teardrops," set into the legs above the pivots. These features are paralleled in the decoration of both actual folding stools from the tomb, which suggests they were made *en suite*. By contrast, the legs of Tutankhamen's imitation folding stool (Obj. No. 83), which was most recently to be seen in the United States in the traveling exhibition "Tutankhamun and the Golden Age of the Pharaohs," lack the panels; and the detailing of the goose heads is different.

The pattern inlaid on the deeply coved seat of the inlaid ebony throne depicts a piebald cowhide, not a leopard pelt. The rectangular panel set into the middle of it imitates a cushion made of animal skins. The colorful decoration of the backrest includes a frieze of uraei across the headrail. Two tiny cartouches identify the sun disk in the center above them as Akhenaten's god Aten. Below, a pair of cartouches topped with sun disks of carnelian flank a vulture with outspread wings. These call the king Nebkheperure Tutankhaten. The names alternate in the vertical ebony and ivory strips in the elaborately inlaid pattern of niches further down. The earlier personal name Tutankhaten is also used in all the texts on the back of the backrest. The later Tutankhamen figures only in the two long, horizontal ebony strips on the front. These are obviously secondary.

The use of the epithet "perfect ruler" (*heqa-nefer*) with the name Tutankhaten dates the manufacture of the inlaid ebony throne to the very beginning of his reign. It was Akhenaten who introduced this title into his protocol to replace the traditional "perfect god" (*netjer-nefer*). Usage reverted to the older "perfect god" not long after Tutankhaten's accession, but nevertheless before the change of his name to Tutankhamen. This is demonstrated by the texts on the stiles and center brace at the back of the gold throne. These inscriptions call Tutankhaten "perfect god."

Aside from its undisputed status as a masterpiece of craftsmanship, the gold throne also provides valuable historical information. Its texts supply unequivocal evidence that Tutankhaten's wife was indeed Akhenaten's and Nefertiti's third-oldest daughter, Ankhesenpaaten. (Egyptologists had suspected as much prior to the tomb's discovery, but proof was lacking.) The inscription on the center brace behind the backrest names Ankhesenpaaten "King's Wife" of Tutankhaten. The cartouche accompanying the inlaid figure of the queen in the scene on the front of the backrest now reads Ankhesenamen, but originally the hieroglyphs here, too, spelled Ankhesenpaaten. The order of the signs which shows Amen at the bottom of the queen's cartouche is unique. All other writings of Ankhesenamen afford Amen pride of place, at the top of the cartouche. By contrast "pa-Aten" always comes last in the writing of Ankhesenpaaten. The craftsman charged with altering the queen's name simply smoothed down the hieroglyphs chased in gold foil in the lower part of the cartouche behind her and replaced "pa-Aten" with "-Amen." The king's Aten-name, in a cartouche behind his figure and on the inside of the left armrest, was similarly altered. But the inlaid cartouche reading Tutankhaten on the outside of the right armrest was left standing, probably because it would have involved more work to cut new inlays and fit them in. All the cartouches with Aten-names on the stiles and center brace would not have been visible to anyone approaching the throne elevated on a dais, which adequately accounts for them being left untouched.

The gold throne conforms to a type of seat whose use was the prerogative of royalty. The lion protomes in particular signal royal ownership. Winged uraei wearing silver- and gold-gilt Double Crowns form the armrests. A total of six more uraei, each with a sun disk on its head, keep watch for any threat that might approach the enthroned pharaoh from the side or behind. The papyrus thicket depicted on the back of

the backrest is also a protective motif, for it was in the papyrus marshes of the Delta that the goddess Isis reared her son, Horus, in safety from Set, the murderer of his father Osiris.

The presence of Akhenaten's god in the form he introduced — a radiant sun disk shining down on the royal couple — implies an early date in the reign of Tutankhaten/amen for the throne's manufacture. This is the last appearance of the icon, even though the existence of a separate cult for the god can be traced down into the early Nineteenth Dynasty.

There are a few other chairs that depict the owner in a scene on the front of their backrests. The earliest example belonged to Queen Hetepheres, the mother of Khufu.[14] Tutankhamen's aunt, Sitamen, the oldest daughter of Amenhotep III and Queen Tiye, is depicted twice in a symmetrical composition on the backrest of her chair from the tomb of her grandparents (KV46).[15] A chair in the Metropolitan Museum of Art shows that such indicators of ownership were not restricted to furniture made for royalty, for an ivory panel set into the backrest depicts the commoner Reniseneb seated before an offering table.[16] The scene showing Ankhesenamen in front of her enthroned husband would seem, then, to document Tutankhamen's ownership of the gold throne.

However, three specialists dispute his ownership, arguing that the gold throne was not originally intended for his use. All of them propose that it was made for Akhenaten. Belgian Egyptologist Claude Vandersleyen based one argument against Tutankhaten's ownership on the size of the throne.[17] Certainly his claim that it is scaled for an adult is correct. But it is no coincidence that the height of the seat above the floor — the highest of any chair or stool preserved from Egypt — equals one Egyptian cubit. The form, as well as the opulent decoration of the gold throne, shows that it had an official, public role to play at court, unlike the child's throne. Such a piece of furniture was surely planned with the context of its use and the status of the owner — rather than his size or age — uppermost in the designer's mind.

Vandersleyen's main argument, however, is that the figures in the scene on the backrest don't "look like" Tutankhamen and Ankhesenamen. To Vandersleyen the king "looks like" Akhenaten; but since the lady does not "look like" Nefertiti to him, she must be another consort: viz. Kiya, whom the Heretic called his "much beloved wife."

Unfortunately, Vandersleyen has forgotten that the creation of an official portrait-type for a new king was not simultaneous with his accession; initially the image of the predecessor exerted a strong influence on artists. It is only to be expected that depictions of Tutankhaten resemble Akhen-

Opposite, The gold throne of Tutankhamen (Obj. No. 91) from the KV62 Antechamber & its companion footstool (Obj. No. 90). Undisputed as a masterpiece of ancient craftsmanship, the throne also provides vauable historical information. Originally from early in the king's reign, the throne was updated following the change of his name from Tutankhaten to Tutankhamen. A few scholars have argued that the throne originally had been made for Akhenaten & only adapted for his second successor. The four spaces between the seat & railings were once filled with an openwork sema-tawy "Unification" motif, which is now missing. The footstool is decorated with Egypt's traditional enemies on its top surface, with rekhyt birds on the two long sides.

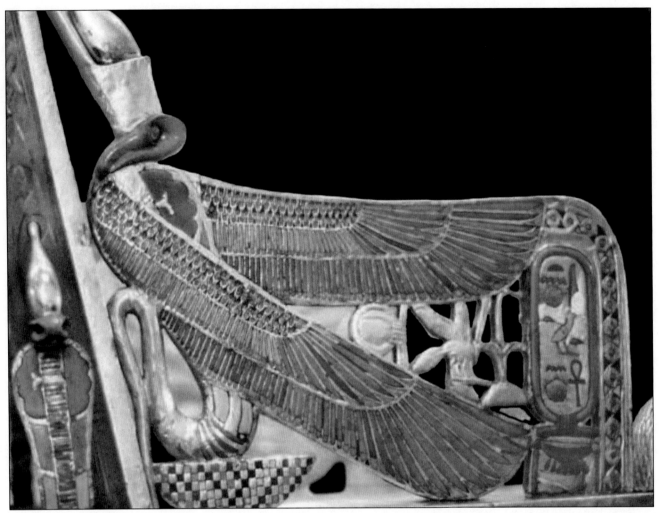

Detail of the heavily inlaid exterior of the right arm of Tutankhamen's gold throne, in the form of a Double Crown-wearing winged cobra presenting the king's cartouche with his Aten prenomen. Photo: Diehl

aten — who was, after all, his father. Vandersleyen also fails to observe that depictions of Tutankhamen and Ankhesenamen vary from one example to the next; even in the several vignettes of a single object, the small golden shrine from the tomb (Obj. No. 108), the figures' faces display considerable variation from scene to scene.[18] Furthermore, in Egyptian art the face of a queen (like those of deities) traditionally resembles the "portrait" of the reigning king to a remarkable degree. The profile of the royal woman on the backrest of the gold throne is in fact the mirror image of the king's opposite her.

Earl L. Ertman also thinks that the king in the scene on the backrest should be Akhenaten, rather than Tutankh-aten/amen. He has argued[19] that the fat folds on the stomach of the king's figure are only appropriate for Akhenaten. Ertman's powers of observation are no better than Vandersleyen's. Fat folds are associated with certain poses (sitting, slouching and bending over), not with the subject's age or sex. There are depictions of Nefertiti and Tiye with fat folds on their stomachs, and they are also present on the tummies of Tutankhaten's (half-)sisters depicted as nude girls sitting on cushions at their partents' feet in the famous painting

176

from the King's House at El Amarna, now in the Ashmolean Museum, Oxford. There is no reason why Tutankhaten should not be shown with them.

Marc Gabolde advances yet-additional arguments against Tutankhaten being the king for whom the throne was made.[20] He believes a passage in the "Restoration Decree" describing Tutankhamen as sitting on the throne of his father should be taken literally. But surely this passage is metaphorical; and, in any case, the same text repeatedly calls the god Amen-Re the king's father. Gabolde is surely correct in asserting that Akhenaten's "revolution" was coeval with him and the restoration of traditional cults well underway at Tutankhaten's accession. He deduces that under those circumstances, no throne would have been made showing Tutankhaten and his wife basking under the rays of Aten. But according to such reasoning, it would have been equally senseless to alter a throne of Akhenaten's with such a scene in favor of Tutankhamen. And even more inexplicable would be altering the texts a second time to name Tutankhamen and Ankhesenamen. Furthermore, the reendowment of the traditional cults, as asserted in the text of the "Restoration Decree," did not mean the sudden and complete rejection of Aten and the cessation of the disk's worship.

In short, there are adequate grounds for rejecting the notions of those who would deny that the gold throne was

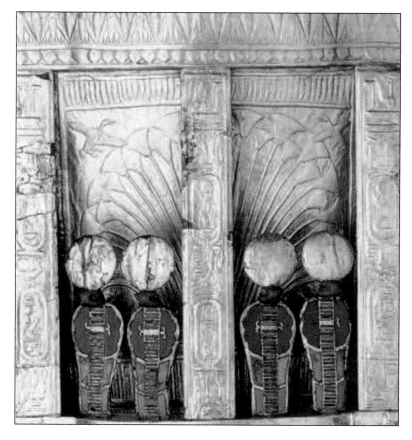

Detail of the exterior back of the gold throne, with four inlaid uraei, each supporting a sun disk. Behind them is a papyrus-thicket motif. Cairo Museum

The Ankhesenamen cartouche on the center brace behind the backrest of the gold throne. Photo: G.B. Johnson

Tutankhaten/amen's and his alone. Where and when he sat upon it are considerably more difficult questions to address. Since, however, evidence for the use and repair of the throne in antiquity is unequivocal, it follows that the gold throne was not made with a single, specific occasion in mind, such as the king's coronation.

In relief and painting, thrones with armrests and lion-protomes feature in the design of royal carrying-chairs; they are also shown, unoccuppied, on a ship's deck. But in comparison to other preserved chairs, the gold throne exhibits structural weaknesses (the absence of angle braces, for example, whose purpose was to minimalize racking stress) that would have made its use on a boat or mounted as a carrying chair impractical.

In a contribution to the *festschrift* for Donald B. Redford, Lyn Green investigates the important role of official feasting in strengthening the bond of loyalty between Akhenaten and his subjects.[21] Some features of the scene on the backrest relate it to depictions of such feasting that are found in the reliefs and paintings of tombs and temples during Akhenaten's reign. Floral collars on stands, like the one behind the queen, are typical furnishings of a banquet halls, while Ankhesenamen's gesture could be interpreted as calling her spouse's attention to the drink she is about to offer him from the chalice in her other hand. The scene would have been visible only when the throne was unoccuppied; perhaps it could substitute magically for the king when he was absent from such an event for whatever reason. But this is speculative.

We must be satisfied, for the present at least, with the certainty that Tutankhamen's subjects were just as impressed by the gold throne — sparkling in the sunshine or glinting in the light of blazing torches — as are modern-day visitors to the Egyptian Museum in Cairo.

Postscript

Summary descriptions of all the furniture from Tutankhamen's tomb are found in the three-volume account of the discovery and clearance by Howard Carter (and Arthur C. Mace, for vol. 1). Hollis S. Baker provided a more-systematic review, category by category, in his *Furniture in the Ancient World: Origins and Evolution, 3100-475 B.C.* (London, 1966), as does Nicholas Reeves in *The Complete Tutankhamun: The King, The Tomb, The Royal Treasure* (London, 1990). Both Geoffrey Killen, *Ancient Egyptian Furniture: 4000-1300 B.C.* (2 vols., Warminster 1980, 1994) and Dan Svarth, *Egyptisk Móbelkunst fra Faraotiden* (Ebeltoft, 1998) have published drawings of some of the seats from Tutankhamen's tomb. However,

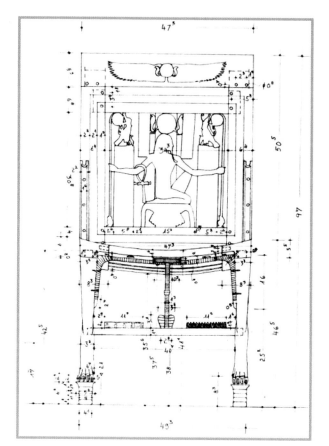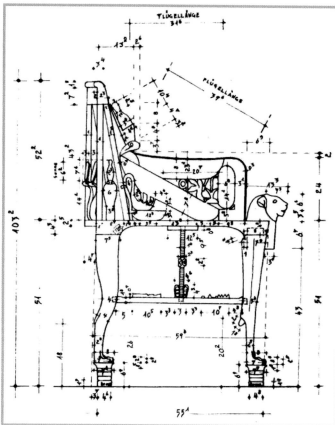

Drawings with detailed measurements made in 1935 by Walter Segal of two of the KV62 seats; on the left the frontal view of the cedar throne, above of the right side of the gold throne.

comparison with the originals reveals errors in their renderings that suggest neither studied each specimen in detail outside its Cairo Museum case, which, as Baker emphasized, would be absolutely essential for an accurate analysis of design and construction.

Although Alfred Lucas remarked in print that the Berlin-born architect Walter Segal (1907–1985) worked — with Howard Carter's knowledge and agreement — on Tutankhamen's seats,[22] Segal's scale drawings and notes on construction have only recently been published. Segal spent the summer and early autumn of 1935 recording all the preserved seats and fragments of them which were in the collection of the Egyptian Museum at that time. Each piece was removed from its case and taken to a temporary laboratory set up for Segal's use on the top floor of the Museum. There he could study, measure, draw and photograph them.

His drawing of Tutankhamen's seats and footstools and his notes on construction provide the starting point for my study of this material entitled *The Thrones, Chairs, Stools, and Footstools from the Tomb of Tutankhamun*, published under the auspices of the Griffith Institute, Oxford. There readers will find a thorough discussion of these summarily presented above, with full bibliographic documentation, as well as publication of all the other seats and footstools from the tomb.

Tutankhamen-Period Battle Narratives at Luxor

by W. Raymond Johnson

Many readers may not realize that the recent sphinx-road excavation project directed by the Egyptian Supreme Council for Antiquities — to clear the entire three-kilometer sphinx-lined road between Luxor and Karnak Temples — continued an earlier program begun in 1958. At that time the Egyptian Antiquities Organization (EAO, now the Ministry for Antiquities and Heritage) initiated the clearance of the large occupation mound (tell) of medieval Luxor that covered the southern end of the sphinx road directly in front of the pylons of Luxor Temple.[1] Hundreds of medieval house-foundations constructed of broken-up stone-block fragments quarried from pharaonic monuments in the area were uncovered by the EAO and dismantled to expose the well-preserved sphinxes beneath. The thousands of stone fragments, many of them inscribed, were eventually stacked all around the temple.

The Epigraphic Survery and Luxor Temple

The University of Chicago's Epigraphic Survey became involved with this material while documenting the inscribed-wall remains of the Grand Colonnade Hall dominating the central part of Luxor Temple. This gigantic structure was started by Amenhotep III, as the third and most-ambitious phase of his building program at Waset (Thebes, Luxor), to commemorate his deification-while-alive, but was actually finished by Tutankhamen several years after Amenhotep III's death. The exquisite wall reliefs within the monument date primarily from the very end of Tutankhamen's reign and are hurriedly executed; the southern part of the hall that Tutankhamen was unable to finish was carved by order of Seti I. The inscribed walls depicted and described rites associated with the annual rejuvenation of the creator god Amen-Re at Luxor Temple during the festival of Opet. The best-known reliefs in the first (lowest) register show the great river-procession of the divine triad of Waset — Amen-Re, Mut and their hawk-headed son, the moon god, Khonsu — from Kar-

Opposite, Watercolor facsimile copy by Nina DeGaris Davies of King Tutankhamen fighting Asiatics from his chariot, detail of a scene decorating one side of the painted chest from his tomb, KV62.

Photo: George B. Johnson

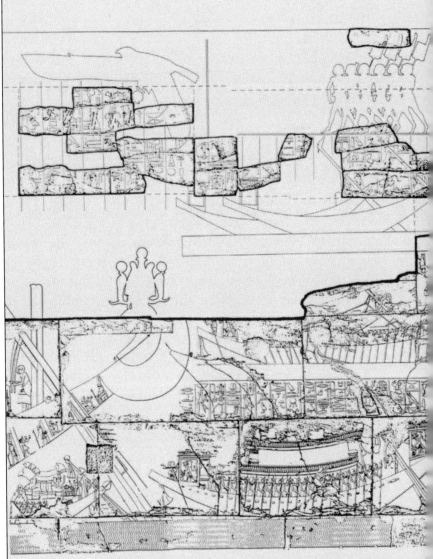

Above, Section of excavated sphinxes lining the ancient avenue extending between the Karnak Complex & Luxor Temple. Below, The eastern blockyard at Luxor Temple, with the Colonnade Hall on the right.

Photos: Kmt/Forbes

nak to Luxor and back again in their magnificent, gilded barques pulled by the royal barges of the king and queen, and many, many oared towboats. While this procession narrative is depicted elsewhere at Luxor (Deir el Bahari, Rameses III's barque sanctuary at Karnak and Khonsu Temple), the Colonnade Hall example is the largest that survives.

Our original purpose in studying the blockyard material was to find fragments of Tutankhamen reliefs from the destroyed upper walls of the Colonnade Hall. Careful scrutiny of the blockyards resulted in the identification and recovery of over 1,500 wall fragments from the hall, hundreds of which were incorporated into the first two volumes of the Epigraphic Survey's Luxor Temple series devoted to this structure.[2] A third volume is planned that will be dedicated exclusively to upper-register fragments and joined fragment-groups. Since then the ES has expanded its program in the Luxor Temple blockyards, to include conservation, protective measures, reconstruction of fragment groups and an open-

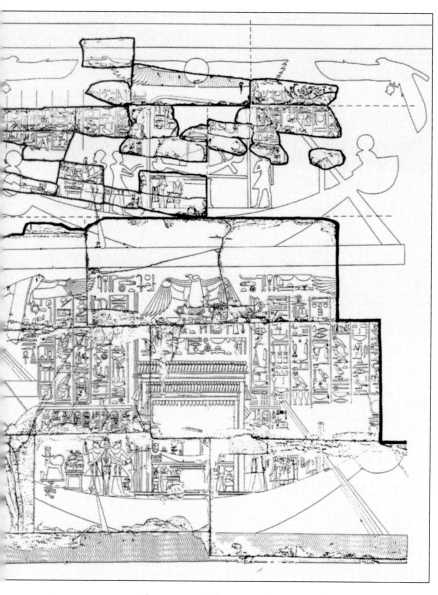

Left, Adaptation of the Epigraphic Survey drawing of a section of the great Colonnade Hall eastern interior wall, depicting the barque of Khonsu (RILT 1, plate 68). Below, top to bottom: Detail of the Colonnade interior west wall, depicting the Opet procession of the barque of the king; details of the same procession on the Colonnade interior east wall. Author's photos

air museum to the east of the temple, completed in 2010.³

In the course of the investigation of the blockyards for Colonnade Hall material, everything related to the reign of Tutankhamen by inscription, style and content was moved to a holding area east of the temple — for documentation, analysis and integration with the standing-wall reliefs. The carving style of Tutankhamen's reign is easy to recognize, since it combines Amarna-period naturalism with the traditional carving-style of his Thutmosid predecessors. As a result Tutankhamen's scenes exhibit a liveliness and energy that sets them apart from temple decoration before and after the late Eighteenth Dynasty. The Opet register fragments were also fairly small in scale, with a rich array of details: boats, sailors in rigging, piles of food offerings, divine barques and barque processions, and small-scale texts that allowed immediate identification. Tutankhamen's upper-register relief fragments are gigantic in scale, but also very easy to recognize by their clean lines, sharp unfinished edges, and a distinct lack of in-

King Tutankhamen is depicted fighting Asiatics & Nubians & hunting from his chariot in four scenes on the famous painted chest or casket found in the Antechamber of his tomb (above) Egyptian Museum *Archaeological artist Nina DeGaris Davies painted watercolor facsimilies of these scenes, shown in details at right & below.*

Photos: George B. Johnson

Right, Block at Karnak Temple from a structure of Tutankhamen's bearing his defaced cartouches & partial image. Photo: Kmt/Forbes

Above, Block inscribed with the cartouches of Nebkheperure Tutankhamen & naming the "Mansion of Nebkheperure in Waset." Below, Reused talatat *block inscribed with the joint cartouches of Ay (left) & Tutankhamen, almost certainly from the latter's mortuary/memorial temple at Waset.* Author's photos

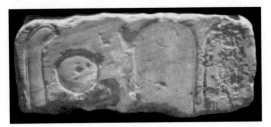

terior carved details (which would have been painted).

Mystery Blocks

Imagine our surprise when the sorting revealed not only the expected fragments from Tutankhamen's Colonnade Hall reliefs, but also a second group of Tutankhamen-period blocks, identical in style and also small in scale, but differing in many ways. There were barque-procession scenes, enshrined barques, offering scenes, river-procession scenes and texts of various sizes — many smaller in scale than the Colonnade Hall reliefs. There were also statue-purification scenes (statues of Tutankhamen, identified by his cartouche) and inscribed doorjamb fragments that clearly bore no relation to the much-larger Colonnade Hall reliefs. Particularly strange were blocks that appeared to depict some sort of battle between Egyptian and Asiatic chariotry forces, also small in scale and late Eighteenth Dynasty in style. One fortuitous block preserved the upper part of a king, cartouches partly preserved, bending forward in his chariot with his bow pulled back, poised to shoot an arrow. The name was clear; the pharaoh leading the Egyptian chariotry forces in these blocks was Tutankhamen! The pose of the king is identical to the chariot scenes found on the famous painted casket from his tomb, showing Tutankhamen hunting lions and desert game with bow and arrow on the vaulted lid, but also routing Nubian enemies on one long side and Asiatics on the other.

A further surprise was the realization that every block from this second group was an Akhenaten *talatat* (roughly 52 x 22 x 26 cm.) that had been turned over and recarved, mostly in raised relief. Original Akhenaten sunk-relief deco-

Above & Below, Talatats *from a Tutankhamen battle-narrative with details of combate with Asiatic enemies.* Author's photos

Above & below, Details on Tutankhamen battle-relief talatat *showing Asiatic & Egyptian soldiers.*

Author's photos

ration was sometimes still preserved on one or more adjacent sides of the raised-relief carving, often upside down, which indicated dismantling and wholesale reuse of the blocks — not simply adding on to a preexisting Akhenaten-period structure. Horemheb is traditionally credited with the dismantling of Akhenaten's Aten complex at Ipet Isut (Karnak), yet the implication was that Tutankhamen had begun the demolition of at least part of that complex for a monument

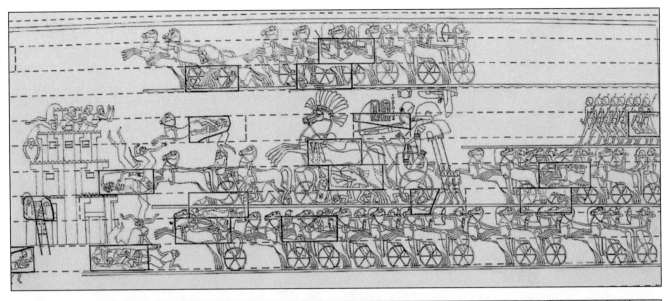

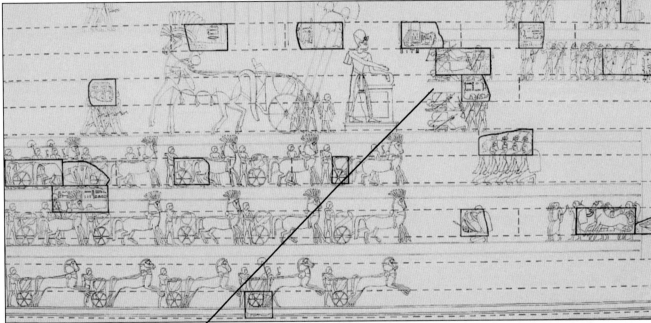

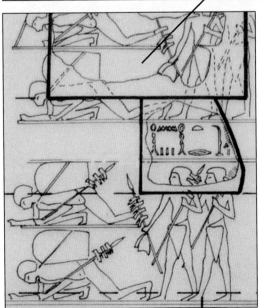

The Author's drawings reconstructing portions of a Tutankhamen battle-narrative. Top, The king & Egyptian forces attack an Asiatic fortified town. Above, The presentation of prisoners & war booty to the king, including the severed right hands of the slain enemy skewered on spears (detail at left). Opposite, Detail in reverse of Tutankhamen in battle, shooting an arrow from his chariot; note similarity to battle scenes of the KV62 painted casket.

of his own. But what was this monument? And what the heck was going on with those battle scenes?

Photographs in the Chicago House archives showed that many of the *talatat* blocks at Luxor Temple had been dismantled from Christian-period structures built inside and around the Rameses II First Court, where a church still stands, supporting the mosque of Abul Haggag above. The raised-relief *talatat* at Luxor Temple had been found with hundreds of sunk-relief *talatat* original to Akhenaten in those same medieval foundations. Texts on the blocks indicate that they were all part of Akhenaten's Karnak Aten-complex. A

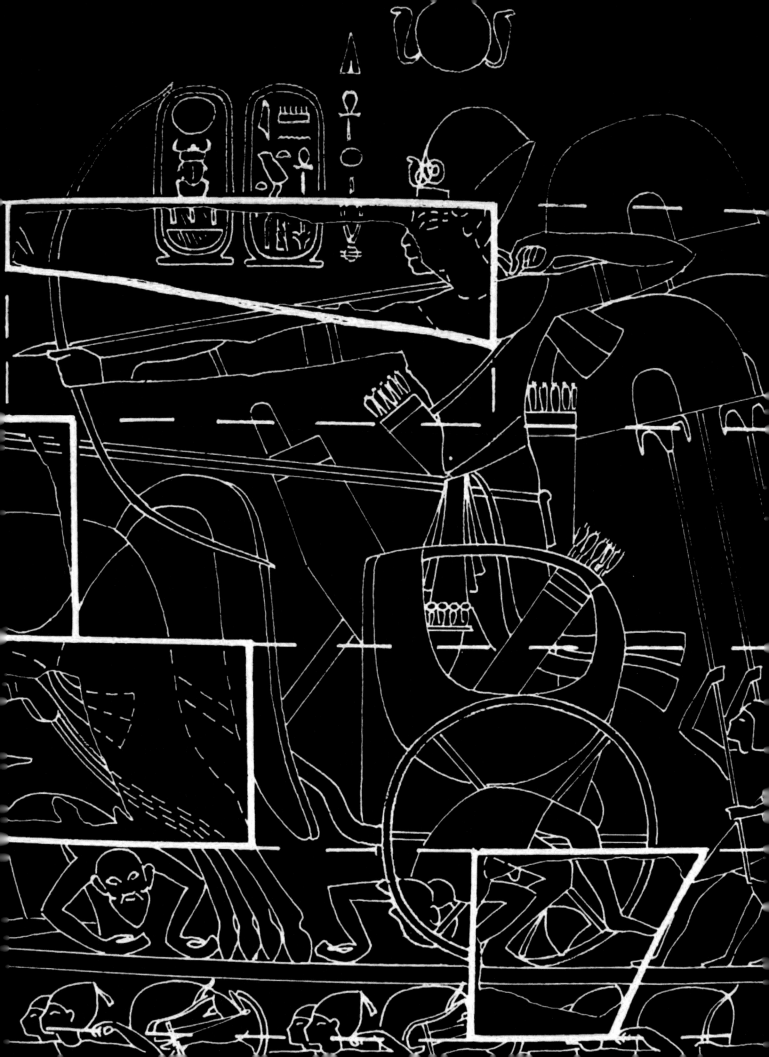

little investigation revealed that the material had all been quarried in medieval times from the Second, Ninth and Tenth pylons at Karnak, where Horemheb had hidden the blocks away after he had demolished Akhenaten's Karnak Aten-temples. When the pylons in their turn were quarried centuries later, Akhenaten's blocks ended up recycled at Luxor Temple, as building material in the medieval settlement. Excavations of this material in the medieval levels of Medamud to the north and Tod even farther to the south show that Akhenaten's blocks, because of their small size, traveled far and wide at that time.

The Mansion of Nebkheperfure, Beloved of Amen, Founder of Waset

Now, years later, and with more than 200 of these enigmatic blocks identified, we know that the reused *talatat* came from a temple started by Tutankhamen and finished by his successor, Ay, called the "Mansion of Nebkheprure Beloved of Amen, Founder of Waset (Thebes)," or, for short, the "Mansion

Left, Talatat *raised-relief detail of the royal vessel returning to Egypt following a campaign in Western Asia. Above, Detail from the same block of a manacled Syrian hanging in a cage suspended from the ship's sail yard.* Author's photos

of Nebkheprure in Waset."[4] The decorative program suggests that the structure was originally begun as Tutankhamen's mortuary temple, and completed after his death by Ay as a memorial temple to the young king, with reliefs of Ay officiating in Tutankhamen's cult as his successor. This may have been one way that Ay legitimized his succession, just as he is shown in Tutankhamen's tomb in the role of Iunmutef priest/son/successor, who conducts the Opening of the Mouth ritual on the mummy of the deceased king. The small blocks join large blocks,[5] many of which were excavated from within the Second Pylon at Karnak in the late 1920s by Henri Chevrier; and more by Ramadan Saad, from the Ninth Pylon in the mid 1970s.[6]

Most recently this corpus was studied and recorded for publication by our colleague Marc Gabolde for the Centre franco-égyptien d'étude des temples de Karnak (CFEETK). Marc and I were delighted to find out that we had elements of the same structure in our respective blockyards; he had noted a few raised-relief *talatat* in the Second Pylon, which

191

Above, Colorfully painted blocks depicting Tutankh-amen's chariot & horses in a hunting scene (note slain bull at bottom) from his mortuary temple, similar to the famous relief on the backside of the First Pylon of the Mortuary Temple of Rameses III at Medinet Habu (opposite). Author's photos

Right, Painted details of the same scene have been wash-ed away by rain in recent years, while the block was in open-air storage at Karnak. Photo: Kmt/Forbes

is the probable origin of most of the *talatat* material in the Luxor blockyard. The large blocks that Marc has document-ed, with square pillars and architraves in sunk relief, and raised-relief wall scenes featuring both Tutankhamen and Ay, are also reused Akhenaten blocks, originally architraves in-scribed for Akhenaten and the Aten. Several of the reused *ta-latat* blocks in the Luxor Temple blockyard establish the connection of the two groups beyond any doubt. One in par-ticular, a *talatat* in sunk relief, preserves cartouches of Tut-ankhamen and Ay facing each other, and was part of a scene which showed Ay venerating his deceased predecessor. Eventually the reused *talatat* from Luxor Temple will be published with the large blocks from Karnak, in a collaborative monograph between our two institutions.

The Battle-Narrative Scenes

I found the battle-themed blocks to be of particular interest — and discovered that between the large and small blocks, two military campaigns were depicted, in the same small scale, but in reverse orientation to each other. Architectural clues indicate that the battle reliefs wrapped around the inside of an open court on either side of a central doorway. A few large blocks preserve sections of a magnificent Nubian campaign narrative; one extraordinary block preserves parts of two scenes: towboats and soldiers arriving from the left, and a scene on the right where the king is presenting manacled Nubian prisoners to the gods.

There are far-more blocks preserved from the Asiatic battle narrative: more than forty small reused *talatat* that I noted in the Luxor and Karnak block-storage areas, and half-a-dozen large blocks from Karnak. Enough has survived to tell us that this was a very special composition indeed, displaying features that are usually associated with the great Ramesside battle-narrative tradition. Preserved were groups of blocks from four distinct episodes in a complex narrative:

(1) the battle proper, with Egyptian chariotry forces led by the king pitched against enemy chariotry and a Syrian-style fortress; (2) the presentation of prisoners, booty and severed hands of the slain enemy to the king; (3) the return trip to Egypt by a flotilla of barges, including the king's royal barge (with a manacled Syrian hanging in a cage from the sail yard!); and (4) the formal presentation of prisoners and war booty by the king to Amen. There are indications that there were other episodes as well, leading up to the battle proper.

This sort of episodic battle-narrative is very common, almost cliché, in the battle reliefs of Seti I, Rameses II and Rameses III. In the past Seti I has been credited by scholars with initiating the entire genre, but this is clearly not the case. Steve Harvey has shown from his work with Pharaoh Ahmose's terribly destroyed mortuary-complex at Abydos that chariot-battle depictions go back to the initial use of the horse and chariot in Egypt, at the very beginning of the Eighteenth Dynasty. Steve's chariot-battle reliefs may even depict the expulsion of the Hyksos from Egypt by the southern Egyptian rulers. Time will tell how elaborate the narratives of these scenes were.[7]

What we can say is that by the time of Tutankhamen — and possibly earlier — the battle-narrative tradition was fully formed. It continued to develop in the reign of

194

Horemheb, whose royal mortuary temple — dismantled and reused by Rameses III in Karnak Khonsu Temple — had elaborate battle-narratives of its own. Horemheb's battle-reliefs form the missing link between the narratives of Tutankhamen and those of the Ramesside kings. The Ramesside battle-narrative tradition, then, marked the culmination and final flowering of a much longer tradition, which was in full flower by the end of the Eighteenth Dynasty.

The Mortuary Temple of Tutankhamen?

A number of details support the identification of the "Mansion of Nebkheperure in Waset" as Tutankhamen's mortuary temple. The architectural evidence indicates that the orientation of the reliefs in the court had the Nubians (southerners) on the left and the Asiatics (northerners) on the right. A west-bank location for the temple puts the Nubians on the south side of the court and the Asiatics on the north, consistent with the Egyptians' sense of artistic and spatial realism. Tutankhamen's temple is very similar in its cultic program to a limestone memorial temple near Medinet Habu that Thutmose III constructed for his father, Thutmose II.[8] There is also the fact that the closest parallel for Tutankhamen's battle-narratives are the similar, larger-scaled narratives from Horemheb's dismantled mortuary temple, which also appear to have wrapped around the inside of his peristyle court. It is possible that Tutankhamen's mortuary complex was located near Horemheb's.[9]

Another piece of evidence relates to the famous bull-hunt scene at Rameses III's mortuary temple at Medinet Habu, on the back of his first pylon, south side. This scene depicting that king hunting wild bulls in the marshes is considered by many to be among the last great original compositions in Egyptian history. But there is at least one earlier example. Among the Tutankhamen-period blocks which Ramadan Saad extracted from the Ninth Pylon are two that join to form the lower part of the young king in his chariot hunting wild bulls in the marshes; the bulls felled with the king's arrows are visible at the edge of the block.[10] Other blocks preserve parts of scenes depicting Tutankhamen hunting game in the desert, another standard Ramesside mortuary-temple genre scene. We have made assumptions of originality based on the better-preserved Ramesside-period mortuary temples — at the expense of the Eighteenth Dynasty mortuary complexes that have not survived. It is possible that the genre scenes we associate with the Ramesside mortuary temples may all derive from earlier Eighteenth Dynasty prototypes.

The Question of Historicity

Some of the details of the Tutankhamen battle narratives are worth noting for their startling originality. The trip back to Egypt from the battleground by royal barge and towboats is not found in the later battle narratives. The detail of the unhappy manacled prisoner in Syrian garb suspended in the cage hanging over the deck of the royal barge is unique in Egyptian art. Another particularly grisly detail is found in the episode after the battle, where the king is presented with prisoners and booty — including horses — but also the severed right hands of the enemy dead. In later Ramesside battle-aftermath accounts, the hands are shown being placed in piles before the king; but, in the Tutankhamen reliefs, the hands are skewered on spears like *shish kabob*(!). That is another detail that does not repeat in the Ramesside battle reliefs.

Which leads to the sixty-four-thousand-dollar question: do these reliefs with their unique details, rendered at a time when truth was strived for in Egyptian art, depict actual events? When Tutankhamen is shown in his battle chariot leading Egypt's chariotry forces against an Asiatic citadel in one narrative — and against Nubian foes in another — does this indicate that the scenes commemorate real, historic episodes in the life of Tutankhamen? Or are they ritual scenes, designed to show the king symbolically triumphing over Egypt's traditional enemies?

That question is not easily answered. But the origi-

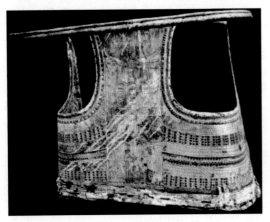

Bodies of the pair of so-called "State" chariots found dismantled in the Tomb of Tutankhamen. Covered in heavily embossed sheet-gold with inlays, these vehicles are probably more ornate than the chariot the young king would have rode into battle; rather they would have been used on the occasion of formal ceremonial parading — unlike others found in his tomb which show more use. Digitally colorized & adapted Harry Burton photos

nality of the scenes strongly suggests that such details could only have been observed and recorded on the battlefield. If the details of the battle and aftermath represent true events, then the presence of Tutankhamen in the composition might indicate that he actually was present. From the wear on many of the objects found in his royal tomb — such as throw sticks, staves, bows and arrows, quivers, a cuirass of leather-scaled armor, slings, swords, axes, spears, daggers and chariots — it is clear that the young king was an active young man. He was certainly old enough to participate in the manly art of war by ancient standards of maturity, and his tomb contains the objects that would seem to support that idea.

The Fatal Accident — on a Military Campaign?
The recent analysis of Tutankhamen's mummy which indicates traumatic injury to his leg — possibly the result of a chariot accident — that appears to have led to infection and premature death,[11] gives one pause. Could Tutankhamen's tragic accident have occurred during a military campaign? If the young king had participated in one of these campaigns — during which the accident happened — and later died of infection (as seems to be the case), one would expect the Egyptian sources to be completely silent. Such things did not happen to Pharaoh, for the wellbeing of the Universe depended on the king being eternally triumphant over the forces of Chaos.

Reliefs in the Tomb of Horemheb at Sakkara, plus Hittite textual sources — such as "The Deeds of Shuppililiuma as Told by His Son Mursili II" — give ample evidence for Egyptian military activity during the latter part of Tutankhamen's reign, as Egypt struggled to regain control of territories lost during the time of Akhenaten.[12] The growing power and influence of the Hittite empire on the Egyptian vassal states required direct military intervention, which was coordinated by Tutankhamen's deputy and military commander-in-chief, General Horemheb. Asiatic and Nubian campaigns are documented in Horemheb's Sakkara tomb, including tantalizing fragments of a military camp being set up in a hilly landscape — alas incomplete. Perhaps more of these scenes will eventually be found, clarifying the question of the young king's participation in these campaigns, or not.

Whether or not Tutankhamen took an active role in the battles commemorated in the "Mansion of Nebkheprure in Waset," his battle narratives, with their vivid realism, mark a major turning-point in Egyptian art. At the very least, these compositions are the true beginning of the great Ramesside battle-narrative tradition.

Beyond the Tomb
The Historical Tutankhamen from His Monuments

by Dennis C. Forbes

Prior to the discovery of Nebkheperure Tutankhamen's Valley of the Kings Tomb in 1922, the last Thutmosid ruler of the Eighteenth Dynasty was an historically ephemeral figure, only known to scholars from a scant few monuments and unrecognized on others which had been usurped by his second successor, Horemheb, concluding ruler of the dynasty.

Since the four (or was it five?) so-called "Amarna" pharaohs — Akhenaten, Neferneferuaten (?), Smenkhkare, Tutankhamen and Ay — had been officially erased from the kings list by Horemheb and the early Ramesside rulers (Seti I and Ramses II), who either dismantled those rulers' monuments or re-inscribed them as their own, it remained for early Egyptologists to reconstitute what could be known of their reigns from fragmentary evidence.

Akhenaten, of course, was the exception, with ruins of an entire city at Akhetaten (El Amarna) — and its badly mutilated so-called Royal Tomb and the nearby well-decorated tombs of his officials — being explored and recorded by Egyptologists as early as the 1880s.

But of the Heretic's first and second coregents — the latter also his probable successor — there were just the barest hints in the known record, such as: the sketch-depiction of Smenkhkare and his consort, Queen Meritaten, in an El Amarna official's tomb: ring bezels with his name; and a box lid bearing both his and Akhenaten's names — all evidence of not much more than his existence.

So little was known of Akhenaten's second successor that, when Theodore Davis discovered a small shaft-tomb (KV58) in the Valley of the Kings in 1909 that contained some gold-foil fragments with Tutankhamen's prenomen and nomen, plus a tiny depiction of that king smiting an enemy in the presence of Queen Ankhesenamen and the courtier Ay, the excavator was satisfied that he had located the shadowy king's actual burial place — having two years earlier uncovered a pit with embalming and funerary-banquet debris, plus

One of the major surviving reliefs depicting a Khepresh-wearing Nebkheperure Tutankhamen, on the north interior wall of the Grand Colonnade Hall of Luxor Temple. Carved in raised relief in the best post-Amarna style, it depicts the young king before offerings to Amen-Re. It was usurped by his second successor, Horemheb, who simply replaced the last Thutmosid's cartouches with his own. Author's photo

The other two Horemheb-usurped relief depictions of Tutankhamen in the Grand Colonnade Hall of Luxor Temple. Author's photos

a scarf bearing the prenomen Nebkheperure and a Year 6 date.

Just prevously in 1906, a small faience cup with the same prenomen had also been found by Davis. Thus, these three minor Valley of the Kings discoveries constituted the total proof of Tutankhamen's existence, along with two granite standing statues from the Karnak Cachette of 1904, where it was recognized that the names of that king had been overwritten by those of Horemheb.

Another uninscribed fragmentary statue-group from the same cache — of a youthful king seated between Amen and Hathor — was cautiously dated as *"Eighteenth Dynasty? Before the period of Horemheb,"* without an actual attribution. Today this is pretty certainly to be seen as the two deities in the company of Tutankhamen.

It is quite apparent today that one of Nebkheperure Tutankhamen's chief efforts in actively fostering a return to religious orthodoxy was the commissioning of numerous statues of the god Amen-Re, who had particularly suffered from the religious persecutions of Akhenaten. As had been the practice of Amenhotep III, the features of the young king were given to the god in these replacement images. Any number of these were later usurped and re-inscribed by Horemheb, so that — before Tutankhamen's unmistakable facial features were confirmed by the multiple depictions of him found in his tomb — it was assumed that the Amen statues

200

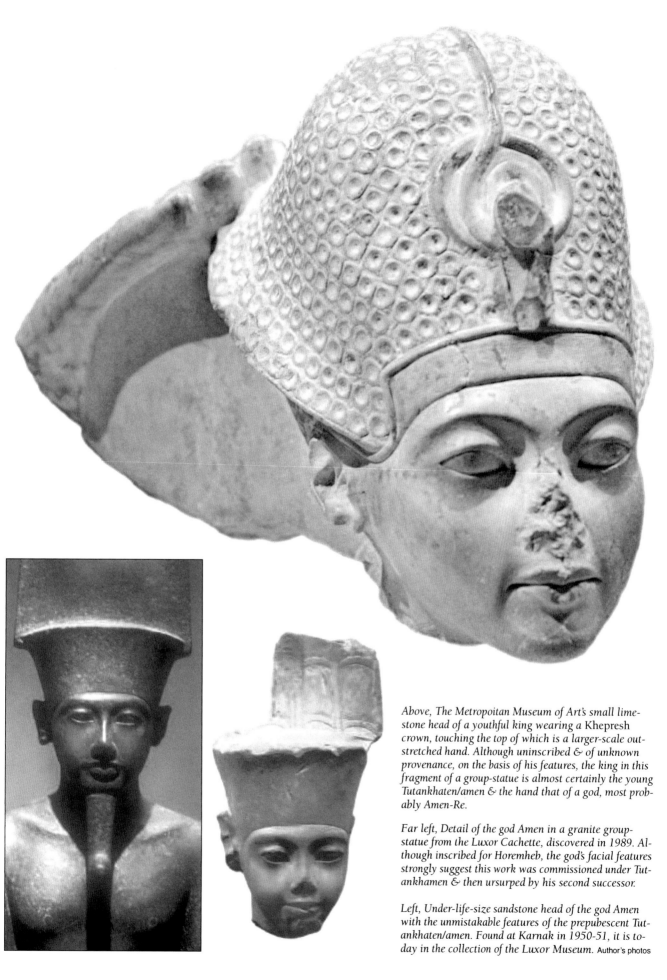

Above, The Metropoitan Museum of Art's small lime-stone head of a youthful king wearing a Khepresh crown, touching the top of which is a larger-scale out-stretched hand. Although uninscribed & of unknown provenance, on the basis of his features, the king in this fragment of a group-statue is almost certainly the young Tutankhaten/amen & the hand that of a god, most probably Amen-Re.

Far left, Detail of the god Amen in a granite group-statue from the Luxor Cachette, discovered in 1989. Although inscribed for Horemheb, the god's facial features strongly suggest this work was commissioned under Tutankhamen & then ursurped by his second successor.

Left, Under-life-size sandstone head of the god Amen with the unmistakable features of the prepubescent Tutankhaten/amen. Found at Karnak in 1950-51, it is today in the collection of the Luxor Museum. Author's photos

Gods with the face of Tutankhamen: Left, A fragmentary quartzite colossus of Amen-Re in situ in the god's temple at Karnak; the tip of the nose was found & restored in 2003. Above, Detail of a life-size limestone statue of Amen-Re found in the Karnak Cachette in 1904 & today in the Luxor Museum. Below, Granite head of Amen-Re in the collection of the Metropolitan Museum of Art, NYC. Opposite, A colossal gray-granite statue of the god Khonsu, discovered in the Karnak Cacchette. The exquisitely carved figure is in the finest post-Amarna style, the refined features unmistakably those of the idealized youthful boy-king. Author's photos

had been commisioned by the commoner-king.

But Amen-Re was not the only beneficiary of Tutankhamen's return to orthodoxy. Also found in the Karnak Cachette was a large gray-granite standing statue of the moon-god, Khonsu (son of Amen), exquisitely rendered in the very best post-Amarna sculptural style and with the idealized-but-recognizable features of the young king.

Additional Karnak Cachette finds were eleven fragmentary sandstone images of a king wearing the *Nemes* head covering which once stood before the chests of crio-sphinxes that had lined the avenue leading from Karnak's Tenth Pylon to the precinct of the goddess Mut. When found it was suggested that these represented Amenhotep IV early in his reign; today, however, it is generally agreed that they are, instead, to be seen as depicting Tutankhamen, whose cartouches have been found on bases of recently excavated sphinxes (these, of course, overwritten by Horemheb, as part of his appropriation of his predescessor's monuments).

Besides taking over Tutankhamen's statuary for himself, Djoserkheperure Horemheb also re-inscribed the for-

Above, Fragmentary uninscribed calcite triad of a youthful ruler seated between Hathor & Amen-Re, found in the Karnak Cachette in 1904 & now in the Cairo Egyptian Museum. Catalogue General, *Statues et Statuettes,* 1906 *Opposite, Detail of the face of the same king, which clearly has the features of the young Tutankhamen.* Author's photo

In the Karnak Cachette were two nearly identical gray-granite standing figures of a king wearing the Nemes head covering (details right & opposite), identified by the inscriptions they bore as Horemheb. The facial features, again, are almost certainly those of Tutankhamen, meaning that the statues were usurped for the later ruler. Because they are so similar, it is probable that the pair originally flanked a doorway in the Amen temple. The full-length view above is of the statue seen in detail at above right, as found, prior to the restoration of its missing parts in painted plaster. The sculptures are today in the collection of the Cairo Egyptian Museum.

Author's photos right & opposite; full-length statue from Catalogue General, *Statues et Statuettes*, 1905

mer's architectural monuments, as well. The chief example of this is the decoration of the Grand Colonnade Hall of Luxor Temple. This unique structure had actually been built by Amenhotep III, who died before its reliefs celebrating the annual Opet Festival could be fully carved. Tutankhamen finished this work, including at least three large-scale raised-relief representations of himself presenting offerings on the interior north wall of the Hall. These are in the best post-Amarna style and the facial features are easily recognizable as the youthful king's; but the accompanying cartouches identify the individual depicted as none other than Horemheb, who thus took credit for his predecessor's completion of the Colonnade Hall's decoration.

Tutankhamen's premature death at eighteen or nineteen assured that, like his intended tomb in the West Valley of the Kings (WV23), the king's memorial temple on the Luxor west bank was doubtless far from being finished, perhaps only just begun. It is likely that the late king's immediate

During the 1931 University of Chicago excavations at the Memorial Temple of Ay & Horemheb, two painted-quarzite colossi were uncovered, which, although usurped in turn by Ay & Horemheb, had originally stood in the unfinished funerary monument of Tutankhamen & depict that king. One statue (right) was allotted to the excavators &, restored, is in the collection of the Oriental Institute Museum, Chicago. The second (below) is in the Egyptian Museum, Cairo, displayed as found.

successor, the commoner-king Ay, began quarrying Tutankhamen's funerary monument in order to construct his own such structure (this later to be appropriated, after his fashion, by Horemheb), so that the greatly denuded site near Medinet Habu is referred to collectively today as the Ay and Horemheb Memorial Temple.

Two features from the Tutankhamen structure were re-inscribed in turn by Ay and Horemheb, for their sequential

Above & detail at right, One of 11 uninscribed fragmentary sandstone Osiride images of Tutankhamen, found in the Karnak Cachette (1904), which were elements of ram-headed sphinxes lining the avenue leading from the Karnak 10th Pylon to the Mut Precinct. When discovered they were thought to depict Amenhotep IV. Author's photos

use: a pair of identical colossal standing king-figures in pigment quartzite, with Tutankhamen's facial features, which were most likely meant to have stood in that king's funerary monument. These were discovered during the 1931 excavations by the University of Chicago at the Ay-Horemheb site, one being alloted to the excavators, the other sent to the Egyptian Museum, Cairo. The former has recently been re-restored and is displayed in the Oriental Museum, Chicago; the latter is on view in Cairo as found.

Besides his memorial temple, Tutankhamen caused at least two other structures to be erected on his behalf in the area of Waset (Thebes, Luxor). One bore the name "Mansion of Nebkheperure in Waset" and the other "Mansion of Nebkheperure, Beloved of Amen, Who Sets Waset in Order." The nature or scale of these two structures is unknown. Both were subsequently dismantled and are only represented today by scattered inscribed stones in the blockyards of Karnak.

Tutankhamen also built beyond Waset. At Mennufer (Memphis) there was apparently a structure called "House of Nebkheperure." Architectural fragments bearing his name were found in the temple precinct of the god Ptah there, as well. An inscribed limestone lintel of the king and a stela depicting him and his queen are known from the Giza area. An Apis Bull burial at Sakkara apparently took place during Tutankhamen' time on the throne, a set of Apis canopic vessels dating to his reign.

Tutankhamen built outside of Egypt, as well, with

Above, small pigmented-calcite sphinx found in the Luxor Temple cachette (1989), the features of the king's head thought to depict Tutankhamen; it is today housed in the Luxor Museum. Below, A naturalistic large red-granite recumbent lion from Gebel Barkal & today in the collection of the British Museum; it is dedicated by Tutankhamen for his "father," Amenhotep III.

temples dedicated by him in Nubia at Kawa and Faras. At Gebel Barkal two red-granite lions were found which had been carved in the time of Amenhotep III, one of these being inscribed by Tutankhamen for his "father," Nebmaatre Amenhotep. These sculptures are now in the British Museum.

Other artifacts of the king include: an uniscribed pigmented limestone bust in Berlin, thought to be of Tutankhamen, found at El Amarna in 1912 (but that identification is disputed); a bronze statuette with gilding in the collection of the University Museum, Philadlphia; a calcite small sphinx found in the Luxor Cachette in 1989 and now in the Luxor Museum; a small painted-limestone statuette of a youthful king found at El Amarna in 1923 and a facial fragment of a limestone sculpture in the style of the reign of Tutankhamen, both in the collection of the Brooklyn Museum; an under-life-size sandstone head in the Museum of Fine Arts, Boston, which is uninscribed but with Tutankhamen's distinctive features; and a number of other unprovenanced small items from the reign in various collections worldwide.

In the southern blockyard at Karnak are a number of Nebkheperure Tutankhamen inscribed blocks (sampling above) from a dismantled large structure (or structures) of the king, original location(s) unknown. With few exceptions (top r. & l.) the prenomen & nomen cartouches have been subjected to erasure. Author's photos

Symbolism in the Decoration of King Ay's Tomb (WV23)[1]

by Earl L. Ertman
Photographs by George B. Johnson

Some of the wall scenes in King Ay's tomb (WV23) are remarkable in several respects, since they do not conform to the usual subject matter found in royal tombs of the New Kingdom. The discussion of these scenes herein will focus first on the west wall of the burial chamber, preceeding from left to right. When one enters this space, the composition above the doorway on the west wall depicts Four Sons of Horus, seated rather than standing (as is usual), flanking a table piled high with food offerings. Their low seats are decorated the same as the seat of the god Osiris at the right end of this wall. The only difference is the Sons of Hours have a maroon cushion behind them, while Osiris has a white one. Also unusual in this scene is the fact that each of these four figures holds a flail. Those of the front figures cross over the forearms of the rear figures, in order not to obscure the hands of the latter.[2] Each Son wears a royal crown: the two on the left the White Crown, with beard straps and a gold brow-band, like that of a living king[3]; the other two the Red Crown, likewise with beard straps. Each crown has a uraeus at the brow. The accompanying inscription, *"To know the names of the four gods,"* is also uncommon.[4] Could the fact that these Sons of Horus are attired like earthly kings, each wearing a royal crown with uraeus and holding a flail, indicate that they were meant to be images or aspects of King Ay himself? This should be considered a possibility.

All of the scenes are placed above a series of red and yellow horizontal bands with black lines separating them. The yellow background may imitate a roll of papyrus with text and figures spread out on the wall; later royal tombs usually have a blue-gray background. Tutankhamen's tomb also used a yellow ground and it was King Ay who officiated at his predecessor's interment. Other similarities between Ay's and Tutankhamen's tomb decoration will be discussed below.

To the right of the Four Sons of Horus, King Ay wears the White Crown, with a gold brow-band, and is embraced

Opposite, Detail of the only unmutilated royal image in WV23, one of Ay's two ka figures in the long west-wall scene of the king in the presence of deities.

213

Right, The Entrance to WV23 in the West Valley of the Kings. Below, The restored sarcophagus of King Ay, in situ *in the WV23 burial chamber.*

Right, WV23 plan & section.

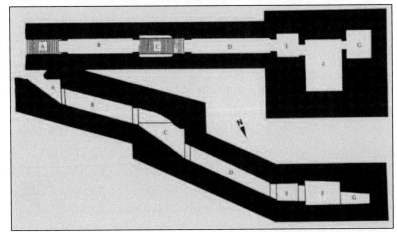

by the goddess Hathor, her right arm around his body. Ay's figure is almost totally obliterated — as are most of his images in the tomb. Hathor, as usual, wears a pair of horns with a sun disk; but, in addition, she has a uraeus on a band around her wig. Like the other two goddeses on this wall, Hathor wears a white sheath-dress supported by two shoulder straps. All three of the female deities wear bracelets, anklets and armlets, except Nun in the center of the wall, who lacks the latter. A white line around much of Hathor's face, hair and body may be the result of the disintegration of paint, possibly the initial red layout lines rather than a drawn out-

Left, A general view of the west wall of the WV23 burial chamber. Below, Scene above the doorway in that wall, depicting the mummiform Four Sons of Horus, atypically seated & wearing the White & Red crowns & false beard of the king, as well as bearing the royal flail-scepter, suggesting that they may be meant as representations of Ay himself.

line. This paint breakdown is best seen on the figure of the Goddess of the West — which will be considered shortly.

Back to back with Hathor is the first of two *ka* images of the king, which will be discussed separately. The next figure of Ay has been mutilated, except for his mid torso, a portion of his arms, plus legs, feet and some of his straight beard — all generic parts that could allude to any king, not

The WV23 burial chamber's long west-wall tableaux, depicting, from left to right: Ay (mutilated) embraced by Hathor; the 1st ka figure; Ay (mutilated) greeted by Nut; 2nd ka figure (mutilated); Ay (mutilated) with an ankh held to his nose by the Goddess of the West; & Ay (mutilated) embracing a seated Osiris.

specifically Ay. The latter is depicted wearing a uraeus on a short wig, cut off straight above the shoulder. He also wears a *shendit* kilt, as he stands before Nut. She is making *nyny*, "a greeting and ritual action."

Back to back with Nut is the second *ka* figure; and in front of the latter is another defaced representation of the king, probably wearing a white *Khat* head covering, broad collar and a multi-colored *sporran* (apron). Ay receives an ankh held to his nose by the Goddess of the West, while she grasps his left hand. Unlike the other goddesses, this one wears a golden browband like a reigning queen, but without

216

a uraeus. For some reason her eye has been hacked out, although the rest of her image has been spared. Her pose is unusual, with her torso frontal, yet her feet and legs facing towards the right. The torso seems to twist impossibly, as if she was meant to have been facing the king, who is shown behind her in the composition. Ay and this goddess may have been intended to be side by side, where she could have more easily offered the ankh to the king across her body. Egyptian rules of the representation made showing this action difficult on a flat surface.

The last scene on this west wall depicts Ay standing

Following two pages: King Ay's unmutilated west-wall ka *figure holding a staff, the king's-head finial of which probably depicts Ay; & the mutilated west-wall figure of Ay wearing a false beard &* the Nemes *head covering &* sporran *apron, as he stands in front of & embraces a seated Osiris, who wears a colorful* Atef *crown & holds crook & flail scepters.*

Top, General view of the greatly damaged east wall of WV23's burial chamber, with tableaux of King Ay fowling & hunting in the marshes, accompanied by Queen Teye. Above, Vignette from the small gold shrine discovered in KV62, with Tutankhamen fowling from a reed skiff, also accompanied by his queen, Ankhesenamen. Right, Detail of 12 pintail ducks flying above a papyrus grove in the east-wall fowling scene, with them possibly symbolizing the 12 hours of the night. Opposite, Detail of the scene of Ay fowling, with raised serpentine throw-stick & four captured ducks. The mutilated figure of the king wears a Khat head covering & a floral broad-collar.

in front of an image of Osiris. The king's left arm encircles the god, who is seated on a raised dais. Osiris wears a very colorful *Atef* crown — rather than the usual White one — topped by a sun disk. He bears a uraeus, seldom seen on this deity — although the figure of Tutankhamen, as Osiris, in the Opening of the Mouth ceremony in KV62, also wears the emblem. Ay is attired in a long red garment of cloth or leather, the surface of which is described by Lyla Brock as *"rows of blue diamonds and white or yellow rhomboids on a red ground."*[5] He also wears a stripped *Nemes* with a uraeus.

In addition to the intended defacement of the king's images on the west wall, his two *ka* figures there have also suffered in varying degrees. Ay's usual Horus Name is "Radiant of Appearances" (*thn h'w*), whereas the tomb scene has

Below, General view of the south wall of WV23's burial chamber, with texts from the Amduat & two depictions of the barque of Re, separated by the goddess Nephthys. Note the level reached by flood debris, which had entered the space through the doorway on the left.

Above, Detail of the righthand barque of Re, the god (far right) companied by 8 other deities. Below, Detail of the goddess Nephthys on the south wall, with descending-canthus treatment of her eye.

General view of WV23's burial chamber north wall, with the depiction of the 12 hours of the Amduat represented by a dozen baboons, similar to the same subject in the Tomb of Tutankhamen (KV62).

"Radiant of Forms" (*thn-hprw*). This is either a variant or simply a mistake in writing the name.[6]

Best preserved is the *ka* figure behind Hathor. The *ka* portraits were undoubtedly created in the official image of Ay himself and they also bear traits first seen in the reign of King Akhenaten: an ovoid pierced earlobe and two fat-fold lines at the neck, plus a line indicating the jaw — all elements found also in Tutankhamen's reign. Both *ka* figures wear beards secured by chin straps and carry ankhs and an ostrich feather — symbol of Maat — in their right hands. In their left they each hold a staff or cane with a small image of a

king's head and shoulders as the finial. This tiny depiction shows Ay wearing a broad collar and a *Nemes* head covering, with a false beard, chin strap and uraeus. To this writer's knowledge, the Egyptian name for these finial figures of kings on a pole or standard is unknown.

Beneath the *ka* sign, following the contours of the back of each head, both of Ay's *ka* figures are wearing two small feathers, like those on the head of the one *ka* figure in Tutankhamen's tomb. These feathers have a dark tip and chevron markings, probably indicating they come from a peregrine falcon.[7] Dual feathers with similar markings are also seen *"...in the well shaft of WV22, Tomb of Amenhotep III, where the deceased pharaoh is accompanied by the ka of his defied father, Tuthmosis IV."*[8] Dee Ann Hoff continues, seeing these feathers as iconographic allusion to the pharaoh's death and the accompanying phrase, *"The Falcon has flown to heaven."*[9] The use of *ka* figures seems to have begun in the reign of Amenhotep III, continuing with Tutankhamen and seemingly ending with Ay, as Horemheb, Rameses I and Seti I have no painted *ka* figures in their tombs. Ay's second *ka* has damage to his face, kilt and one foot.

On the left end of the burial chamber's opposite long wall, the east one, Ay is shown fowling in a reed boat, wearing a white *Khat* wig cover, with a uraeus, as he grasps four live ducks — possibly pintails — in his right hand. With his left he holds a serpent-headed throw stick above his head. A long white sash descends from his waist, and he wears a broad collar decorated with white flower petals interspersed by red dots.

There are differing views regarding Ay's use of the subjects of fowling and harpooning in the marshes on his tomb's wall. It is frequently asked why, as king, he would include such scenes — common in the tombs of New Kingdom nobles — in his royal resting-place. The answer sometimes offered is that, as a nobleman, Ay had enjoyed these pastimes and wished to continue them in the Afterlife, even though such depictions are not found on the walls of any other royal tombs of the New Kingdom. Suggested solutions to this anomaly may clarify the inclusion of these hunting scenes by King Ay.

Tutankhamen is seen in a similar tableau, not on his tomb walls, but on the right side of the small golden shrine found in KV62.[10] The symbolism of the scene has been discussed by Gay Robins, who indicated that the *"...pintail ducks with the spread wings grasped in the king's hand are not just an allusion to pA(w)t, 'primordial time,' but also to pAwr, the primorial god who came into existence through himself and created the world. Their presence, therefore, underscores the king's role as creator god in this scene."*[11]

The position of Tutankhamen is reversed from that of Ay and the objects he holds also differ. Behind him on the papyrus boat of the shrine scene is Ankhesenamen, who holds the lily scepter. There is not enough room for her to wear tall plumes — as Ay's wife does in the WV23 scene — so a modius with dual uraei topped with sun disks flank an ointment cone. Tutankhamen also grasps four ducks in one hand and a throwstick in the other hand held high above his head.

On the WV23 wall behind Ay is a papyrus thicket, from which the ducks he grasps must be assumed to have come. Of the twelve birds flying above the stylized plants, three groups of four birds have their heads colored similarly.

Detail of the Amduat baboons in WV23. There is variation in their depiction & one group of 6 faces towards the second group of 6. Because of the greater wall-space, they are more widely separated than is the case for the equivalent baboons in KV62.

One wonders whether these birds allude to the twelve hours of the night or have some other symbolic reference.

Thinking that this scene merely copies or continues a theme frequently found in private New Kingdom tombs is incorrect, as it does not recognize the royal associations of the depiction. Fragments of a fowling scene from the reign of King Sahure in the Fifth Dynasty have survived,[12] as well as a sketch from the verso of a drawing board dated to the New Kingdom and possibly to the coregency of Hatshepsut/Thutmose III.[13] The scene in question shows that the subject of a king fowling was used during the New Kingdom and that it continued as a royal tradition known at least as early as the mid-Old Kingdom.

Little remains of a second figure of Ay on a boat to the right of the marsh thicket. Part of the king's kilt, broad collar and short wig survive, along with portions of his arms, indicating his posture on the small vessel. It appears that Ay is holding or pulling a papyrus stalk. If this is so, then Arielle Kozloff's statement in *Egypt's Dazzling Sun*, citing Lana Troy's source for the word *seshesh*, might be referenced here: *"Troy translates* seshesh *as 'pulling' the papyrus, and describes this act as preliminary to hunting in the marshes with a boomerang."*[14] Ted Brock pointed out to me a scene of Amenhotep III performing this ritual in a relief at Luxor Temple.[15] Emily Teeter discussed this scene on a votive bed, stating, *"The boating scene is known from the Old Kingdom reliefs as a ritual of pulling or shaking papyrus for Hathor, a deity associated with birth. The pleasant sound that rustling papyrus made was equated with the sound of the sistrum, a ritual rattle sacred to Hathor."*[16]

On the wall of Ay's tomb, his wife, Teye (Tey), holding a lily scepter and wearing a red sash, stands behind him on the boat, facing the marsh. Her partially defaced cartouche is seen in front of her. She wears two tall plumes, often associated with Hathor.

The next scene, oriented towards the right, is heavily damaged, but the few remaining details help determine the original subject. Queen Teye, again sporting double plumes, stands behind her husband. He wears a white *Khat* with uraeus and a broad collar, and raises his arm to plunge a harpoon into an animal which embodied evil forces, presumably a hippopotamus, now lost along with the boat on which the royal couple were standing when the lower part of the wall collapsed. T. Säve-Söderbergh stated regarding regarding New Kingdom hippo-hunting scenes that *"...earlier representations of hippopotamus hunting clearly shows the scenes in Theban tombs of the early Eighteenth Dynasty go back, not to the corresponding scenes in private tombs of the New Kingdom, not to corresponding scenes in the private tombs of the Old Kingdom,*

The Amduat-baboons tableau in the burial chamber of Tutankhamen's tomb. In this instance all 12 animals are identical & face in the same direction.

There is a distinct possiblity that the same artist worked on the decoration of the burial chambers of both KV62 & WV23, as evidenced by a similar seeming "error" in both tombs. In Ay's (above left) the bill of one of the ducks the king holds in the marsh-hunting tableaux extends around the corner onto the abutting north wall. In Tutanhkamen's case (above right), the end coil of the rope used to pull the king's coffin-sledge likewise overlaps onto the adjoining wall. Rather than lack of "planning ahead," these similar anomalies may be an individual artist's personal "signature" or hallmark.

but to a royal tradition, in which the chief actor is the king, capturing by himself the ferocious animal. Thus in the Theban scenes the deceased plays a role originally reserved for the king and this explains both his royal dress and the...impossible method of hunting singlehanded on an old fashioned raft."[17]

The fact is that the subject of the Egyptian king harpooning a hippopotamus is documented as early as the First Dynasty. Petrie illustrated a seal impression found at Abydos from that period, showing King Den not only harpooning a hippo, but seemingly wrestling with one.[18] There may have been royal hippo-hunting scenes in the Fourth and Fifth dynasties; but the earliest surviving example is that of the Sixth Dynasty's Pepi II, from his funerary temple.[19]

Wives are not present in these hunting scenes until the New Kingdom, in both nobles' tombs and the few royal examples. The short answer to this, for royal depictions, is that — starting with Amenhotep III, continuing with Akhenaten, then Tutankhamen and here Ay — queens were included in scenes that previously depicted only the king, inasmuch as their status obviously had changed — probably due to the expanded roles of first Tiye and then Nefertiti. While neither Ankhesenamen nor Teye enjoyed such elevated importance, the tradition of accompanying their sportsmen spouses continued, if briefly.

In terms of the probable short interval between the decoration of KV62 and WV23, one might expect more stylistic similarities than are apparent between their burial-chamber scenes. In both tombs are walls with depictions of a dozen squatting baboons representing the twelve hours of the night. In Ay's tomb, on the north wall of the burial chamber, the first hour of the *Amduat* ("The Book of What is in the Underword") is illustrated by the god Khepri on a solar barque, which is placed almost centrally in the top register. To the left of the barque are five divinities facing left (or west), led by two goddesses, followed by three male deities.[20]

A similar scene in Tutankhamen's tomb has the solar barque bearing Khepri in the top register, but on the left half of the wall rather than being centered.[21] Additionally the five deities which lead the barque are preceded by two goddesses, but the whole group faces right (north) in this instance, instead of west, as in Ay's tomb. There the baboons are divided into left and right groups, these facing towards the center of the wall; and only in the top one of the three rows of animals do the baboons have a red face, like those in Tutankhamen's tomb, the others with lighter faces. These figures in WV23 probably originally had red outlines, if the tomb's Four Sons of Horus tableaux can be the deciding factor. It is conceivable that black paint had originally covered the red strokes, as an outline, and that both colors have since deteriorated and fallen off.[22]

Eyes with descending canthi are seen several times where eyes are preserved in WV23.[23] They exist in KV62, as well. Unusal and important are two distinct features observed in both tombs: the bill of one of the ducks held up by Ay in his marsh scene and the rope attached to Tutankhamen's funerary sledge[24] both wrap around the wall in their respective tombs, continuing on the abutting perpendicular wall, which strongly suggests the same artist may have painted both scenes and that this seeming failure to plan ahead was, in fact, intentional and may have been the artist's "hallmark" in both tombs. So we would seem to have a master painter, whose name is lost. Anonymous artists throughout the centuries have been given a name based upon one of their major works or aspects of their style. So here we are taking about an artist whom we might call the "signature painter," whose painting details extend from one wall to the adjacent one.

Gay Robins has studied the proportions of the figures in each of the royal tombs, noting that the south wall of Tutankhamen's burial chamber was laid out using the 18-square grid, whereas the north wall of the WV23 burial chamber was executed on a 20-square grid.[25] The decoration in each tomb is non-traditional in both subject matters and arrangement for New Kingdom royal sepulchers. There was more wall area in Ay's burial chamber for compositions, while limited room in Tutankhamen's corresponding space (as well as limited time to complete it) necessitated the simpler subject matter seen there.

Notes to the Essays
Forbes & Johnson: "Given Life"
(Originally published in *Kmt* 18:3, fall 2007)

1. Alan Gardiner, *Egypt of the Pharaohs* (Oxford, 1964), 205.
1. William Moran, *The Amarna Letters* (Baltimore, 1992).
3. The same divine conception by Amen, during a visit to the bed-chamber of Queen Ahmes in the guise of Thutmose I, was proclaimed by Hatshepsut in her temple at Deir el Bahari.
4. Translation after J.H. Breasted, *Ancient Records of Egypt*, Vo. 2, 369-370.
5. Ibid., 353-355.
6. Howard Carter and A.C. Mace, *The Tomb of Tut·Ankh·Amen*, Vol. 1, 79.
7. T.G.H. James, *Howard Carter, The Path to Tutankhamun* (London and New York, 1992), 174-175.
8. Elizabeth Thomas, *The Royal Necropoleis of Thebes* (Princeton, 1966), 83-87.
9. Sukuji Yoshimura and Joro Kondo, "The Tomb of Amenophis III: Waseda University Expeditions 1989-2000, *Annales du Service des Antiquités de l'Égypte* 78 (Cairo, 2004), 205-209.

Kozloff: "Plague"
(Originally published in *Kmt* 17:3, fall 2006)

1. This essay is an expanded version of a paper presented at the annual meeting of the American Research Center in Egypt, April 23, 2005. I am grateful to the following individuals for discussing with me the nature of plague, in particular Bubonic Plague, and providing references for me: Dr. Jerald S. Brodkey, professor emeritus of Case Western Reserve University School of Medicine; Dr. Joe Hinnebusch, investigator, and Dr. Tom Schwan, senior investigator, National Institutes of Health, Rocky Mountain Laboratories; and Dr. Kent L. Gage, research biologist and former chief of Plague Section, Centers for Disease Control.
2. A.I. Sadek, *Popular Religion in Egypt during the New Kingdom* (Hildesheim, 1987), 29. He notes that her cult arose in the New Kingdom, becoming especially strong during the reign of Amenhotep III.
3. He is thought to have created more than 700 Sekhmet statues. An informal count suggests that large statuary of all other deities combined from this reign is fewer than 200. One thousand whole or partial statues of Amenhotep himself are known today (B. Bryan in A. Kozloff and B. Bryan, *Egypt's Dazzling Sun: Amenhotep III and His World* (Cleveland, 1992), 125.
4. Letter EA 11, W. L. Moran (trans.), *The Amarna Letters* (Baltimore, 1992), 21. This queen was not Tiye, because Tiye would continue to be mentioned in subsequent letters.
5. Ibid., Letter EA 23, 61-62.
6. L. Berman in Kozloff and Bryan, eds., 58-59.
7. Letter EA 35, Moran, *Letters*, 107-109.
8. H. Goedicke, "The Canaanite Illness," *Studien zur Ältägyptischen Kultur* 11 (1984): 91-105, esp. 92, fn.3.
9. M. Meiss, *Painting in Florence and Siena after the Black Death* (Princeton, 1951).
10. C.A. Smith, "Plague in the Ancient World: A Study from Thucydides to Justinian" (on-line 1996), 8-9.
11. John Julius Norwich, *Byzantium: The Early Centuries* (New York, 1988), 233, 362.
12. Thucydides, *History of the Peloponnesian War II*: 48-65.
13. D. Raoult, et al., "Molecular identification by 'suicide PCR' of Yersinia pestis as the agent of Medieval Black Death," *Proceedings of the National Academy of Science* 97, no. 23 (November 2000), 12,800-12,803.
14. M. Achtman, et al., "Yersinia pestis, the cause of plague, is a recently emerged clone of Yersinia pseudotuberculosis," *Proceedings of the National Academy of Science* 96, No. 24, (November 1999), 14,043. The word "recently" in the title of this article is in geologic not historical terms. It refers to an event that occurred between 1,500 and 20,000 years ago, with a median date being the year 8750 BC. See further discussion of Bubonic Plague below.
15. E. Panagiotakopulu, "Pharaonic Egypt and the origins of plague," *Journal of Biogeography* 31, 2 (2004), 269-275.
16. Why and how plague disappears and reappears is not known. According to Schwan (personal communication) some scientists have suggested that the organism can remain in the soil; this theory is controversial however.
17. C.W.C. Oman, "The Hundred Years War," *Encyclopaedia Britannica* XI (Chicago, 1943): 888b.
18. Meiss, 65. 19. Ibid., 64-65; 20. Ibid., 7; 21. Ibid., 27; 22. Ibid., 38; 23. Ibid., 44-45; 24. Ibid., 77-78; 25. Ibid, 67-70; 26. Ibid., 67-70.
27. Achtman, *PNAS* 96, 14,043; Raoult, *PNAS* 97, 12,803.
28. Achtman, 14,043.
29. Norwich, 233.
30. Smith, 6; 31. Ibid., 2; 32. Ibid., 2.
33. Thucydides: 48-65.
34. BBC News On-Line, "Typhoid 'caused fall of Athens,'" Jan. 24, 2006. Report of the University of Athens team which "analyzed DNA from dental pulp found in a burial pit dating back to 430 BC and linked it to the organism that causes typhoid.
35. N. Axarlis, "Plague Victims Found: Mass burial in Athens," *Archaeology* On-line News, April 15, 1998.
36. A. Kozloff and D. G. Mitten, *The Gods Delight: The Human Figure in Classical Bronze* (Cleveland, 1988), 35.
37. A.D. Trendall, *Red Figure Vases of South Italy and Sicily* (London, 1989), 17.
38. Panagiotakopulu, 260.
39. Berman in Kozloff and Bryan, 56-59, 68.
40. B.G. Davies (trans.), *Egyptian Historical Records of the Later Eighteenth Dynasty* V (Warminster, 1994), 44-45; 41. Ibid., 23.
42. P. Lacau, "Suppressions et modifications des signes dans les textes funéraires," *Zeitschrift für Ägyptische Sprache* 51 (1913), 1-64; A. J. Spencer, *Death in Ancient Egypt* (Harmondsworth, 1982), 156 ff.
43. T. Säve-Söderbergh, "Preliminary Report of the Scandinavian Joint Expedition," *Kush* 15 (1967-68), 237-240. He discusses Adams's and Trigger's observations on this phenomenon as well.
44. J. Vercoutter, "The Gold of Kush: Two Gold-washing Stations at Faras East," *Kush* 7 (1959), 120-153; D. Klemm, R. Klemm, A. Murr, "Ancient Gold Mining in the Eastern Desert of Egypt and the Nubia Desert of the Sudan," in R. Friedman, ed., *Egypt and Nubia: Gifts of the Desert* (London, 2002), 216-218, and fig. 4. These authors do not accept Vercoutter's identification but illustrate many other gold-working sites both along the Nile and in the eastern desert.
45. Meiss, 67.
46. C. Aldred, *Akhenaten: King of Egypt* (London, 1988), 149, 283.
47. See A. Dodson and J. J. Janssen, "A Theban Tomb and its Tenants," *Journal of Egyptian Archaeology* 75 (1989), 125-138, for discussion and previous citations.
48. Axarlis, on-line.
49. Porter and Moss I (2), 2, 562-564 (KV 46).
50. Berman in Kozloff and Bryan, 312-317.
51. Porter and Moss I (2), 1, 16-18 (TT 8).
52. Earl Ertman of the KV63 team was kind enough to discuss the finds with me.
53. S.T. Smith, *Wretched Kush* (London, 2003), 85-86.
54. Sadek, 29-33; 55. Ibid., 100.
56. Kozloff in Kozloff and Bryan, 409.
57. Hans Goedicke, *Problems Concerning Amenophis III* (Baltimore, 1992), 18-23, 86-88.
58. J. Houser-Wegner, "Khonsu," in D. B. Redford, ed., *The Oxford Encyclopedia of Ancient Egypt* II (Oxford, 2001), 233.
59. Porter and Moss III (2), 2, 704; E.F. Wente, "The Gurob Letter to

Amenhotep IV," *Serapis* 6 (1980), 209-215.

60. It is worth noting that later Theban tombs, such as the 19th Dynasty's Sennedjem (TT1), show the deceased actually working in the fields rather than sitting grandly on a cushioned chair watching his field hands, as in the 18th Dynasty.

61. W.R. Johnson, "Images of Amenhotep III in Thebes: Styles and Intentions," in L. Berman, ed. *The Art of Amenhotep III: Art Historical Analysis* (Cleveland, 1990), 26-46.

62. Kozloff in Kozloff and Bryan, 261-283.

63. Porter and Moss I (2): 1, 105-111 (TT 55).

64. M. Bierbrier, *The Tomb-builders of the Pharaohs* (New York, 1984), 65.

65. G. Andreu, "Le site de Deir el Médineh," in C. Ziegler et al., *Les artistes de Pharaon: Deir el-Médineh et la Vallée des Rois* (Paris, 2002), 24.

66. Ibid., 274-275.

67. Kozloff in Kozloff and Bryan, 376-378.

68. Berman in Kozloff and Bryan, 58.

69. Charles van Siclen, "The Accession Date of Amenhotep III and the Jubilee," *Journal of Near Eastern Studies* 32 (1973), 290-300; Goedicke, 28 ff.

70. M Jørgenson in H. E. Nørregärd-Nielsen et al., *Ancient Art to Post-Impressionism: Masterpieces from the Ny Carlsberg Glyptotek, Copenhagen* (London, 2004), no. 12, 39, 214.

71. J.E. Johnson, III, "Yersinia (Pasteurella) Infections, Including Plague, " in Petersdorf et al., eds., *Harrison's Principles of Internal Medicine* (New York, 1983), 979-980.

72. This statement was reconfirmed in discussions with Hinnebusch, Schwan and Gage, who state that the "recent" onset of Bubonic Plague in East and Central Africa is recent only in geologic terms, and according to Gage *"it likely pre-dated the onset of Egyptian civilization."* Telephone conversation October 27, 2005.

73. Halioua and Ziskind, 123-124.

74. Several New Kingdom texts, including the *Hearst Medical Papyrus* (dated ca. 1520 BC) and *London Medical Papyrus* 15 (ca. 1350 BC), refer to "the Canaanite or Asiatic (Amu) illness." Goedicke's identification of Bubonic Plague was rejected by Bardinet, who argued the disease was leprosy. Leprosy would not have had the cataclysmic effect of Bubonic Plague. The *Ebers Papyrus* (dated ca. 1500) describes a bubonic-like illness.

75. Panagiotakopulu, 271

76. According to this hypothesis, the ancient Egyptians would have recognized a new color of rat coming off the ships from the East, just as we notice that in Toronto squirrels are black, in Cleveland they are brown, and in Philadelphia gray. When foreign black rats died in large numbers in Egypt, the ancient Egyptians would have blamed these immigrant rodents for transporting the disease from the East, from Canaan.

77. Panagiotakopulu, 272 .

78. Conversation with Schwan, October 20, 2005. Gage confirmed this point October 27, 2005.

79. G. A. Reisner, *Canopics*, Catalogue Gènèral, nos. 4001-4740, 4977-5033 (Cairo, 1967), 392-394.

80. Conversation with Gage, October 27, 2005, who noted that camels — which did not exist in Egypt during Amenhotep III's time — are highly susceptible to Bubonic Plague, suffering outbreaks in recent decades in Saudi Arabia, Pakistan and other areas.

81. A. Dodson, "The Canopic Equipment from the Serapeum at Memphis," in A. Leahy and J. Tait, eds., *Studies on Ancient Egypt in Honour of H. S. Smith* (London, 1999), 59-75.

82. In the U.S. the disease exists in "prairie dogs" (desert rodents) and is rarely transmitted to humans. Gage feels that in Africa the disease probably cycled through desert rodents in earlier (geologic) times and spread to grassland rodents such as the *Arvicanthus* during times of stress.

83. In more desolate areas without the easy transport provided by a great river and heavy international trade traffic, *Y. Pestis* moves very slowly. The disease traveled to the U.S. west coast from China in 1900, and took 50 years to reach the South Dakota line. *"Then it stopped and didn't go further until last year when it went into the Black Hills."* (Dean Biggins, research biologist with the U.S. Geological Survey, quoted in J. Robbins, "Endangered, Rescued, Now in Trouble Again," *New York Times*, April 18, 2006.

84. *"Non-traumatic pathological destruction of soft tissues are rare finds in Egyptian mummies. Frequently they can not be authenticated because of the poor state of preservation of the bodies...."* W. Pahl, W. Undeutsch, "Differential Diagnosis of Facial Skin Ulcerations in an Egyptian Mummy," *SÅK* Band 1, Beihefte 1-5 (1985), 283.

85. Raoult, 12,800-12,803.

86. Z. Topozada, "Les deux campagnes d'Amenhotep III en Nubie," *Bulletin de l'Institut Français d'Arachaeologie Orientale* 88 (1988), 153-164.

Johnson: "Tiye Plaque"
(Originally published in *Kmt* 21:4, winter 2010-11)

1. N. Reeves, *The Complete Tutankhamun* (London & New York, 1990), 47-48.

2. Ibid., 48.

3. N. Reeves & J. Taylor, *Before Tutankhamun* (London, 1992), 119.

4. Personal communication with Nicholas Reeves, April 18, 2002.

5. H.E. Winlock, *The Treasure of Three Egyptian Princesses* (New York, 1948).

6. G.B. Johnson, "Seeking Nefertiti's Tall Blue Crown,"*Amarna Letters* I (San Francisco, 1991), 50-61.

7. Ibid., 54, 61.

8. W.V. Davies, *The Statuette of Queen Tetisheri. A Reconsideration.* Occasional Paper No. 36 (British Museum, 1984). See also Davies, "Queen Tetisheri Reconsidered," *Kmt* 2:4 (winter 1991-1992), 54-61.

9. C. Lilyquist, J.E. Hoch, A.J. Peden, *The Tomb of the Three Foreign Wives of Thuthmosis III* (New Haven, 2004).

10. E. Teeter, "Fakes & Forgeries in the Collection of Chicago's Oriental Institute Museum," *Kmt* 19:4 (winter 2008-09), 53-60.

11. T.G.H. James, *Howard Carter, The Path to to Tutankhamun* (London, 1992), 135.

12. Drovetti Collection, Museo Egizio, Turin, No. 1379.

13. An English-language edition of E. Prisse d'Avennes's work was published as *Atlas of Egyptian Art* (Cairo, 1997).

14. As seen in Sitamen's depictions on two different chair backs from the Tomb of Yuya and Thuyu (KV46).

15. L. Borchardt, *Portrats der Koningin Nofretete* (Leipzig, 1923).

16. Personal communication with Emily Teeter, 2010; and Teeter, *Kmt* 19:4.1.

Martin & Bedman: "Long Coregency"
(Originally published in *Kmt* 25:2, summer 2014)

1.Our first report on the results of excavations and other issues concerning the findings and provisional conclusions in relation to Vizier Amenhotep-Huy was published in summer of 2011: Francisco J. Martín Valentín & Teresa Bedman, "Excavations in Tomb 28 at Asasif, Luxor West Bank, belonging to Vizier Amenhotep called Huy," *Kmt*, Vol. 22, No. 2 (summer, 2011), 42-53. Our team in the Season 2013 was comprised of: Gustavo Cabanillas, Maria Dolores Corona, Ahmed Baghdady, Juan Martin Rojo, Ana de la As-unción, Mahmoud Abdellah, Yaser Abd El Rasik, Mohamed El Azaab, Mari Fe San Segundo, Delfina Redondo, Gregorio Francisco,Alejandro Serrano, Daniel González, Lucia Fernández, Verónica Robles, Esther Fernández, Fernando Báez, José Luis Garcia-Vicioso, José Miguel Sánchez-Vicioso, Mario Pérez, Ana Quesada, José Luis Rodríguez, Raquel Pérez, Mahmoud Abd El Rasik.

2. Francisco J. Martín Valentín & Teresa Bedman, "The Tomb of the Vizier Amenhotep-Huy in Asasif (AT 28): Preliminary Results of the Excavation Seasons 2009-2012," *Archaeological Research in the Valley*

of the Kings & Ancient Thebes. Papers Presented in Honor of Richard H. Wilkinson, Pearce Paul Creasman, ed., University of Arizona Egyptian Expedition Wilkinson Egyptology Series, Vol. I (Arizona, 2013), 181-199

3. Francisco J. Martín Valentín & Teresa Bedman, 2013: 194 and fig. 11.

4. The latest known date for Vizier of Amenhotep-Huy is the first day of the first month of *Shemu*, in Year 35 of Amenhotep III. See Ricardo Caminos, "Amenophis III's vizier Amenhotep at Silsilah East," *Journal of Egyptian Archaeology* 73 (1987), 210 and note 1.

5. This fourth column was the first to be discovered during the seasons of 2010 and 2011. See Francisco J. Martín Valentín & Teresa Bedman, 2011: 50, 53.

6. "Hrw Hr TnTAt 'Als Thronestrade auf (Hr) der der König', 'Horus... auf dem Thronestrade,'" *Wb.* V, 384, (I, 9), 385, (1).

7. Marie-Ange Bonhème & Annie Forgeau, *Pharaon. Les secrets du Pouvoir* (Paris,1988), 300.

8. *The Epigraphic Survey, The Tomb of Kheruef: Theban Tomb 192.* OIP 102 (Chicago, 1980), Pl. 27-28, 34, 43-45. *Urk.* IV, 1867, 2-4.

9. Wolfgang Helck, *Urk.* IV, 1869, 14-18.

10. Helck, *Urk.* IV, 1871, 7-8.

11. Such is the case of the mention of both sovereigns in TT55 of Ramose. See Helck, *Urk.* IV, 1878, 13-14.

12. The Epigraphic Survey, *The Tomb of Kheruef: Theban Tomb 192*, Pl. 8-9 y 11-13. B. Porter & R. Moss, *Topographical Bibliography, Vol. I, Part I, The Theban Necropolis* (Oxford, 1960), 298 (5), II; 299 (6).

13. Francisco J. Martín-Valentín, *Amen-Ho-tep III, el esplendor de Egipto: Una tesis de reconstrucción histórica* (Madrid, 1989), 180- 181.

14. The document with the highest date attested to the reign of Amenhotep III is a jar seal found in Malkata which makes mention of the fifth epagomenic day in Year 38 of his reign. See Williams Hayes, "Inscriptions from the Palace of Amenhotep III," *Journal of Near Eastern Studies* 10 (1951), pp. 35-40, fig. 11, no. 143. See also H.W. Fairman, *The City of Akhenaten*, Vol. II, Chap. 6 "The Inscriptions," 103-104: "....It is obvious that this is not conclusive evidence, but it is a point which must be reckoned with, and is of the highest significance when taken in conjuction with the slowly, but steadily increasing evidence, that Amenhotep III not only lived on after the accession of Akhenaten, but lived with him at Amarna."

15. The idea that the two sovereigns reigned in common for a long period was launched by Ludwig Borchardt in *Amenophis IV Mitkönig in den letzen Jahren Amenophis III? Allerhand Kleinigkeiten*, 1933, 23-29. The problem of the coregency has ignited a huge debate among specialists. See: H. Schlögl, *Echnaton-Tutanchamun, Fakten und Texte.* (Wiesbaden, 3rd. Ed. 1989); F. Aling, *Prosopographical Study of the Reings of Thutmosis IV and Amenhotep III*, 1976, 224-229; and William J. Murnane, *Ancient Egyptian Corregencies*, SAOC, 40 (Chicago, 1977), 231-233; also Donald B. Redford, *History and Chronology of the Eighteenth Dynasty of Egypt* (Toronto, 1967). The greatest defender of the long coregency (between eleven and twelve years), was Cyril Aldred, *Akhenaten, King of Egypt* (London & New York, 1988), 169-182. See also Francisco J. Valentin-Martín, "Indications et évidences d'une corégence entre Amenhotep III et Amenhotep IV dans la nécropole Thébaine," *Proceedings of the Seventh International Congress of Egyptologists Cambridge, 3-9 September 1995*, C. J. Eyre,ed. (Leuven, 1998), 741-757. See the exhaustive study of Claude Vandersleyen, in *L' Égypte et la Vallée du Nil*, Vol. 2. (Dés la fin de l'Ancien Empire à la fin du Nouvel Empire), (Paris, 1995), 402-407. Also to be considered are the very important publications of W. Raymond Johnson: "Images of Amenhotep III in Thebes: Styles and Intentions," L. M. Berman, ed., Cleveland Museum of Art (Bloomington, 1990), 24-26; "The Deified Amenhotep III as the Living Re-Horakhty: Stylistic and Iconographic Considerations," *Sesto Congresso Internazionale di Egittologia*: 2 (Turin, 1993), 231-236; "Amenhotep III and Amarna: some new Considerations," *JEA* 82 (1996), 65-82. "Monuments and Monumental Art under Amenhotep III: Evolution and Meaning," *Amenhotep III. Perspectives on His Reign*, David O'Connor & Eric H. Cline, eds. (Ann Arbor, 1998), 63-94.

16. J.D.S. Pendlebury, "The Desert Altars," *The City of Akhenaten*, Vol.

II, Chap. V, 102: *"...This coregency will also allow Amenhotep III to be the father of Tutankhaten and simplifies the whole chronology of the period."*

Kozloff: "Chips Off Old Statues"
(Originally published in *Kmt* 23:3, fall 2012)

1. An abbreviated form of these findings was first published by this author in "Chips Off the Old Block: Amenhotep IV's Sandstone Colossi, Re-cut from Statues of Amenhotep III," *Millions of Jubilees: Studies in Honor of David P. Silverman*, Z. Hawass and J.H. Weg- ner, eds. (Cairo, 2010), 279-294. Lisa Manniche's monograph, *The Akhenaten Colossi of Karnak* (New York, 2010), describes their discovery and summarizes the work of art historians and scientists who have studied the statues in the nearly nine decades they have been available to scholars. Although Dr. Manniche learned of my work and requested notes from me, I could not analyze my evidence in time for her publication date.

2. R. Freed, "Observations on Some Amenhotep IV Colossi from Karnak," *Memnonia* 10, 195-200, pls. LV-LVIII.

3. This author's previous publications on re-cut statuary include "Enthroned Amenhotep III Recut by Ramesses II," *Egypt's Daz- zling Sun, Amenhotep III and His World*, A. Kozloff and B. Bryan, eds. (Cleveland, 1992), 172-175, no. 14; "A Masterpiece with Three Lives," *Studies in Honor of William Kelly Simpson*, P. Der Manuelian, ed. (Boston, 1996), 477-485; "Statue of Queen Arsinoe," *Miho Museum: South Wing*, T. Umehara, ed. (Kyoto, 1997), 34-37. With Edmund S. Meltzer, this author presented a paper, "Have Ramose's Statuary and Sarcophagi Been Right under our Noses All This time?," at the American Research Center in Egypt annual meeting, April 23-25, 2010, Oakland, CA.

4. Freed recorded many instances of paint and gesso traces in her *Memnonia* article. See note 2.

5. A short *Khat* is also worn by the head in the Alexandria Museum, A 2.

6. See similar carving on JE 55938 below.

7. See also JE 99065 below.

8. See also JE 55938. Two torsos in storage in Egypt bear the same decoration. See Manniche, *Akhenaten Colossi*, Figures 2.63 and 2.75

9. On the red-quartzite statue several features were blocked out in the form of roughened surfaces to accommodate the attachment of overlaid gilding. These spaces include a broad collar, armlets and a pectoral with its supporting chain.

10. JE 49529 and JE 98894 of this group show the same tool marks.

11. See this author's discussion of the Louvre's statue of Rameses II recut from one of Amenhotep III, note 3 above.

12. Ibid.

13. Christie's New York, *Antiquities*, 6 December 2007, lot 19, pp. 20-23.

Ertman: "Smiting"
(Originally published in *Kmt* 17:4, winter 2006-07)

1. For a good illustration in color, see R. Schulz and M. Seidel, eds., *Egypt: The World of the Pharaohs* (Köln, 1998), 21, pl. 26. At the inception of this research I was unaware of Emma Swan Hall's *The Pharaoh Smites his Enemies* (Munich, 1986). Many of the original citations reflect this fact, and once I was able to obtain a copy of this publication, the citations in her published research were added to the end notes of this article. I thank E.C. Brock for obtaining a copy for me.

2. A.J. Spencer, *Early Egypt: The Rise of Civilisation in the Nile Valley* (Norman, OK, 1993), pl. 32, and in numerous books dealing with ancient Egypt. At the time of my initial writing, I was unaware of the calcite palette scene of King Zer from Sakkara (Hall, fig. 7). However, this scene does not depict the person delivering the intended blow as a king through specific identifying regalia or inscription.

3. Spencer, pl. 67.

4. Among many sources see K. Lange and M. Himmer, *Egypt, Architecture, Sculpture, Painting in Three Thousand Years* (London, 1956), pl 139; also Hall, fig. 28.

5. Hall, fig. 37, after R.M. Saad, "Les travaux d'Aménophis IV au IIIe pylône du temple d'Amon Re^c a Karnak," *Kêmi* 20 (1970), fig. 2.

6. D. Redford, "Studies on Akhenaten at Thebes II: A Report on the

Work of the Akhenaten Temple Project of the University Museum, The University of Pennsylvannia for the Year 1973-4," *Journal of the American Research Center in Egypt* XII (1975), pl. VI, b).

7. R. Smith and D. Redford, *The Akhenaten Temple Project* I, *Initial Discoveries* (Warminster, 1976), 76, 81, pl. 23, 3; 140.

8. Ibid., 81, n. 38, pl. 23.2; and no. 0121 09810; also Redford, *JARCE* XII, pl. V, b. There are other Karnak *talatat* scenes in which Nefertiti is placed behind Akhenaten in smiting scenes. The examples cited are merely to illustrate this change.

9. J. Cooney, *Amarna Reliefs from Hermopolis in American Collections* (Brooklyn, 1965), 80-81; also Hall, fig. 40.

10. Ibid., 84, drawing and block, 82-83); also Hall, fig. 39.

11. Ibid, drawing, 82; block, 83.

12. Ibid., 84-85. John Cooney "...*with considerable hesitation*..." identified this smiting figure as Akhenaten, which initially I accepted without hesitation. After presenting this paper in Luxor, Egypt, in January 2006, Raymond Johnson pointed out that the enemy being dispatched was female by evidence of a breast between this figure's right arm and torso. As to the fact that Nefertiti's garment usually touched the ground, Johnson suggested that the hem would naturally rise when the arm was raised. I thank him for this observation and the resulting correction to this paper.

13. M. Raven, "Meryneith: High Priest of the Aten," *Minerva* 13 (July/August 2002), 31-34, esp. 32, figs. 4-5.

14. I am grateful to Maarten Raven and Rene Van Walsem for permission to publish the line drawing of the smiting scene from the Leiden Expedition excavation of the Tomb of Meryneith at Sakkara.

15. The *talatat* discussed earlier which included a child in one and perhaps more scenes are now in Boston (MFAB) and New York (MMA); they came from El Amarna and date at least after Year 5, and probably later.

16. Smith and Redford, 2, pl. 23 (instances of Nefertiti smiting a foe; and No. 0121 09810 (not pictured), 81, n. 38.

17. Following the Tucson lecture, Peter Brand suggested that the images of the king smiting on the side of a ship's kiosk(s) may have been made on an "open work" or "lattice-like" base rather than being painted on fabric or a pliable material. I thank Peter for his comments.

18. J. Baines, "The Dawn of the Amarna Age" in D.O'Connor and E. Cline, eds., *Amenhotep III: Perspectives on his reign* (Ann Arbor, MI, 1998), 293. Stelae of the royal family found in private house shrines also functioned as "*something that could be worshipped by the nonroyal.*"

19. My thanks to Maarten Raven for this additional information, and for his assistance related to the Meryneith relief scene.

20. T. Davis, *The Tombs of Harmhabi and Touatânkamanou* (London, 1912), 128, fig. 4; also Hall, fig. 41.

21. Hall, fig. 66; also The Epigraphic Survey, *Reliefs and Inscriptions at Karnak* I, II (Chicago, 1954), pl. 88.

22. Hall, fig. 82; also The Epigraphic Survey, *Temple of Khonsu* I, *Scenes of King Herihor in the Court* (Chicago, 1979), pl. 20. The scene illustrates the royal barque being towed during the Opet Festival, the fore and aft kiosks containing smiting scenes.

23. I appreciate Raymond Johnson's analysis and his pointing out that these later smiting scenes were copied from the Luxor Temple Opet Festival scenes of Tutankhamen, rather than from *talatat* blocks.

24. Following the Tucson presentation, David O'Connor suggested that Ankhesenamen might merely be handing the king the next scimitar for his use, similar to the scene on the KV62 small golden shrine, where she hands him another arrow as he is shooting birds in a marsh.

Krauss: "Final Secret"
(Originally published in *Kmt* 20:2, summer 2009)

1. M. Mode, *Hallesche Beiträge zur Orientwissenschaft* 6 (1984), 37-45.

2. R. Krauss, *Kmt* 19:3 (fall 2008), 50-52.

3. J. Meier-Graefe, *Kunst und Künstler. Monatsschrift für bildende Kunst* 28.12 (September 1930), 479-482.

4. G. v. Paczensky and H. Ganslmayr, *Nofretete will nach Hause: Europa – Schatzhaus der dritten Welt* (Munich, 1984), 276f.

5. R. Krauss, *Jahrbuch der Berliner Museen* 33 (1991), 7-36.

6. See n. 4.

7. A. Fricke, in *Imperialism, Art and Restitution*, J.H. Merryman, ed. (Cambridge, 2006), 178 (Art. 4), 190 (Art. 11).

8. See note 2.

9. Letter from A. Erman to H.O. Lange, November 4, 1920; Lange's correspondence, Royal Library Copenhagen, Manuscript-Dept.

10. R. Krauss, *Jahrbuch Preussischer Kulturbesitz* 24 (1988), 107.

11. Ibid.

12. W. Kaiser, in *Das Deutsche Archäologische Institut. Geschichte und Dokumente*, Vol. 3 (Mainz, 1979), 101f.

13. H. Schäfer, *Amtliche Berichte* 35 (1913/14), 140f.

14. See note 2.

15. L. Borchardt, *Porträts der Königin Nofretete* (Leipzig, 1923), 15.

16. C.Aldred, *Akhenaten and Nefertiti*. Exhibition catalogue (Brooklyn, 1973), 102.

17. W. Davis, *American Journal of Archaeology* 82 (1978), 389.

18. Letter to the author dated October 9, 1988.

19. W.M.F. Petrie, *Illahun, Kahun and Gurob* 1899-90 (London, 1891), Pl. XXIV.

20. Borchardt, *Porträts*, 17.

21. Ibid., 8.

22. CG 34174, see for example G.T. Martin, *The Royal Tomb at El-Amarna. I. The Objects* (London, 1974), Pl. 54.

23. E.S. Bogoslovskij, *Göttinger Miszellen* 61 (1983), 56; I. Munro, *Göttinger Miszellen* 94 (1986), 83.

24. C. Andrews, *Ancient Egyptian Jewellery* (London, 1990), 117; A. Wilkinson, *Ancient Egyptian Jewellery* (London, 1971), 108.

25. See note 13. 26. See note 18.

27. "Most ugliest" is paraphrased from Homer Simpson's "most dumbest."

28. Borchardt, *Porträts*, 4. 29. See note 13. 30. Borchardt, *Porträts*, 13.

31. http://www.enemigosdelaegiptoloia.com/newsletter_ emc003.pdf: *Egyptian Museum Newsletter* No. 3, September-December 2008.

32. For beeswax as painting material, see A. Lucas, *Ancient Egyptian Materials and Industries*, 4th. ed., J.R. Harris, ed. (London, 1962), 352f. Borchardt explained the patina of the Cairo stela thus: "*By oxidation what is blue has developed into a darker, greenish hue.*" Analysis of small samples of stela paint taken in 1985 showed precisely the mixture of pigments cited in my text in imitation of oxidation.

33. L.Borchardt & H. Ricke, *Die Wohnhäuser in Tell El-Amarna* (Berlin, 1980), 91, 95-98.

34. A. Erman, *Amtliche Berichte* 9 (1888), LXII, XXXXVIII.

35. L.Borchardt, *Sitzungsberichte der Preussischen Akademie der Wissenschaften 1888* (I), 129-137

36. A. Erman, *Mein Werden und mein Wirken. Erinnerungen eines alten Berliner Gelehrten* (Leipzig, 1929), 230.

37. Letter from A. Erman to Eduard Meyer, dated January 2, 1888; papers of E. Meyer, Archive of the Berlin-Brandenburgische Akademie der Wissenschaften.

38. MLC 2078 (no provenance) in the Babylonian Collection at Yale; see J. Friberg, *Reallexikon der Assyriologie* 7 (1987-1990), 547.

39. J.D. Cooney, *The Bulletin of the Cleveland Museum of Art* (January 1965), 2-4.

40. G. Maspero, *Guide du visiteur au Musée du Caire*, 4th ed.(Cairo, 1915), 145.

41. Borchardt sent letters and telegrams from Cairo on December 21,

28, 1912 and January 1, 9 and 14, 1913.
42. Borchardt, *Porträts*, 3.
43. Ibid., 13. 44. Ibid., 24.

Dodson: "Nefertiti-Tutankhaten Coregency?"
(Originally published in *Kmt* 20:2, summer 2009)

1. B. Porter and R. Moss, *Topographical Bibliography of Ancient Egyptian Hieroglyphic Texts, Reliefs and Paintings, IV: Lower and Middle Egypt* (Oxford, 1934), 213–214.
2. A photograph of the squeeze is published in S. Moseley, *Amarna: The Missing Evidence* (Calshot, 2009), 144, fig. 7.8, albeit accompanied by some bizarre interpretations. The visible traces are included in the copy of the scene published with this essay.
3. P.E. Newberry, "Akhenaten's Eldest Son-in-Law 'Ankhkheperure," *Journal of Egyptian Archaeology* 14 (1928), 3-9.
4. W.M.F. Petrie. *Kahun, Gurob and Hawara* (London, 1890), pl. xxiii; 1894: pl. xv.
5. H. Beinlich and M. Saleh, *Corpus der Hieroglyphischen Inschriften aus dem Grab des Tutanchamun* (Oxford 1989), 4[1k].
6. Porter and Moss, *Top. Bib.* I² (1960), 253[5].
7. Newberry, *JEA* 14.
8 Cf. W.J. Murnane, *Ancient Egyptian Coregencies* (Chicago, 1977); J. Allen, "The Amarna Succession," in P. Brand (ed.), *Causing His Name to Live: Studies in Egyptian Epigraphy and History in Memory of William J. Murnane* (http://history.memphis.edu/murnane/).
9. J.R. Harris, a. "Neferneferuaten," *Göttinger Miszellen* 4 (1973), 15-17; b. "Neferneferuaten Rediviva," *Acta Orientalia* 35 (1973), 5-13; c. "Neferneferuaten Regnans," *AO* 36 (1974), 11-21; d. "Akhenaten or Nefertiti?," *AO* 38 (1977), 5-10.
10. Cf. Newberry *JEA* 14, 7; D. Montserrat, *Akhenaten: history, fantasy and ancient Egypt* (London, 2000), 168–173.
11. On which there is of course a vast literature!
12. J. Samson, a. "Nefertiti's Regality', *JEA* 63 (1977), 94; b. "Akhenaten's Coregent Ankhkheprure-Nefernefruaten," *GM* 53 (1982), 58.
13. R. Krauss, *Das Ende der Amarnazeit* (Hildesheim, 1978), 43-47.
14. Dodson, "Why did Nefertiti disappear?," in W. Manley (ed.), *Seventy Mysteries of Ancient Egypt* (London, 2003), 127-131.
15. Allen, in *Causing His Name to Live*; M. Gabolde "Under a Deep Blue Starry Sky," in *Causing His Name to Live*, 17-23.
16. C. Loeben, "No Evidence of Coregency: Two Erased Inscriptions from Tutankhamun's Tomb," *Amarna Letters* 3 (1994): 105-109.
17. Depending on whether or not Neferneferuaten is given an independent reign.
18. While only the "durbar" scenes are formally dated to Year 12, other private tomb decoration can be dated by either the form of the name of the Aten or by the presence of Princess Meketaten, who would seem to have died not long after Year 12.
19. Either mery(et)-Neferkheperure or mery(et)-Waenre: the former seems to have been paired with the nomen Neferneferuaten-mery(et)-Waenre, the latter with Neferneferuaten-akhetenhaes.
20. For example we have Rameses VI adding Meryamun to Amenhotep III's old "Nebmaatre" and Rameses VII adding the same epithet to Rameses II's "Usermaatre-setpenre." Besides similar additions to historic prenomina in the late Twentieth Dynasty, we also find the accretion of epithets to nomina during the mid Twenty-second Dynasty (cf. Dodson, "A New King Shoshenq Confirmed?," *GM* 137 (1993), 55). This is only reversed towards the end of the Third Intermediate Period, with the archaizing simplicity of the names of Shoshenq V and his contemporaries.
21. E.g. G. Roeder, *Amarna-Reliefs aus Hermopolis: Ausgrabungen der Deutschen Hermopolis-Expedition in Hermopolis 1929-1939* (Hildesheim, 1969), pl. 18[340-VIA, 652-VIIIA], 106[451-VIIC], 127[783-VIII], 159 [364-VIII]; cf. Gabolde, *D'Akhenaton à Toutânkhamon* (Lyon, 1998), 121-122, n.997.
22. A block from Karnak preserves what was clearly once part of an inscription reading '[...-ta]sherit, born of [...] born of the King's Great Wife [...]' (D. B. Redford, "Studies on Akhenaten at Thebes. II. A Report on

the Work of the Akhenaten Temple Project of the University Museum, The University of Pennsylvania, for the Year 1973-4," *Journal of the American Research Center in Egypt* 12 (1975), 11-12, pl. vii; note that the restoration provided there is pure speculation, as we have no idea of the context of this isolated block on the original wall).
23. Mentions of Meryetaten and Ankhesenpaaten in connection with children in the Ashmunein reliefs derive from the usurpation of depictions of Akhenaten's junior wife, Kiya, alongside her daughter: there are no original representations of Meryetaten and Ankhesenpaaten with a child. Also, the alleged "death in childbirth" of their sister, Meketaten, as shown in the Royal Tomb at Amarna, is probably nothing of the kind: see J. van Dijk, "The Death of Meketaten," in *Causing His Name to Live*.
24. In KV55: here is not the place to once again recount the interminable debate on that deposit!
25. On the basis of blocks from a relief, found at Ashmunein, that name him as a "King's Son" in conjunction with one of Akhenaten's daughters (see most recently "Editor's Report," *Kmt* 20:1 [2009], 2).
26. Allen, in *Causing his Name to Live*.
27. Krauss, *Ende*; Gabolde, *D'Akhenaton à Toutânkhamon*.
28. Cf. Murnane, "The End of the Amarna Period Once Again," *Orientalistische Literaturzeutung* 96 (2001), 18, contra Gabolde, *D'Akhenaton à Toutânkhamon*, 178–183)
29. Cf. Samson, *JEA* 63; E.L. Ertman, "Is There Visual Evidence for a 'King' Nefertiti?," *Amarna Letters* 2 (1992), 50-55.
30. See A. Van der Perre, "The Year 16 graffito of Akhenaten in" Dayr Abū Hinnis, "A Contribution to the Study of the Later Years of Nefertiti," *Journal of Egyptian History* 7 (2014), 67-108. Nefertiti's death and burial as a queen has been argued from the existence of a queenly ushabti of Nefertiti (Loeben, "Eine Bestattung der großen königlichen Gemahlin Nof-retete in Amarna," *Mitteilungen des Deutschen Archäologischen Instituts, Kairo* 42 [1986], 99-107; "Une inhumation de la grande épouse royal Néfertiti à Amarna? La figurine funéraire de Néfertiti," *Égypte Afrique et Orient* 13 [1999], 25-30; cf. J.-L. Buvot, "Un chaouabti pour deux reines amarniennes?," *Égypte Afrique et Orient* 13 [1999], 31-34; and Allen in *Causing his Name to Live*, 14). However, like all Egyptians, Nefertiti would have certainly had her principal items of funerary equipment made long before she could have contemplated ending her life as a king. The "problem shabti" should most likely be seen as stray from some palace storeroom, abandoned at Nefertiti's change of status, rather than from her burial.
31. Cf. L. Troy, *Patterns of Queenship in Ancient Egyptian Myth and History* (Uppsala, 1986).
32. J. Pendlebury, *City of Akhenaten III*, pl. xcv (279); cf. Krauss, "Zur Chronologie der Nachfolger Achenatens unter Berucksichtigung der DOG-Funde aus Amarna," *Mitteilungen der Deutschen Orientgesellschaft* 129 (1997), 242-244.
33. W. L. Moran, *The Amarna Letters* (Baltimore, 1992), 114-115.
34. Harris, "Akhenaten and Neferneruaten," in C.N. Reeves (ed.), *After Tut'ankhamun* (London and New York, 1991), 60.

Eaton-Krauss: "Thrones"
(Originally published in *Kmt* 19:2, summer 2008)

1. "Die Throne Tutanchamuns: Vorläufige Bemerkungen", *Göttinger Miszellen* 76 (1984), 7-10.
2. "Royal Mummies of the Eighteenth Dynasty: A Biologic and Egyptological Approach," in *After Tutankhamun. Research and Excavations in the Royal Necropolis at Thebes*, C.N. Reeves, ed. (London and New York, 1992), 11.
3. Both types of compositions are included in the paintings on the so-called painted box from the tomb, Obj. No. 21; see Nina M. Davies, *Tutankhamun's Painted Box*, reproduced in color from the original in the Cairo Museum, with explanatory text by Alan H. Gardiner (Oxford, 1962).
4. For a thorough study of this kind of chair, see Henry G. Fischer, "A Chair of the Early New Kingdom," in his *Varia Nova, Egyptian Studies* III (New York, 1996), 141-175.
5. CG 51111: The armrests of this chair are also filled with openwork; see William Stevenson Smith, *The Art and Architecture of Ancient*

Egypt, 3rd (sic) edition, revised, with additions by William Kelly Simpson (New Haven and London, 1998), fig. 281 (where the caption gives the incorrect provenance "Malqata").

6. MMA 36.3.152: illustrated in the exhibition catalogue *Hatshepsut. From Queen to Pharaoh*, Catharine H. Roehrig, ed. (New York, New Haven and London, 2005), 95.

7. As I observed in my publication of a stool of this type from the Tomb of Sennedjem: "Three Stools from the Tomb of Sennedjem, TT 1," in *Ancient Egypt, the Aegean and the Near East: Studies in Honor of Martha Rhodes Bell*, Jacke Phillips, ed. (San Antonio, 1997), 185-186, 191-192.

8. For monuments documenting this policy, see M. Eaton-Krauss, "Tutankhamun at Karnak," *Mitteilungen des Deutschen Archäologischen Instituts Kairo* 44, 1988, 1-11; Eaton-Krauss and William J. Murnane, "Tutankhamun, Ay, and the Avenue of Sphinxes between Pylon X and the Mut Precinct at Karnak," *Bulletin de la Société Égyptologie Genève* 15 (1991), 31-38.

9. Christian Loeben was the first to call attention to this fact which he discussed in detail in his unpublished MA thesis (*Die beschrifteten Truhen und Kästen des Tutanchamun*, Freie Universität, Berlin, 1986); compare now the entry in the exhibition catalogue *Tutanchamun: Das goldene Jenseits. Grabschätze aus dem Tal der Könige*, André Wiese and Andreas Brodbeck, eds. (Basel, 2004), 340-341. For an English translation of the "Restoration Decree,"see William J. Murnane, *Texts from the Amarna Period in Egypt* (Atlanta, 1995), 212-214.

10. Details of the depictions of bound captives on the footstool are well illustrated in Christiane Desroches Noblecourt, *Tutankhamun. Life and Death of a Pharaoh* (New York and London, 1963), pl. XIa-c. Desroches-Noblecourt's book was one of the first on Tutankhamen to be published with good color illustrations and is still worth having for that reason alone.

11. Sella Curulis, *The Folding Stool, an ancient symbol of dignity* (Copenhagen, 1980).

12. Smith, *Art and Architecture*, n. 5, 204.

13. For most of the examples, see the list that Deborah Sweeney compiled when she published one of the two examples that come from Levantine sites: "The Man on the Folding Chair: An Egyptian Relief from Beth Shan," *Israel Exploration Journal* 48, 1998, 38-53.

14. As reconstructed by George B. Johnson, "The Mysterious Cache-Tomb of Fourth Dynasty Queen Hetepheres," *Kmt* 6:1(spring 1995), 40, 50 (illus.).

15. CG 51113: This chair has frequently been included in traveling exhibitions of objects from the Egyptian Museum, and it is among those objects from the Valley of the Kings currently on tour in the exhibition "Tutankhamun and the Golden Age of the Pharaohs." In Zahi Hawass's catalogue of the exhibition as shown in America, *Tutankhamun and the Golden Age of the Pharaohs* (Washington, D.C., 2005) it is no. 55 on p. 145.

16. MMA 68.58. This chair is the subject of Henry G. Fischer's study cited above in Note 4.

17. For references to Vandersleyen's publications of his theories on the ownership of the gold throne, see his contribution "Royal Figures from Tutankhamun's Tomb: Their Historical Usefulnesss," in *After Tutankhamun* (Note 2), 73-78.

18. See the plates in M. Eaton-Krauss and Erhart Graefe, *The Small Golden Shrine from the Tomb of Tutankhamun* (Oxford, 1985).

19. "The Identity of the King and Queen on Tutankhamun's Gold Throne," in *Egyptology at the Dawn of the Twenty-first Century. Proceedings of the Eighth International Congress of Egyptologists* (Cairo, 2000, Zahi Hawass and Lyla Pinch Brock, eds., vol. II (Cairo and New York, 2003), 209-214.

20. See, most recently, his popularizing booklet *Akhenaton – du mystère à la lumière* (Paris, 2005) and my review in *Egyptian Archaeology* 30 (spring 2007), 42-43.

21. "Some Thoughts on Ritual Banquets at the Court of Akhenaten and in the Ancient Near East," in *Egypt, Israel, and the Ancient Mediterranean World: Studies in Honor of Donald B. Redford*, Gary N. Knoppers and Antoine Hirsch, eds. (Leiden and Boston, 2004), 210-217.

22. "Notes on Some of the Objects from the Tomb of Tutankhamun," *Annales du Service des Antiquités d'Égypte* 41 (1942), 147.

Johnson: "Battle Narratives"
(Originally published in *Kmt* 20:4, winter 2009-10)

1. For the only published record of that work see Muhammad Abdul Qader Muhammad's report in *Annales du Service des Antiquites d'Egypte* 60 (1968), 227-79.

2. *The Epigraphic Survey, Reliefs and Inscriptions at Luxor Temple Volume 1: The Festival Procession of Opet in the Colonnade Hall*, Oriental Institute Publications 112 (Chicago, 1994); *Epigraphic Survey, RILT Volume 2: The Façade, Portals, Upper Register Scenes, Columns, Marginalia, and Statuary in the Colonnade Hall*, OIP 116 (Chicago, 1998).

3. The Luxor Temple blockyard open-air museum is funded in part by the World Monuments Fund and a Robert W. Wilson Challenge to Conserve Our Heritage grant. For ongoing reports on recent blockyard-activities, see "The Epigraphic Survey," in the *Oriental Institute Annual Reports* for the last few years.

4. See Donald Redford in the *Akhenaten Temple Project Volume 2: Rwd-Mnw and Inscriptions*, 20, n. 98. for the equation of the two temple names, with whom I agree. The Ninth Pylon blocks appear to be from the sanctuary of the Tutankhamen temple, where Ay is shown accompanying Tutankhamen as a high official (his figures were later erased). The Second Pylon material appears to be from the front of the temple, including a square-pillared forecourt, with reliefs showing Ay as king.

5. The small blocks formed the upper courses, the large blocks were from the lower courses and foundations.

6. See the reports of Henri Chevrier in *ASAE* 1926-1956, and of Ramadan Saad in *Karnak* 5 (1975), 93-109.

7. Steve Harvey will soon be publishing his study of this material in the Oriental Institute Publication series.

8. See the article by Luc and Marc Gabolde in the *Bulletin de l'Institut Français d'Archéologie Orientale* 89 (1989), which examines the similar nature and function of the two complexes.

9. In my study of the Tutankhamen material, I have recorded twenty-two of Horemheb's battle-themed mortuary-temple blocks reused at Khonsu Temple; but undoubtedly there are many, many more built into the walls of Khonsu Temple itself. All of the material that is visible will all be recorded and published by the Epigraphic Survey in a future volume of the Khonsu Temple series. The Architectural Survey of the Oriental Institute excavated Horemheb's mortuary temple (appropriated from Ay after the old king's death); see Uvo Hölscher, *The Excavation of Medinet Habu Volume 2, The Temples of the Eighteenth Dynasty*, OIP 41 (Chicago, 1939). Hölscher noted colossal mud-brick walls to the north of the temple, which he speculated could be another mortuary complex, possibly that of Tutankhamen.

10. This block, when found, was bright with painted detail — which is now completely missing, due to changing weather conditions and greatly increasing humidity in Luxor.

11. A.R. Williams, "Modern Technology Reopens the Ancient Case of King Tut," *National Geographic Magazine*, June 2005, 2-21.

12. For a recent reevaluation of Egypt's foreign affairs at this time, see: John Darnell and Colleen Manassa, *Tutankhamun's Armies: Battle and Conquest during Ancient Egypt's Late 18th Dynasty* (New Jersey, 2007).

Ertman: "Ay's Tomb Decoration"
(Originally published in *Kmt* 20:3, fall 2009)

1. This essay was initially presented as a paper at the anual meeting of the American Research Center in Egypt in New Jersey, April 2009. My thinks to Otto Schaden for his assistance and permission to publish this tomb's decoration, and to George Johnson for his excellent

photographs.

2. This detail was pointed out to me by Heather Alexander, one our our Amenmesse Project photographers, and it is unusual in its composition.

3. Earl Ertman, "Another Look at a Relief of King Akhenaten from the Harer Family Trust Collection and the Use of Streamers During the Amarna Period, *Journal of the Society for the Study of Egyptian Antiquities* 20 (1990), 108-112, especially 110 and pl. VIII; also Ertman, "More Comments on New Kingdom Crown Streamers and the Gold Temple-band They Held in Place," *JSSEA* 23 (1993), 51-55. The chief queen seems also to have worn this brow band.

4. I am grateful for this information from Hans Goedicke, and for other suggestions regarding this essay.

5. Lyla Pinch Brock, "The Royal Red Fabic," *JSSEA* 25 (1995), 7, also 10 and fig. 3

6. My thanks to Otto Schaden for pointing this change out to me: see: Schaden, *God's Father Ay* (University of Minnesota, 1977), 218, 230. He also indicated it appears that the variant writing of Ay's *ka* name may have been spared because it was not on the workmen's "list" of names to be erased; see Schaden in *Amarna Letters* 4, 99 and n. 16; and Schaden, *Journal of the American Research Center in Egypt* 21 (1984). 39-64, esp. 42 and note 10. See also L. Bell, "Luxor Temple and the Cult of the Royal Ka," *Journal of Near Eastern Studies* 44 (1985), esp. 258.

7. My thanks to Dee Ann Hoff for providing me with some of her unpublished research material related to the use of two feathers, especially those found on the heads of *ka* figures. See Schaden, *AL* 4, 88.

8. Personal correspondence, Dee Ann Hoff.

9. Ibid. Her correspondence to me from June 12, 2006, and following. She cites the slightly later use of the falcon having flow to heaven from J. Cerny, *The Cambridge Ancient History*, vol 2: "History of the Middle East and Aegean Region c. 1380-1000 BC," Chapter 35: "Egypt from the Death of Rameses III to the End of the Twenty-first Dynasty," 1975.

10. M. Eaton-Krauss and E. Graefe, *The Small Golden Shrine from the Tomb of Tutankhamun* (Oxford, 1985), pl X, side B, BR-1.

11. Gay Robins, *Tenth International Congress of Egyptologists, Abstracts of Papers*, 22-29 May, 2008.

12. L. Borchardt, *Das Grabdenkmal des Königs Sa3hure'* II (Leipzig, 1913), pl. xvi.

13. J. Galán, "An Apprentice's Board from Dra Abu el-Naga, *Journal of Egyptian Archaeology* 93 (2007), 95-116, esp. Fig. 2, 4 and 9.14.

14. A. Kozloff and B. Bryan, *Egypt's Dazzling Sun: Amenhotep III and His World* (Cleveland, 1992), 353, n. 1.

15. For an example of Amenhotep III performing this ritual, see W. Wettengel, "Zu Den Darstekkungen Des Papyrusrascheins," *Studien zur Alt Ägyptischen Kultur* 19 (1992), Abb 3, 337, pl. 3. I thank E.C. Brock for this reference.

16. E. Teeter, *Baked Clay Figurines and Votive Beds from Medinet Habu* (Chicago, 2008).

17. T. Säve-Söderbergh, *On Egyptian Representations of Hippopotamus Hunting as a Religious Motive* (Uppsala, 1953), 24; also in W.B.Emery, *Archaic Egypt* (Baltimore, 1963).

18. Ibid., 16, fig. 7.

19. Säve-Söderbergh, fig. 9.

20. Schaden, *AL4*, illustration p. 99.

21. George B. Johnson, "KV62, Its Architecture and Decoration, " *Kmt* 4:4 (winter 1993-94), 47.

22. Schaden, *AL4*, 100. This eye form as initially discussed in my paper, "Yellow Face Masks from KV63 Coffins and the Use of the Eye with Descending Canthi," *The 58th Annual Meeting of the American Research Center in Egypt Program and Abstracts*, Atlanta (2007), 45-46. For a preliminary analysis of this eye shape, see Ertman, "Nefertiti's Eyes — Did the queen's distinctive feature become a symbol of Egyptian royalty?", *Archaeology* 61, No. 2 (March/April, 2008), 28-32.

24. Schaden, *AL4*, 90. Midway between the shoulders of King Ay and his feet the alternating colors of the curving end of the line used to pull the funerary sledge can be seen.

25. G. Robins, "The Proportions of Figures in the Decoration of the Tombs of Tutankhamun (KV62) and Aye (WV23)," *Göttinger Miszellen* 72 (1984), 27-32. She notes that A. Piankoff's remarks that the decoration of Ay's tomb was "...a rather superior version of the decoration of the tomb of Tutankhamun" (29), citing A. Piankhoff, *Mitteilungen des Deutschen Archäologischen Instituts* 16 (1958), 247-251, pls. 21-25.

About the Authors

Dennis C. Forbes is the founding editorial director of *Kmt, A Modern Journal of Ancient Egypt*, and the author of *Tombs. Treasures.Mummies. Seven Great Discoveries of Ancient Egypt*, as well as *Imperial Lives, Biographical Sketches of Significant New Kingdom Egyptians*, Vol. One. **George B. Johnson**, following a career in banking, discovered a second career in archaeology photography and has worked with several missions in Egypt, most recently the KV10 and KV63 projects. He is special projects editor for *Kmt*, to which he has contributed numerous articles and photographs since the early 1990s. **Arielle P. Kozloff**, an independent scholar, was formerly curator of Ancient Art at the Cleveland Museum of Art and co-curator of the 1992-93 exhibition "Egypt's Dazzling Sun, Amenhotep III and His World," as well as co-editor of the exhibition catalogue of the same title. **Dr. Francisco J. Martin Valentin** has been director of the Instituto de Estudio Egipto (IEAE, Madrid) since 1997, of which Egyptologist **Teresa Bedman** is manager; they work together on the Project Vizier Amenhotep-Huy (TA28). **Earl L. Ertman** is an art historian and emeritus professor of the University of Akron (OH). A specialist of the Amarna period, he was also the associate director of the KV10 and KV63 missions to the Valley of the Kings. Egyptologist **Dr. Rolf Krauss** was employed by the State Museums in Berlin (the Egyptian Museum and the Museum for Pre- and Early History) from 1982 until his retirement in 2007. He has published extensively on the Amarna period. **Marianne Eaton-Krauss** has her PhD from the Institute of Fine Arts, New York University, and has held positions at universities in Berlin, Muenster and Marburg, Germany. Her areas of specialization are Old Kingdom sculpture and the history and art of the Amarna and post-Amarna periods, with focus on Tut-ankhamen and his reign. **Dr. W. Raymond Johnson** has been director of the University of Chicago's Oriental Institute Epigraphic Survey, based at Chicago House in Luxor, Egypt, since 1997, having been on the staff of the Survey since 1978. His specialty is Amenhotep III and his reign. **Dr. Aidan Dodson** teaches Egyptology at the University of Bristol, U.K., and is a contributing editor of *Kmt*. He is the prolific author of several books and numerous articles on a wide range of subjects Egyptological, with a special focus on the Amarna period.

Made in the USA
San Bernardino, CA
31 January 2020